Nazism, War and Genocide

From the reviews of the hardback edition:

"**Nazism, War and Genocide** will be essential reading for students of the period."
Richard Evans in *BBC History*

"Taken together, the essays presented in this collection do a splendid job of summarising and criticising the state of our knowledge of the field they cover. All are further characterised by a very accessible style and great readability. . . this book is an ideal way for undergraduates, graduate students, lay people or specialists in other fields to quickly learn the essentials of our current knowledge of some of the central issues surrounding the history of the Third Reich."   Bruce B. Campbell, H-Net: *H-German*

"[The essays] form an interesting, informative and scholarly collection. . . As an introduction to the subject, the book is excellent."
Jewish Chronicle

"The result is a richly-defined overview of the historiography of Nazi Germany in the early 21st century, which reveals how the focus of historical investigation and evaluation of issues have changed and developed."
History Teaching Review Year Book

"These essays are highly informative and are to be recommended for both scholars and students as starting points to the topics to which they do such justice."
German Studies Review

Neil Gregor is Reader in Modern German History at the University of Southampton. His previous publications include *Daimler-Benz in the Third Reich* (1998), which won the Fraenkel Prize for Contemporary History and was short-listed for the Longman/*History Today* Book of the Year); *Nazism: A Reader* (2000) and *How to Read Hitler* (2005).

Cover illustrations

Front cover: Nazi formations marching through Nuremberg during a Party rally. (Source: Stadtarchiv Nuremberg, LR-434-F2-1a; reproduced with permission of the Stadtarchiv Nuremberg.)

Back cover: Women inmates in bunks at Auschwitz. (Sourced from and reproduced courtesy of The Wiener Library, London.)

Nazism, War and Genocide

New Perspectives on the History of the Third Reich

edited by

NEIL GREGOR

UNIVERSITY
of
EXETER
PRESS

First published in 2005 by
University of Exeter Press
Reed Hall, Streatham Drive
Exeter EX4 4QR
UK
Paperback edition with new Introduction
first published by University of Exeter Press in 2008

www.exeterpress.co.uk

British Library Cataloguing in Publication Data
A catalogue record for this book is available
from the British Library.

ISBN 978 0 85989 806 5

Typeset in 10½pt Plantin Light
by XL Publishing Services, Tiverton

Printed in Great Britain by Antony Rowe Ltd., Chippenham

Contents

Introduction to the Paperback Edition

Nazism, War and Genocide: as the title of this volume suggests, a frighteningly simple set of stories lies at the heart of the history of the Third Reich. At a particular historical juncture a mass movement of radical nationalism and virulent racism captured power in Germany; once in power it prepared and unleashed a war at which it had been aiming from the outset; at the same time it perpetrated a continent-wide genocide—a genocide, moreover, which had been clearly intimated in the early ideological writings of its leadership. The devastating human and material consequences of these events were such that, by the end of the century in which they had occurred, they had become a near-universal moral yardstick for debating the nature of crimes against humanity, and a negative ethical norm against which the standards of civilised society could be defined.

Yet precisely because of the vast dimensions of the crimes, and precisely because of the moral and political challenge they continue to pose, the Third Reich remains one of the most hotly contested periods of world history. Historians continue to argue over the relative prevalence of consent and coercion in sustaining the regime in power, the nature of the decision-making process in the Third Reich, and the nature of the underlying motive force of its radicalism. Similarly, the degree to which Nazi ideology penetrated German society and gave the 'people's community' meaningful cohesion, the breadth of popular and institutional participation in the crimes of the regime, and the extent of wider social knowledge of those crimes remain key areas of disagreement.

This volume brings together some of the world's leading scholars of the Third Reich to offer a series of interpretative essays which address these and related themes. Drawing both on their own research and the latest findings of the wider community of historians in this field—findings summarised and discussed in the editor's opening historiographical survey—they offer a snapshot of the state of scholarship on central aspects of the Third Reich. As individual essays they represent significant contributions to the particular topics on which they focus. Read together, alongside and in the context provided by the others, they provide an insight into the key areas of debate, contention, and, in some cases, ongoing disagreement in this crucial area.

The integrative power of the 'people's community', and the extent to which that integrative power was rooted in the exclusion of persecuted minorities, is examined by Robert Gellately in his essay on social outsiders in the Third Reich. As he emphasises, Nazi terror was not arbitrary, but was focussed overwhelmingly on the persecution of the 'enemies of the people', or, in the racialised vocabulary of the Nazis, 'community aliens'. These outsiders—habitual criminal offenders, gypsies, homosexuals and others widely regarded as sexually deviant, 'asocials' and the supposedly workshy—were defined, in the first instance, by Nazi ideology. But this ideology reflected wider social prejudices, resentments and hatreds harboured by broad sectors of the population. Precisely for this reason the persecution of these outsider groups was not only accepted but also often welcomed by the conformist mass of the ordinary German population. As such, it played an important role in generating the sense of community which the Third Reich aimed to establish. The significance of these outsiders and the centrality of their stigmatisation to the consolidation of the Third Reich after 1933 is underlined for Gellately by the telling fact that down to the late 1930s—until the mass arrests of Jews in the wake of *Kristallnacht*—major German concentration camps such as Buchenwald or Sachsenhausen incarcerated more of these social outsiders than they did Communists or Jews. It was, indeed, the persecution of these groups, rather than the initially less popular attacks on the Jews, that for Gellately contributed so strongly to the strengthening of the dictatorship in the eyes of ordinary people.

Gellately's emphasis on the real affective and ideological bonds under-pinning the 'people's community' during the 1930s is, despite the very different focus of his essay, confirmed by Norbert Frei's compelling account of the development of Auschwitz during the war—as a concen-tration and extermination camp, as a site of economic activity, and as a model colonial settlement for thousands of Germans. Forcefully chal-lenging the popular image of Auschwitz as a sealed-off space, an isolated centre of unimaginable horror deep in Poland, Frei reminds us that it was located on territory fully integrated into the German Reich before 1945. The ever-expanding complex of camps, factories and 'model town' thus became home not only to thousands of SS men and their families, but also to many more German administrators, planners, businessmen, party functionaries and, indeed, to other, even more prosaic agents of colonial domination such as builders, guesthouse proprietors and teachers. These people were part of the shared enterprise of the 'Germanisation' of the town; they shared the ideological understandings of why they were there—and what this meant for the pre-existing residents of the town, including its Jews. The Germans' mass presence both here and at the multitude of other killing fields also gave rise to shared knowledge of genocide, a shared knowledge which represented the open secret of German society after 1945. It follows that when some ordinary Germans began to address the Holocaust in the early 1960s, the explosiveness of this did not lie in the fact that things were being revealed about which most Germans had hitherto been ignorant—rather, they were daring to speak openly on a subject on which a strong social consensus in favour of silence had hitherto prevailed.

As Dick Geary's timely essay on the experience of the working class under the regime reminds us, however, the ties that bound the 'people's community' were not always strong and they were far from universal. Acknowledging the findings of recent research which demonstrate that the workers were far from immune from the material, symbolic and ideological blandishments of Nazism, he nonetheless cautions against pushing the evidence too far, and reminds us gently of the political conditions under which workers were forced to respond to the regime. As his piece shows, to the fault lines between 'majority' and 'minority' which Gellately describes in his piece should be added the fissure which ran more firmly down the centre of German society before 1933—that between bourgeoisie and working class. The organised Left were, after all, the first victims of the Nazi regime. While only a small minority of German workers were actually killed or imprisoned in 1933, the effects of the terror were felt far more widely, and the terror apparatus remained a real, constant threat from 1933 onwards. Under these circumstances it is unsurprising that many, indeed most, German workers chose the path of circumspection in their relationship to the regime. Their silence should not, however, necessarily be taken to have represented consent. Rather, it reflected the realities of life under a dictatorship. The limits of the regime's ability to break down working class identities and capture the workers with the surrogate offerings of the 'people's community' is also demonstrated, for Geary, by the speed with which the traditional parties of the German working class re-emerged out of the wreckage of the Third Reich in 1945.

Moreover, as Jill Stephenson's study of relations between ordinary Germans and forced foreign workers in rural areas shows, it was not only those social groups with strong traditions of organised, politically-focussed opposition to Nazism which maintained a certain distance to the regime. In rural southern Germany responses to the various categories of newcomer who arrived in hitherto socially homogeneous village communities were shaped less by the dictates of Nazi ideology than by long-standing traditions and habits of mind with regard to 'outsiders'. Forced Polish workers were often welcomed by local peasant families as a valuable source of much-needed agricultural labour, treated with respect and fairness, and offered the customary familial and social intimacy accorded to all workers on the farm. Religious solidarities between

German and Polish Roman Catholics proved stronger than the supposedly natural ethnic hatreds insisted upon by the Nazis; the sparse
population density of rural areas and the lack of Nazi functionaries in some
regions made it almost impossible for the regime to police ordinary
Germans' behaviour, even on an issue so ideologically crucial. Incoming
German evacuees from urban areas suffering as a result of bombing were,
by contrast, often resented for their alleged arrogance and their refusal to
'muck in' to village life. Here, again, deeper seated social, cultural and
sometimes religious antagonisms between different milieus and different
regions of Germany proved stronger than the regime's constant invoca-
tions of community and shared sacrifice.

These four essays offer, then, a differentiated picture of the relationship between German society and the Nazi regime, and of the extent to
which the regime was able to realise the vision of community it espoused.
The purchase of the regime clearly varied greatly according to locale,
context, issue and moment. Nonetheless, aspects of its offerings were
sufficiently alluring for the 'people's community' to have been perceived
and experienced as real by many, and clearly served to mobilise significant numbers of ordinary Germans behind the regime's destructive
agendas.

The other four essays focus on the regime itself, both in the extended
and the narrower sense. Jane Caplan and Nikolaus Wachsmann address
aspects of the terror system, a feature of the Third Reich which, arguably,
has been paid insufficient attention in some recent studies of the period.
In her study of the emergence of the concentration camps, Caplan emphasises that, for all the improvisation and arbitrariness that characterised the
early history of the terror apparatus, there were numerous continuities
with the regimes of punishment and discipline developed in earlier periods
of German history. The powers of arbitrary arrest conferred upon the
Gestapo drew upon long-standing traditions of police detention during
states of emergency. There were strong institutional continuities too, as
local police and local government functionaries adapted to the demands
(and opportunities) of the new situation by expanding or modifying pre-
existing institutions such as workhouses. There were, moreover, strong
rhetorical continuities in the language which surrounded the newly
extended apparatus of punishment and repression, as local officials and
Nazi leaders drew upon the traditional associations of 'work', 'discipline'
and 'order' to legitimate the new penal regime. For Caplan the regime's
remarkable success in naturalising the concentration camp system within
the framework of the wider penal system rested precisely on officials'
ability to draw upon the established, the familiar and that which was
regarded as 'normal' even as they radically expanded and altered the
boundaries of the terror apparatus. Only as Himmler and Heydrich grad-

ually brought the police system under their control did the concentration camp system evolve into the massive SS 'empire' which it was to become during the later 1930s and the war.

Caplan's emphasis on the breadth of Nazi terror is reinforced by Nikolaus Wachsmann's study of the role of the judicial system in the administration of Nazi terror during the war years. Whereas an older literature emphasised the increasing marginality of the traditional apparatus of state in the face of a burgeoning array of special Nazi agencies, and explained the 'cumulative radicalisation' of persecution as a function of that, Wachsmann stresses that the 'legal' terror administered by the conventional judiciary remained central to Nazi penal policy throughout. Legal officials, no less than SS officers, wished to contribute to victory in the war; they may not have been radical Nazi ideologues, but their outlook was still deeply nationalist. During the war, as Wachsmann demonstrates, the terror apparatus expanded and its application increased greatly. However, it was subject to a complex dynamic which affected different categories of victim differently at various stages of the war. In the first half of the war, the main focus of its activities was on foreigners—both on those who lived in territories now annexed to the Reich and those deported to Germany as forced labour. The ongoing popularity of the regime amongst ordinary Germans, which was rooted in the military successes of the first half of the war, meant that the regime felt no need to extend its terrorisation of the German population. In the second half of the war, however, the ever-growing prospect of defeat—and the regime's desire to clamp down on manifestations of defeatism—led to a greatly increased incidence of terroristic justice towards the German population too; the judiciary's need to prove its reliability in the face of Hitler's criticisms also led to a radicalisation of sentencing. In the last year of the war the dynamic changed again. On the one hand, the establishment of flying courts martial represented the final abandonment of anything which might be termed due legal process, and led to a final frenzy of terror on the part of a minority of remaining fanatics. On the other hand, other judges sought to distance themselves from the regime in anticipation of its collapse, and avoided harsh sentencing, so that harsher directives from the regime at the top did not, in practice, necessarily translate into increased terror on the ground overall.

Both Caplan's study of the role of civil service officials and Wachsmann's examination of the judiciary remind us that the translation of the regime's agendas into practice rested, to a great extent, on the willingness of large numbers of functionaries across the state apparatus to act out its daily demands. But the policy drive itself did not come from the echelon of mid-ranking collaborators who facilitated the Nazis' measures, however agreeable to those measures they often undoubtedly were. Rather, it came from the top—from an extended group of leaders, drawn from the 'old fighters' of the movement, at the centre of which stood Hitler himself. For this reason, two of the contributions to this volume revisit the decision-making processes right at the top of the regime—one in respect of Nazi foreign policy, the other in relation to the unfolding of the genocide. Ian Kershaw traces the policy options—if policy options they were—of Hitler and the military leadership during the era of 'strategic vacillation' following the defeat of France in June 1940. Acknowledging the overarching ideological imperative which drove Nazi foreign policy, Kershaw reminds us that nonetheless, in the short- and mid-term, decisions had to be made on the basis of military and strategic necessity, and that various possible scenarios presented themselves as practical means to the ideological ends. The navy, in particular, sought to impress upon Hitler the desirability of the 'peripheral' strategy, which was based on defeating Britain not via a direct attack on the imperial motherland but instead by weakening her hold on the Empire through challenging her in the Mediterranean. This strategy was a more practical version of alternative visions of Germany's path to world domination which held sway in sections of the German navy, visions drawing on those strains of an older German imperialism which emphasised the pursuit of overseas colonies via *Weltpolitik* rather than continental expansion. However, Hitler was only interested in the 'peripheral' strategy as a means of preparing for the attack on the Soviet Union, which always remained his ultimate goal— and it was Hitler, not the navy, who set the military priorities. In any case, diplomatic considerations, centred on the impossibility of balancing out the competing interests of France, Italy and Spain in the Mediterranean, made the pursuit of this strategy impossible. Ultimately, the presence of alternatives was illusory—ideological, political and strategic factors pointed in the direction of the attack on the Soviet Union.

Mark Roseman's contribution, finally, centres on the decision-making process during the crucial phase of transition to the systematic mass murder of the Jews. In particular, he places the protocol of the notorious Wannsee Conference of January 1942 against the background of the evolution of Nazi Jewish policy as revealed by the latest archival research. Here, the focus is on the agendas of the top leadership of the SS, and, in particular, Reinhard Heydrich, whose motives for organising the conference have troubled historians for decades. As Roseman makes clear, the transition to mass murder took place via a series of incremental steps over the course of 1941 and 1942, undertaken in a series of related but nonetheless distinct killing operations in a wide range of localities in the occupied east, rather than as a result of a single directive. As such, the search for the 'smoking gun' document which enables historians to pinpoint a decision by Hitler will probably always prove fruitless. To that extent, it is also clear that the Wannsee conference was not the moment at which the decision for genocide was taken, but rather one at which the issues of who was in charge, and how it was to proceed, were addressed. Heydrich—and by extension Himmler—were establishing the primacy of their jurisdiction over that of the civilian ministries which were also involved at the very same time that they were ensuring the complicity of those ministries by informing them clearly of what was envisaged.

In focussing on decision-making processes among the elites of the regime neither the authors of the individual pieces nor the editor wish to give succour to the exculpatory agendas of those who wish to pin blame on a small minority of actors only. That is absolutely not the point. If nothing else, Kershaw's and Roseman's essays make abundantly clear that the war was co-prosecuted by a broad military leadership caste which overwhelmingly supported the political leadership's ambitions, and that the genocide was implemented by a very large range of agencies, including, again, broad elements of the traditional ministerial bureaucracy, representatives of which attended the Wannsee meeting itself. The other essays in this volume offer ample evidence of the broader complicity of various agencies and countless individuals in the multiple crimes of the regime.

The point, rather, is to stress that despite all the recent emphasis on the mobilisation of popular fanaticism by the regime, and despite all the insights offered by studies of mass collaboration in the crimes of the Third Reich, a firm understanding of the mechanics and processes of the Nazi state, and of the intentions, decisions and actions of its leading members remains essential to understanding how the policies of the regime unfolded. For this reason, the editor suggests, recent attempts to explain the radical fanaticism of the era as a manifestation of 'political religion' do not do justice to the complex relationship which existed between regime and society during the Third Reich. Neither do they enable us to attribute accurately and carefully the degree of responsibility born by each, or to understand properly the interplay between the two.

The hardback version of this book was produced to honour the career of Jeremy Noakes, one of the most distinguished historians of the Third Reich to have worked in the English language in the last forty years. An appreciation of his career, together with a full list of his publications, can be found in that edition, which was published in 2005. One of its key aims was to produce a set of essays which did justice to both sides of Jeremy Noakes' career—to the contributions he has made as a pioneering scholar and to his work as a communicator of scholarly history to a wider audience. We are correspondingly delighted that, in keeping with the spirit of the original enterprise, the publishers have agreed to make it available in paperback form, thereby improving greatly the accessibility of the essays to students and other readers for whom the original hardback may have been prohibitively expensive. We should like to take this opportunity to renew our thanks to University of Exeter Press for their support of the project, and, of course, to reaffirm our admiration for Jeremy Noakes' exceptional achievements as both historian and teacher.

NG, Southampton, January 2008

Abbreviations

DAF Deutsche Arbeitsfront (German Labour Front)
FAD Freiwillige Arbeitsdienst (Voluntary Labour Service)
GDR German Democratic Republic
Gestapa Geheime Staatspolizeiamt (Secret State Police Office)
Gestapo Geheime Staatspolizei (Secret State Police)
HSSPF Höherer SS- und Polizeiführer (Higher SS- and Police Leader)
IKL Inspektion der Konzentrationslager (Inspectorate of the Concentration Camps)
KdF Kraft durch Freude (Strength through Joy)
KPD Kommunistische Partei Deutschlands (Communist Party of Germany)
Kripo Kriminalpolizei (Criminal Police)
KZ Konzentrationslager (Concentration Camp)
NSDAP Nationalsozialistische Deutsche Arbeiterpartei (National Socialist German Workers Party)
RSHA Reichsicherheitshauptamt (Reich Security Main Office)
SA Sturmabteilungen (Storm Detachments)
SD Sicherheitsdienst (Security Service)
SPD Sozialdemokratische Partei Deutschlands (Social Democratic Party of Germany)
SS Schutzstaffel (Protection Squad)
WVHA Wirtschafts- und Verwaltungshauptamt (Economic Administration Main Office)

1

Nazism—A Political Religion?

Rethinking the Voluntarist Turn

Neil Gregor

I

Sixty years after the end of the Second World War, and over seventy years after the Nazi seizure of power, the scholarly and public fascination with the history of the Third Reich continues unabated. The profusion of academic writing on the subject is now such that, if one turns one's back for a moment, one quickly finds a volume of new literature so great that one struggles to master even that which relates to one's own immediate specialism. There cannot be a small town in Germany which has not now been the focus of a study of the rise to power;[1] it feels as if there is hardly a German business which has not had its use of forced labour or its complicity in other criminal acts probed;[2] local and regional studies of the terror apparatus[3] or the experience of bombing[4] seem to multiply in the night. More broadly, the ubiquitous presence of the war and the Holocaust in the popular culture of the western world, saturated as it is with a constant diet of new documentaries, films, novels and popular histories, suggests the presence of a market for such products which verges on the insatiable.

It has often been suggested that this relentless interest is to be seen as the product of a peculiar cultural moment. For some, the end of the Cold War and the reduced predictability of the present have fostered a need to take nostalgic refuge in a more easily comprehensible past.[5] For others, the growing profusion of literature is to be explained in terms of the obsessions of academia itself. According to this view, the over-internalization of the mantra of 'publish or perish' leads historians to produce the same piece of work several times rather than once, while the fact that the broad outlines of the history of the Third Reich are well-known forces scholars—

especially new entrants to a crowded field—to take refuge in ever more locally focused case studies. As David Blackbourn has shown, it is easy to satirize the profession's ability to generate endless books with neatly alliterative titles such as 'Politics in the Palatinate' or 'Sexuality in Saxony', whose tendency is either to confirm for the tenth time the well-known thesis of a canonical study or, taking refuge in the author's unique familiarity with some obscure local archive, to argue knowingly that 'it was all much more *complicated* than that.'[6]

No doubt both of these perspectives capture partial truths. But it is important to note that, independent of such cultural, institutional, or professional pressures, the proliferation of local case studies of Nazi Germany also contains its own logic in terms of how historians' interpretations of the period have gradually been changing. Indeed, the growth of the close study of local events or moments in the history of the Third Reich has been both symptom and cause of a growing understanding over the past fifteen years that many central assumptions of the historiography which pertained until quite recently are in need of substantial revision.

In the first place, much recent scholarship has been devoted to exploring the huge range of sites upon which the Holocaust and the associated crimes of the Third Reich were perpetrated. A literature which up until the late 1980s was patchy in coverage and quite general in focus has expanded immeasurably in the last fifteen years. Most obviously, the history of the main extermination camps—which, up until surprisingly recently, generated iconic images of mass murder more than they provoked close scholarly analysis—has now been largely written. The Institute for Contemporary History in Munich, for example, has run a large project focused on the history of Auschwitz;[7] the history of the Operation Reinhard camps has been written;[8] other well-known sites, such as Theresienstadt, have been the subject of extensive attention.[9] Similarly, we now have not only studies of most of the major concentration camps on German and Austrian soil—Dachau,[10] Neuengamme,[11] Oranienburg,[12] and numerous others[13]—and of many of the sprawling network of 'subcamps' (*Aussenlager*) which grew during the war to satisfy the economy's demands for forced labour at existing or new production facilities,[14] we also have an extensive literature on the hundreds of smaller, hitherto more obscure camps which existed in both Germany and across occupied Europe.[15] To these have been added numerous individual studies of the huge variety of ghettos, work camps, transit camps, work education camps and, most recently, regular prisons.[16]

Alongside this literature on the full range of stationary killing sites in operation during the Third Reich, much recent scholarship has also deepened our understanding of the nature and extent of the mobile killing actions of numerous Nazi agencies. The role of the *Einsatzgruppen* has been known about, of course, since the Nuremberg Trials, and the precise role of the orders governing their deployment in the broader evolution of genocide in 1941 has been debated for many years.[17] Yet it is only in recent years that the killing acts themselves have come into sharp focus and it is only recently that the interaction of the SS/SD (*Sicherheitsdienst*—Security Service), other German agencies and various local collaborators has been explored. At the same time, crucial studies of individual massacres, both large and relatively small, have added further to our awareness of the diverse manner in which the genocide of the Jews was implemented.[18] The cumulative effect has been to underline that the Nazi campaign of genocide was, in many respects, a far more de-centred process, or set of processes, involving mutually reinforcing interactions between the leadership and its often quite autonomous agents on the ground, than an older historiography, with its one-sided focus on decision-making in Berlin and on implementation at a few, major killing sites, led us to believe.[19]

This is even more clearly the case when one recognizes that a key achievement of the historiography of recent years has been to embed our understanding of the genocide of the Jews firmly within the broader context of the Nazis' pursuit of a visionary racial utopia, with all its murderous consequences for those deemed to be enemies of the 'people's community' (*Volksgemeinschaft*).[20] The connections between the euthanasia programme and the genocide have been demonstrated by a number of scholars,[21] while close study of the practice of 'mercy killing' of so-called 'ballast existences' in Germany's hospitals and asylums has further underlined how the murderous behaviour of the Third Reich was implemented in a range of spaces and places across the whole country.[22] Similarly, studies of the appalling mistreatment of the 5.7 million Soviet prisoners of war taken captive in the Second World War, 3.3 million of whom died of starvation, exposure and disease, or of the millions more foreign forced labourers who toiled under punitive, and sometimes murderous, conditions in the German war economy, have enabled us to connect the history of genocide to the broader programme of racial barbarism pursued by the regime.[23]

This emphasis on the huge range and diversity of the killing sites has, in turn, re-focused historians' understandings of the identity of the perpetrators of the crimes of the Third Reich.[24] In the same way that an often hazy, two-dimensional image of the major extermination camps has finally given way to a much more sharply delineated picture of these sites, an understanding of the SS dominated by stereotypes and assumptions has been challenged, modified and refined by extensive research into its different branches and functions. The image of the brutish, sadistic SS guard has been unpacked by Karin Orth's study of the 'Camp SS', in which she explores the integrative power of violence and its enactment on innocent victims for the group identity of the guards. Exploring the social-izing function of a series of interlocking social and professional networks within this milieu, she demonstrates how the collective practice of violence within the camp system forged shared understandings of how the camps were to be run and their inmates treated.[25] A very different kind of SS perpetrator, meanwhile, has been analysed at length in numerous studies of the SD or the Reich Security Main Office (*Reichsicherheitshauptamt*— RSHA), founded in 1939 as an umbrella organization for the various policing functions which were now brought together under Himmler's control. One such is Ulrich Herbert's biography of Werner Best, who fulfilled, variously, the roles of SD functionary, *Einsatzgruppen*-organizer, Head of Administration in the Military Government of France, and Reich Plenipotentiary in Denmark—and who was thus, clearly, the opposite of the caricature of mindless, brutal sadist of the camps. Another is Michael Wildt's collective biography of the leadership of the RSHA. These have both demonstrated that for many in the 'war youth generation' a profound radical nationalism learned in the immediate post-war years combined with a commitment to secondary virtues such as coldness, hardness, deter-mination and 'objectivity', and with an exceptional talent for organization to produce figures who were both 'theoreticians of destruction' and effective, unquestioning organizers of it, equally at home writing journal papers on population planning or heading up one of the murder squads in the East.[26] A different picture again has been painted of the economic 'experts' in the Economic Administration Main Office (*Wirtschafts- und Verwaltungshauptamt*—WVHA), so that a much more differentiated understanding of the SS is now available.[27]

It was not just the SS/SD-*Einsatzgruppen* who were responsible for the mass murder of the Polish or Russian Jews. Various branches of the police, both regulars and reservists, were also closely implicated in the rounding up and shooting of Jews and other 'enemies of the Reich'. This was espe-cially the case after the invasion of the Soviet Union in 1941. Estimates of how many policemen were involved and what proportion of the murdered Jews they were responsible for vary, and the figures were doubtless different in different areas of the occupied East, but it is clear that a very substantial proportion of such killing activity was the responsibility of the police.[28] They, in turn, were aided by collaborators of one kind or another in just about every country the Germans occupied between 1939 and 1945.[29] Even more significant in terms of what it implies about the numbers of ordinary Germans involved in the crimes of the Third Reich, however, the last fifteen years have witnessed an explosion of irrefutable scholarship demonstrating the close involvement of the *Wehrmacht* in the Holocaust. Building on established knowledge of the army's complicity in the drawing up of criminal orders and its prime responsibility for the deaths of Soviet prisoners of war, historians have demonstrated that German soldiers were also responsible for mass shootings of Jews in the Soviet Union.[30] In Serbia the *Wehrmacht* played a leading role in the initiation of genocidal practices before their expansion by the SS—in particular mass executions of Jews in reprisal for partisan attacks on Germans—and was closely involved in the establishment of concentration camps in that region;[31] Christian Gerlach has calculated that the army was responsible for the deaths of around half of all civilians and POWs in White Russia, and has shown the extent to which a quasi-genocidal population policy underpinned its 'anti-partisan' warfare.[32] Contrary to received wisdom concerning the relative distance of the army to the atrocities of the SS in Poland, it is now apparent that the army participated widely in war crimes against Jews and Poles from the beginning of the war onwards.[33] Controversial and painful as it has sometimes been, the cumulative effect of this scholarship has been to destroy for good the notion that the army fought a decent, conventional war in the East, and that atrocities committed by soldiers were isolated, unrepresentative incidents or acts of legitimate, preventative self-defence. Indeed, *Wehrmacht* soldiers were willing volunteers for reprisal shootings of innocent civilians, so much so that on occasion more volunteered than were needed.[34]

In addition to underlining that the range of military and quasi-military agencies actively involved in the killing was significantly greater than an earlier generation of writing implied, historians have also demonstrated that the implication of civilian agencies in the criminal dimensions of occupation was much greater than previously thought. In place of an image of occupation characterized by simple power hunger, plunder and mindless brutality in a chaotic 'frontier' environment, Christian Gerlach has argued powerfully that a more consistent, long-term vision of colonial domination and restructuring was being pursued by a wide range of agencies. Limited disputes over specific policy issues or groups of victims—such as the minority of Jews not murdered immediately but retained in the local economy for work—should not divert our attention from the essential fact that the policy of genocide did not stand in conflict with that of economic exploitation, but rather complemented and reinforced it, and that the vision of population decimation through starvation and deportation was shared by SS and army, labour and agricultural authorities alike. The implication of this is that the civilian occupants of the bureaucratic apparatus broadly shared the vision of exploitation, plunder and murder once thought the preserve of the SS, and collaborated actively in its implementation.[35]

Lest anyone be deluded, finally, into drawing clear lines between criminal acts perpetrated by men at the front and the maintenance of innocence by women at home, recent work on the perpetrators of Nazi crimes has also tended to reach much less comfortable conclusions about women's involvement.[36] The suggestion that women's contribution to the crimes of the Third Reich lay in their willingness to create private environments which accorded with Nazi notions of domesticity and family life—which was itself an important challenge to earlier convenient notions of universal female victimhood—has been supplanted by the recognition that in their roles as social workers, nurses and administrators German women were closely involved alongside their male colleagues in the implementation of euthanasia, and were thus participants in criminal acts in public places.[37] Moreover, some women were agents of war and colonial domination too. By the end of the war, there were some 500,000 women employed in the German army, and, as Gudrun Schwarz argues,

> they lived and worked in an atmosphere of murder and crime, were bystanders and, as such, witnesses. Many were profiteers, some became accomplices, and still others became perpetrators themselves. When employed as assistants to the military staff, female *Wehrmacht*, SS and '*Kriegshelferinnen*' police helpers were charged with typing the reports of crimes perpetrated by those formations. Those who were signal corps helpers were responsible for communicating criminal orders by way of radio, telephone or telex.[38]

Similarly, in occupied Poland, many women, acting as teachers, Kindergarten workers or party functionaries, embraced and actively pursued policies of racist segregation and persecution against Jews and Poles.[39]

The overwhelming thrust of recent literature, therefore, has been to emphasize that the panoply of organizations actively involved in occupation and murder, the number of German men and women who participated in these crimes, and the range of places in which they committed them, was much, much greater than has hitherto been acknowledged. This, in turn, has naturally had profound implications for historians' understandings of the extent to which ordinary Germans became aware of the crimes not *after*, but *as* they were being committed. For, the more historians have recognized that acts of murder were not confined to a few hidden extermination camps, but perpetrated across Germany and occupied Europe, and the more they have realized that they were committed not just by a few SS rogues but by tens, indeed hundreds of thousands of Germans from all walks of life, the less credible has it become to sustain the idea that the genocide occurred in secret and the bulk of German society remained largely ignorant.

Again, evidence that suggested that many Germans witnessed the crimes of the regime was available from the Nuremberg trials onwards. Hermann Gräbe's famous description at Nuremberg of a mass shooting near Dubno in the Ukraine mentioned not only his own building firm, which was engaged in construction projects under contract to the army, and the SS men and Ukrainian militia who were carrying out the killing, but uniformed postmen who were allowed to watch the horrific spectacle.[40] It is only recently, however, that historians have begun systematically to explore the nature and extent of ordinary Germans' witnessing of such crimes.

Jens Schley and Sybille Steinbacher, for example, have explored the relationships of the concentration camps Buchenwald and Dachau to their respective local communities, demonstrating that all manner of people entered or observed the camps on a regular basis—delivering food, or carrying out repairs—or came into contact with their personnel.[41] Similar observations have been made about ghettos in the East. Writing of White Russia, again, Christian Gerlach has noted that 'what happened in the ghettos was not only known to a handful of functionaries. . . Soldiers and officers, railway workers, members of the Organisation Todt and other members of the *Wehrmacht* retinue indulged in a form of Ghetto tourism';[42] when the Pinsk ghetto was liquidated, it was apparently observed by 'unknown members of the then Reich railways and Reich post service, who had come to the place of execution out of curiosity and sensationalist desire'.[43] Similarly, the liquidation of the Lublin ghetto was common knowledge among Germans in the area;[44] the fact that the wives of SS men stationed in the camp often joined them for extended periods also indicates that many women, as well as men, witnessed the most brutal aspects of Nazi barbarism.[45] When put alongside existing evidence that a broad range of officials were routinely taken on tours of hospitals, where they witnessed the horrors of the child 'euthanasia' programme, and examined alongside the damning evidence of German soldiers' letters home from the front—in which they describe, often graphically and with approval, appalling crimes against Jews and others—it becomes clear that the idea that most Germans were unaware of the crimes being committed by their colleagues, neighbours, friends and family members can simply no longer be believed.[46] In general, it is difficult to dissent from Saul Friedländer's recent assessment that 'the everyday involvement of the population with the regime was far deeper than has long been assumed, due to the widespread knowledge and passive acceptance of the crimes, as well as the crassest profit derived from them.'[47]

Perhaps only indirectly related to the historiographical shifts outlined above, but connected to them insofar as they have also helped to undermine older interpretative models of the Nazi regime, many studies in recent years have focused on the broader, consensual dimensions of Nazi rule and the role of ritual, propaganda and display in mobilizing and enforcing this.[48] Whereas once historians were inclined to see the Nazi

party rallies merely as the artificial staging of a fictitious 'people's community', at which assertions of unity, conformity and commitment papered
over the ongoing political divisions of a conflict-ridden class society, they
are now more willing to entertain the notion that for millions of Germans
the *Volksgemeinschaft* embodied something subjectively real. According to
this view, the rallies were both constitutive and expressive of a genuinely
integrative regime, which drew its strength not only from its capacity to
terrorize, but also from the attractive offer of inclusion in a community
whose 'enemies' were defined as much by 'healthy popular sentiment' (*das
gesunde Volksempfinden*) as by the ideological obsessions of a minority of
radicals. Propaganda, it follows, did not so much dupe ordinary Germans
into believing things which they might otherwise reject, as articulate back
to broad sections of the population that which they already intuitively
knew; rituals and displays enforced their sense of belonging to a community whose 'outsiders' were defined by ethnic, political, social and cultural
resentments that the bulk of the population shared.

The integrating and mobilizing power of the regime's achievements in
the 1930s (the rescue of Germany from the Left, the return to work, the
restoration of 'German pride' through diplomatic successes) and the
ability of the regime to harness the popularity of many of its measures in
the reinforcement of Hitler's charismatic aura were such that, according
to the prevailing consensus, terror played a much lesser role than was once
thought, and the regime's strength rested on a popular acclaim rooted
deep in the population.[49] Moreover, through their willingness to denounce
neighbours to the Gestapo,[50] to enjoy the spoils of 'aryanization',[51] or
otherwise to participate in and benefit from the actions of the regime, ordinary Germans became willing collaborators in a culture of unprecedented
criminality in the 1930s, which explains the apparent willingness of so
many to commit the deeds outlined above. Resistance, by contrast, was
isolated.

In summary: where once historians focused on the coercive dimensions
of Nazi rule, they are now inclined to see it as rooted in consensus; where
once state and society were deemed to be 'in conflict', they are now seen
as collaborators enacting a shared vision. Where once historians enter-
tained the idea that most Germans were passive bystanders to the crimes
of a relatively small number of activists, they now focus on the participation of the many. And if it was possible until relatively recently to argue
that most Germans remained ignorant, such a view is clearly no longer
possible: Germans were not only aware of the crimes being committed
across occupied Europe—in many cases they approved. If intentionality
was once conceived so narrowly that the ideological drive behind the
Holocaust was seen as the preserve of Hitler and a few leading Nazis, the
mass murder of Europe's Jews, alongside millions of others, is now

described as the enactment of the Führer's 'genocidal fantasies' which 'came to be shared by millions of Germans'.[52]

II

How might historians integrate this wealth of new empirical research and the insights it affords into a more general history of the Third Reich—one which takes account of the plebiscitary dimensions of the regime's rule, the integrative power of its material and ideological offerings, and the willing participation of many in crimes inspired by a leader who was widely adored? One recent attempt has been made by the leading scholar of Nazi euthanasia, Michael Burleigh. Resurrecting ideas first fashionable in the 1930s, Burleigh has sought in his 'New History' of the Third Reich to characterize National Socialism as a 'political religion'.[53]

There is, indeed, much of potential interest in this model, which never completely went away.[54] It offers a starting point for thinking about the nature of closed systems of belief, the fervent commitment they can generate, and the things they can lead people to do; it prompts reflection on the relationship between thinking and feeling, between the rational and the emotional in politics; it offers a way of approaching the meanings embedded in the cult forms, mystic initiation rites and acts of celebration; and it prompts consideration of the relationship between those who formulate, interpret and communicate dogma and those who receive it. Perhaps most tantalizingly, it provides the possibility of an interpretation which combines recognition of the presence of uncontested authority with acknowledgement of the fact that people willingly submitted to it. As Omer Bartov has recently argued,

> obedience to authority among those whose collaboration is most necessary, the educated professional elites, men and women of religion and faith, teachers and technicians, generals and professors, comes from accepting the fundamental ideas that guide that authority and wishing to help realise them in practice; and. . . this becomes possible only if both the authority and those who obey it share the same prejudices, the same view of the world, the same fundamental perception of reality.[55]

The apparent similarity with religion would seem obvious.

Yet Burleigh's approach is not without its problems. In the first place, much of his account is couched in the language of analogy, rather than analysis—of *Mein Kampf*, for example, he says that 'Hitler's refashioned and selective account of his own life consisted of a series of dramatic awakenings like Paul on the road to Damascus. . . .'[56] This is typical of a prose style which, through constant insertion of the language of 'faith' as a synonym for quite secular 'belief', through open-ended questions ('for what else was the Führer than a Messiah?')[57] or through vague comparisons (the SS as 'a sort of secular priesthood')[58] seeks to suggest the applicability of a model rather than demonstrate it rigorously.

Secondly—though this is of course a problem with the book, rather than the model it espouses—for a study which claims to offer a new history of the Third Reich Burleigh's account is often focused on quite different targets. Most obviously, there are substantial digressions into the history of the Soviet Union. What starts out as a potentially stimulating attempt to rehabilitate a language of 'totalitarianism' through analysis of the aggressive tyranny which mass conformity and shared fervent belief can generate over the minority of those who wish, happen, or are deemed to be different, thus turns into a quite conventional rehearsal of outdated Cold War models.

The accompanying jibes at left-wing scholars whom Burleigh sees as blind in one eye are typical of a style which misses few opportunities to take passing shots at the apparently related forces of Maoism, left-liberalism and 'political correctness'.[59] There are digs at contemporary believers in social ownership,[60] digs at 'hippies gone to seed in seaside towns';[61] even a description of the RSHA man Alfred Six turns into mockery of the 'faux radicalism' of the generation of 1968.[62] Precisely what was 'faux' about the radicalism of one who played a leading role in Einsatzgruppe B Burleigh does not explain. When he tells us that prejudices against gypsies in 1930 were understandable because, amongst other things, 'their children had odd habits' and 'property values were depreciating' the boundary of good taste has been reached;[63] it is symptomatic of the absence of analytical rigour in the book that Burleigh does not consider whether falling property values were in fact a symptom of the Depression, and resentments against gypsies a manifestation of a wider tendency to blame the ethnically and culturally different for a crisis whose roots lay completely elsewhere. As the late Tim Mason observed, 'if historians have a public responsibility, if hating is part of their method. . . it is necessary that they should hate precisely', and Burleigh falls short here.[64]

It is not, however, just in these passing attacks that Burleigh reveals his politics. Far more interesting, and ultimately far more problematic—because indicative of a problem not just with the book but with the model—is the ideological script which resonates through his own account of the regime as a manifestation of 'political religion'. Both his characterization of the context which produced Nazism and his identification of the perpetrators reveal a partial, one-sided perspective on the period which sits at odds with much of the most compelling recent scholarship.

Firstly, the characterization of the Nazi movement and regime as a 'political religion' has unmistakeable echoes of an older theoretical literature on nationalism which described its emergence primarily as a product of secularization. Indeed Eric Voegelin, the author of one of the canonical texts of the theory of political religion, cited extensively by Burleigh, argued in his 1938 tract that

> this world is in a deep crisis, in a process of withering away, which has its cause in the secularization of the spirit. . . It is appalling to keep on hearing that National Socialism is a retreat into barbarism, into the dark Middle Ages, to times prior to the new progress towards humanity, without the speakers being aware that the secularization of life which the idea of humanity brought with it is precisely the ground on which anti-Christian religious movements such as National Socialism could first grow.[65]

As a great deal of research on both twentieth-century nationalism and Christianity has shown, however, these were far from mutually exclusive discourses. Modern 'scientific' antisemitism did not so much supplant older forms of Christian antisemitism as co-exist or elide with them. For one, Christian leaders were quite capable of articulating a highly racialized language of antisemitism which was at times indistinguishable from the utterances of the Nazi leadership,[66] and it is well known that parsons were among the opinion formers in Prussian villages who led the rural embrace of the new movement.[67] Conversely, the antisemitic caricatures of *Der Stürmer* contain many images of Germany being crucified, Christ-like, on the cross of reparations, or of the commercialism of greedy Jews undermining a proper, traditional German Christmas; much Nazi propaganda continued to contrast 'Jews' with 'Christians', not 'Jews' with 'Germans', and thus to draw on older notions of otherness.[68] In *Triumph of the Will*, Hitler famously descends from the skies in a plane whose fuselage makes the shadow of the cross on the ground; echoes of traditional Christian antisemitism, alongside more general elements of providentialist rhetoric, can be found in *Mein Kampf* itself, which is in many ways a very nineteenth-century text.[69] Nazi ideology, indeed, provides a perfect illustration of Paul Gilroy's suggestion that, for all their apparent modernity, more recent representations of the Jew 'have a lengthy history and that modern inventions, elaborations of that figure were reworked from ample materials inherited from a previous time in which the cosmos, the global and the divine were quite differently configured'.[70]

Recent scholarship has shown, then, how Nazism drew much of its rhetorical force from conventional Protestant nationalism and otherwise drew on religious language; the embrace of the 'national uprising' by

Christian leaders who saw in the Weimar Republic the triumph of alien cosmopolitanism and moral laxity is well known; many Protestants took the movement's claims to be fostering a 'positive Christianity' very seriously.[71] Many Catholic observers, despite their traditionally greater distance to the German state, were similarly impressed by the movement's anti-Bolshevism and promise of a return of order.[72]

It is, however, ultimately unsurprising that Nazism drew—among other things—on the rituals, iconography and rhetoric of Christian tradition, since the latter continued to provide one of the most, if not the most, familiar verbal and visual vocabularies of western society. The construction of Hitler as a 'saviour', and the 'populistic exploitation of naïve "messianic" hopes and illusions of a society plunged into comprehensive crisis' does not add up to an argument that Nazism was a 'political religion'—it merely reminds us that much of the political imagery of western society has its roots in Christian discourse.[73] The blunt caricature of 'political religion' does not do justice to a movement which, as Burleigh acknowledges, sometimes drew intentionally on Christian language, sometimes used it unawares, and sometimes sought to replace it; fuzzy terms such as 'quasi-religious' or 'pseudo-religious' do not provide sufficiently rigorous means with which to analyse the intersections of religious and secular, Christian and racist, traditional and novel discourses and/or practices, or their connotations for the development of the Nazi movement.

A further problem with the 'secularization' thesis lies in its inability to explain the peculiar nature of the immediate crisis which brought Hitler to power. Secularization had been occurring since the eighteenth century; nationalism had been emerging since the beginning of the nineteenth century, and radical, populist nationalism in the last decade or two before 1900. Yet even those historians who retain some fondness for explanations of the Nazi rise to power which begin in the nineteenth century would now acknowledge that its ultimate causes were more short-term than was once thought, and are to be found in the multi-dimensional crisis brought about by the First World War and its aftermath—in the mutually reinforcing ideological, political, social and cultural legacies of a conflagration whose long-lasting impact on German society made attempts to foster a democratic republican system almost impossible.

It is not the place here to rehearse the complex material and psychological motives which led broad sections of German society to channel their anger against the upheavals of the revolutionary era, the Treaty of Versailles, the hyperinflation or the Depression into support for the Nazi movement, nor to outline why crucial sectors of big business, the military and the social elites were willing to use the crisis of the late 1920s and 1930s to engineer the paralysis of a system whose downfall they felt the essential precondition for the pursuit of their reactionary agendas; the mobilization of quite diffuse and diverse cultures of protest and visions of renewal has been explored at length elsewhere too.[74] Suffice it to say that the image of a 'political religion', when applied to the Nazi movement in the 1920s, shoehorns into a crude single mould a social, political and ideological movement whose essential characteristic was its incredible heterogeneity. To force the various ambitions of disorientated rural protestors, middle-class nationalists, elite interest groups, radical young *völkisch* intellectuals and violent SA militia into one bracket and to characterize the diverse ways in which the support or participation of these various groups was elicited and maintained into one overarching term is arguably to impose upon the Nazi movement a unifying coherence which it did not possess, or at least did not possess in this way.[75]

Consideration of the role played by sections of the elites in Hitler's rise to power and the subsequent unfolding of the regime, or of the contribution made by younger, radical *völkisch* intellectuals to genocide, leads on to another key weakness of Burleigh's analysis which betrays the presence of an ideological script, namely his attribution of social responsibility for the phenomenon of Nazism. Writing of an older generation of scholars, he informs us that

> while structuralist historians have told us much about the involvement of Germany's elites in bringing Hitler to power in 1933, they also tended to marginalize as 'hangman's assistants' (*Schergen*) the men who implemented Nazi policy during the war, either for reasons of fastidiousness regarding their gruesome actions or because such inquiries might upset an implicit desire to see non-elite groups as less culpable, an approach whose other aspect was a keen interest in the relative immunity of non-elite classes to National Socialism.[76]

Burleigh aims, clearly, to redress this imbalance by integrating the story of popular fanaticism into the history of Nazism's crimes.

To counter the allegedly excessive focus on 'the elites' which governs this one-sided scholarship, therefore, Burleigh moves centre stage the impulsive radicalism of 'the mass' or, as the telling quote from Goethe's *Faust* in the book's frontispiece puts it, 'the mob'. Attacks on Jews or other 'enemies' are depicted as the releasing of 'low instincts' which eroded the 'customary politics of decency, pragmatism, property and reason';[77] pogrom-style attacks, and by implication the dynamic activism of the regime's genocidal drive as a whole, are characterized, essentially, as a form of mass hooliganism.

At its best, such a characterization captures well the moments when such impulsive violence did, indeed, erupt, as with the 'Night of the Glass' of November 1938. Yet ultimately it fails to recognize the key role ideology played in structuring such violence, which, after all, was not indiscriminate in its choice of targets; it fails to capture the ways in which such forms of abuse interacted with other, legalistic and bureaucratic methods of attack; and it does not attribute adequate agency to the regime itself, which was behind all such attacks. Above all, the characterization of Nazism's unfolding antisemitic radicalism as an extended act of 'mob violence' gives inadequate recognition to the findings of an impressive amount of recent scholarship which makes abundantly clear that the perpetrators of Nazi crimes, far from coming from the fringes of German society, came from its very centre.

Studies of the RSHA, for example, which played a crucial role in planning and implementing anti-Jewish policy in the war, have shown that the generation of young right-wing student radicals of the 1920s who learned their political beliefs and styles in the nationalist paramilitary *Freikorps,* and later turned up as heads of the *Einsatzgruppen,* were for the most part anything but downwardly mobile or *déclassé* members of the *Lumpenproletariat*: most came from lower middle- and middle-class backgrounds, which, for all the inherent instability of the 1920s and early 1930s, were sufficiently solid to enable many to complete doctorates. Most were, if anything, on an upwardly mobile trajectory.[78] Writing of the variety of perpetrators of the Holocaust more generally, meanwhile, Gerhard Paul has concluded that the perpetrators came from all segments of the population, and that no age cohort, social background or confession proved itself to be immune.[79] Either way, whether it stresses the strong anchoring of key perpetrator groups in a firmly *bürgerlich* milieu, or emphasizes more the representative nature of the killers as a 'cross-section' of German society, recent scholarship has rendered conclusively redundant the old idea, beloved of post-war conservatives, that Nazism's violent urges be attributed to an ill-defined 'mob', and that Nazism represented the triumph of socially *déclassé* thugs, psychotic sadists and marginal brutes from outside the mainstream of 'civilized' German society— although something of that characterization doubtless applies to very specific groups of perpetrator.

Finally, what is perhaps most troubling about the language of 'political religion', and its use to explain genocide, is what it implies about the nature of the act of killing. Whether or not one accepts that the intoxicating experiences of the Nuremberg party rallies were akin to the sensation of religious fervour, for the model to work as an explanation of mass murder the genocide must, implicitly, have been unleashed in a state of collective ecstasy, with individual killings being carried out in a similar state of mind. Such an explanatory model, which seems to be driven as much by a

critique of contemporary, mostly non-western forms of religious funda-
mentalism as by an understanding of the very diverse patterns of belief,
piety and worship of Christian communities in the first half of the twentieth century, greatly mistakes the nature of religious effect.

It also, for the most part, overstates the impact of the rallies and the
directness of their connection to genocide. There is, of course, occasional
evidence which suggests that the intoxicating experience of party ritual
led some young Germans enthusiastically to carry out the Führer's wishes,
as in the case of the 900 members of the German Girls' League who
returned home pregnant from the 1936 party rally. However, as Elizabeth
Heineman reminds us, this tells us only that young people are prone to
having sex when away from parental control.[80] In any case, most Germans
did not spend most of their time at party events, and those doing the killing
in the East were scarcely synonymous with the party faithful.

Those who were asked to kill were as likely to have been called up to
the army from their farm in rural Bavaria as to have come from a meeting
with Hitler, and found themselves suddenly exposed to the pressures of
the killing moment which several scholars have sought to analyse recently.
As outlined above, there was, of course, a very broad range of killing situations, and a very diverse range of participants; the evidence which allows
us to interrogate the motives of such killers is also highly ambiguous. It is
small wonder, then, that historians have reached quite different conclusions when seeking to explain why it was that 'ordinary men', and not a
few ordinary women—both German and non-German—were co-opted
into the killing process with such apparent ease. Some have stressed ideological factors, derived either from political commitment or longer-term
socialization in agencies such as the army and Hitler Youth; others have
been more inclined to stress a blend of ideology, the presence of authority,
pressure to conform, routinization and brutalization, and emphasized that
the blend of motives differed not only from situation to situation but from
soldier to soldier or policeman to policeman.[81] Either way, when
describing any one of the countless acts of murder which together made
up the Holocaust, few if any historians have found 'political religion' a
useful tool to explain the killers' behaviour.

III

How, then, might we best continue to try to make sense of the Third
Reich? In the first place, much of the superficial attraction of the 'political religion' analogy undoubtedly derives from the fact that historians
have been busy re-inserting ideology into the centre of their explanations
of Nazi genocide. In recent years, historians have stepped back from what

now seems to be an excessively one-sided emphasis on conflict within the regime, in favour of a set of interpretations which stresses the presence of consensus and co-operation too. Whilst recognizing the crucial impulses brought to the historiography by the 'structuralist' school of thought from the 1960s through to the 1980s, most historians now accept that it offered too narrow an understanding of the nature of ideology in the Third Reich and of the ways in which ideology set the goals of the system. It tended to suggest that one had Hitler at the top, defining the ideological intentions (either closely or more generally) and that beneath him there was merely a mass of competing institutions or individuals with no goals of their own beyond fulfilling the Führer's wishes. Most of all, in stressing internal institutional conflict as the motor of the radicalization of Nazi policy it mistook the presence of competition over jurisdiction for competition over the goals themselves. For all the competition for control, however, there was shared understanding there too, shared understanding which was provided by Nazi ideology. Antisemitism was not simply a set of views held by Hitler: it was the emotional foundation of the entire Nazi regime.[82]

There are a number of indicators of this 'return of ideology'. Whereas once it was fashionable to dismiss *Mein Kampf* as a guide to the future development of Germany, its 'inherent genocidal thrust' has now been more firmly acknowledged.[83] The reissue of Hitler's *Second Book* in an improved translation in 2003, making it available in English for the first time for some forty years, is further evidence of this renewed willingness to take Hitler's ideas seriously.[84] Moreover, a compelling body of research has explored the ways in which ideological commitment drove the actions of the hundreds of second- and third-tier organizers of murder. Once caricatured as bureaucratic desk-perpetrators with no commitment to anything but the discharge of their own functions, figures such as Adolf Eichmann have been portrayed in more recent studies as independent-minded radical anti-semites who believed very firmly in what they were doing.[85]

The continued tendency to see the Nazi genocide of the Jews as an event *sui generis*—a quite legitimate tendency, albeit one in need of constant questioning—has, perhaps, encouraged those historians interested in ideological explanations to focus on those elements of ideology which were themselves more or less peculiar to the Third Reich too: its biological-racial antisemitic utopianism. This has often, although not always, occurred within an interpretative framework which stresses, in various ways, the alleged peculiarities of modern German history.[86] More recently, however, historians have begun to reframe their exploration of ideology to include racism more generally, with a view to offering a more convincing explanation of why it was that millions of Polish and Soviet citizens, and hundreds of thousands of Sinti and Roma (to name but the most obvious other victims) were also murdered under the auspices of Nazism's campaign of genocide.

In his study of the genocide in Serbia, which offers such a fascinating case study because of the leading role the regular *Wehrmacht* played in its implementation, Walter Manoschek drew the conclusion that deep-seated memories of the Austro-Hungarian empire's occupation of the region structured German, and especially Austrian soldiers' attitudes to the inhabitants; moreover, they 'maintained a pronounced, racially-tinted revanchism against the Serbs, whom they regarded as the "gravediggers of the Austro-Hungarian Monarchy"'; in order to put them in the right mood to fulfil their mission, General Böhme, who was responsible for combating partisan resistance in 1941, reminded his troops that '"rivers of German blood" had flown in Serbia in the First World War and that the *Wehrmacht* was to regard itself as avenging these deaths.'[87] Similar thoughts have been advanced by Christopher Browning, who has emphasized that 'the negative stereotypical image of the native population held by many Germans, particularly within the military, predated and anticipated National Socialism. . . In their view, European civilization ended at the old borders of the Austro-Hungarian Empire, and the uncivilized Orient began in Serbia.' The supposed 'hot-bloodedness', greater cruelty and capacity for treachery of the Serbs, a product of their so-called 'Balkan mentality', allowed Germans to apply different moral standards to their own conduct of warfare and occupation, with appalling results.[88]

Much work on the 'low-level' perpetrators of genocide has sought to make our consideration of the act of killing more morally challenging by explaining it in terms of everyday processes, pressures and temptations, rather than solely as a product of extreme commitment to ideological positions which find little counterpart in our own society. It is worth noting that such focus on more generic forms of racial discrimination and ethnic arrogance also has the function of bringing closer to home the mental dispositions which made killing an easier choice than it might otherwise have been. One might, indeed, go further, and explore more rigorously the extent to which nationalism itself was a sufficient preconditioning determinant of ordinary Germans' willingness to kill. Scholars have often pointed to a peculiarly violent or aggressive dimension to the rhetoric of German nationalism going back to before the First World War. The purpose of this, again, has been to sustain a set of arguments regarding the peculiarity of Germany's development from the late nineteenth century onwards. It may, however, be worth formulating the point about continuity the other way around, namely, by pointing to the extent to which Nazi propaganda and rhetoric drew upon much more traditional, ostensibly much less harmful 'mainstream' languages of nationhood, nationalism and national belonging. It is striking that the imagery on Nazi

banknotes and postage stamps, for example, replete as it obviously sometimes was with peculiarly Nazi symbols, also relied very heavily on much
more conventional pictorial symbols of the nation which were in use in
the pre-1914 era. A thorough examination of the ways in which the visual
languages of nationhood deployed by the Nazis drew upon those in broad
circulation since the nineteenth century remains a desideratum of scholarly research. For the moment, it is at least worth asking the question of
how far mentalities best explored under the heading of 'banal nationalism',
as opposed to specifically racial superiority or hatred of the Jews, led to
the crucial lowering of the sense of shared humanity with the victim which,
in turn, facilitated the radical lowering of the moral barriers to killing other
human beings upon which the genocide ultimately depended.

Ideology was of course one thing; its translation into action another. In
recognition of this, historians have given increasing intention recently to
the complex ways in which the experience of violence, the rhetoric of
violence and the practice of violence interacted to create a political culture
in which ends were pursued with increasingly aggressive and, ultimately,
murderous means. For this reason as well, explanations of the origins of
Nazism have tended to refocus on the cultural legacies of the First World
War—of the experience of violence in the trenches, and of its subsequent
mythologization by a younger generation of right-wing activists who
wished to make up for having missed out on the war by demonstrating
their own brutal hardness; links between these, the later development of
the SA, the violence of 1933, the normalization of barbarism in the 1930s
and the brutalizing context of renewed war have all been suggested as ways
of helping to explain why the moral barriers to mass murder were so radically dismantled.[89]

The path from the violence of the First World War to the genocide of
the Second World War was obviously not a straight one.[90] What mattered
was not only the experience of killing itself, but the ways in which ordinary returning soldiers—in all combatant nations—made sense of the
violence and drew their conclusions from it. In this regard, it is worth
bearing in mind that of some thirteen million German men who served in
the *Reichswehr* from 1914 to 1918, only 400,000 joined the *Freikorps* after
the war; this, itself, was only half the number who joined the largest paci-
fist veterans' league.[91] Yet one can agree with Michael Burleigh when he
argues that 'some vital moral threshold was crossed during the war, transforming the conduct of German politics'.[92] The new styles of political
activism which were so characteristic of extremist politics in the 1920s,
and which did so much to undermine the fostering of a republican political culture, would have been unthinkable without the experience of the
First World War. Neither was the coarsening of the tone of German politics confined to the streets. As a recent study of the Nazi membership of

the Reichstag in the 1920s has demonstrated, individual Nazi Reichstag members did not shy from initiating fist-fights with their opponents, and proclaiming that it would be better if their antagonists 'were no longer alive'.[93] Again, it is surely no coincidence that two-thirds of the party's Reichstag deputies in the 1920s were war veterans.[94]

Moreover, the 1920s witnessed an upsurge of violence directed specifically against Jews. The highly assimilated position of Germany's Jews should not deflect our attention from the fact that acts of violence, which were very rare in the pre-1914 era, became increasingly commonplace. Jewish-owned shops became the focus of demonstrations and riots against price rises in the inflation era; rabbis or prominent Jews such as Magnus Hirschfeld were beaten up; synagogues were attacked and cemeteries desecrated (some 200 individual attacks of this kind occurred in the mid-1920s).[95] As early as 1919 the Prussian *Ministerpräsident* Paul Hirsch warned in the Prussian Landtag that 'quite systematically. . . an atmosphere is being generated against Jews which is so storm-laden, that it must come of its own accord—even without external trigger—to an explosion, to a discharge of the zealously gathered dynamite.'[96]

Violence, finally, was absolutely central to the seizure and consolidation of power. For all the recognition of the dynamic, mobilizing, celebratory and congratulatory dimensions of the 'national uprising', and for all the acknowledgement that *'Gleichschaltung'* was a complicated process of adaptation by which the organs of a pluralist society transformed themselves into agents of the new regime as much as were transformed against their will, the story of 1933 has violence at its very heart.[97] There has been a tendency in some recent literature to understate this, and to underestimate the impact it had in shaping the terms on which state and society related to one another from that point onwards. One only needs to consult the reports of the Social Democratic Party in exile (SOPADE) for the early years of the Nazi regime to remind oneself that broad sections of German society were cowed into submission by the wave of violence of 1933, and that this act of submission was the precondition for much of the consensus-building which came thereafter.[98]

This leads to a final, necessarily very brief, set of points, concerning the nature of the Nazi regime itself. For all that one recognizes that the First World War left a multitude of negative legacies for the political culture of the 1920s, we should remember that the state monopoly of violence remained largely intact, if fragile and precarious, and that down to 1933 it was deployed, however questionably, against extremist uprisings and in defence of democratic politics. The politics of the 1920s were also co-determined by powerful, alternative political traditions and parties who played a crucial role in defending the rule of law and the constitutional state. In 1933 this changed fundamentally. Alternative political traditions were largely extinguished, insofar as they were not absorbed into the regime on the regime's own terms, and continued a tenuous separate existence only in the form of a largely ineffective, because marginal, resistance. The state monopoly of violence was no longer deployed in the defence of civility—it was put into the service of the state's own agenda of barbarism. Those engaged in murder now did so with the knowledge that the state was both behind them *and* above them.

For all the emphasis on mobilization, willing participation and voluntarism which has characterized the literature of recent years, therefore, it is also necessary to retain a strong sense of the powerful agency of the regime, a regime whose status as a totalitarian dictatorship, Richard Evans reminds us, 'has been too often underplayed in recent years'.[99] Much as we recognize that the implementation of the regime's criminal agendas was carried out by the local agencies of the state—whether they were hospital staff in Germany or ordinary soldiers in Russia—we need to retain a focus on the crucial drive provided by the regime in a narrower sense. References to the generally violent context of war or to pervasive attitudes of racial superiority explain why atrocities occur—as they did in Vietnam, for example—but they do not suffice to explain genocide.[100] For this, the drive of a regime whose leaders were, on some profound level, deeply committed to it, was necessary.

This, in turn, demands modification of some of the wilder claims concerning the 'voluntary' or 'willing' participation of ordinary Germans in mass murder. Before we can make full sense of the moral challenge posed by the fact that many ordinary Germans did, self-evidently, agree to participate in quite unspeakable acts, we need to ensure that we have a firm understanding of the pressures being brought to bear on them from above. It is one thing to recognize that old-fashioned defensive references to 'higher orders' are completely unjustified, but quite another to suggest—as some scholars seem to edge towards doing—that individual killers were faced with completely free choices, the outcomes of which were determined only by their own personal convictions, moral codes, or desire for blood. To reiterate: this is not merely to restate older, exculpatory positions. As Tim Mason pointed out in a different context, 'human agency is defined or located, not abolished or absolved by the effort to identify the unchosen conditions.'[101] As members of police or army battalions individuals were not only embedded in hierarchically structured organizations governed by both formal and informal codes of obedience, and implementing tasks dispensed locally by immediate figures of authority. They were taking measures which they knew were not being implemented in isolation, but which were occurring as part of the state's broader, unfolding agenda of murder. Any consideration of the situational pressures faced by those offered the choice of whether or not to participate needs to take these direct and indirect pressures from above fully into account.

Ideology, violence, the regime (however interpreted): if we are to explain how it was that so many ordinary Germans came to be co-opted into the machinery of genocide we need to give full consideration to the problems posed by these headings not in isolation but with reference to their mutually interacting function. A full understanding of the varieties of German antisemitism, racism and nationalism in the early twentieth century, an understanding of the increasingly brutal forms which politics took in the 1920s and above all after 1933, and an awareness of the organizing agency of the regime from 1933 onwards are all essential if one is to understand how the constitutional, political, cultural and moral barriers to mass murder were removed so easily. These ideas are not new, but their constant reappraisal in the light of new research provides the key to understanding the nature of 'voluntary obedience' in the Third Reich in a way that misleading old analogies with religion cannot.

2

Political Detention and the Origin of the Concentration Camps in Nazi Germany, 1933–1935/6

Jane Caplan

In June 1933 Hugo Krack, director of the provincial workhouse in Moringen, reported to his superiors in Hanover on the current situation in his institution.[1] He began by describing the ongoing strike by some sixty 'police prisoners' (*Polizeigefangene*), who were refusing food and work in protest against their detention and the conditions in which they were being held: 'They say they are better men than the workhouse inmates and therefore deserve to be better fed.' Krack went on to report the number of women in his charge—thirteen 'correctional inmates' (*Korrigendinnen*), four paupers (*Pfleglinge*), and five police prisoners— who had now been assigned to the women's quarters. This reorganization of accommodation had freed up the possibility that the workhouse 'might admit more female police prisoners. If I may remark,' Krack continued, 'the female police prisoners impose no extra burden of costs for guarding or clothing, which means that we do relatively well out of these women. For this reason it would be desirable for us to admit as many female police prisoners as possible.'

What is going on here? Five months into the Nazi seizure of power, in the middle of the new regime's crackdown on its political opponents, a Prussian workhouse is housing a group of political prisoners, alongside paupers for whom they apparently feel some disdain, and who are confident enough to mount a protest strike. Meanwhile the director of the workhouse, evidently in charge of both prisoners and paupers, is touting for additional business on the grounds that it will be a good bargain 'for us'. So what exactly *is* going on?

I

To answer this question, let us start by standing back and moving to a higher vantage point from which we can survey the topography of political detention without trial in Germany in the summer of 1933. The new regime was granted its providential opportunity to legitimize its long-planned political crackdown when the Reichstag building was set on fire on the night of 27 February. The resulting presidential decree 'for the Protection of People and State' (the Reichstag Fire Decree) suspended constitutional civil rights, including the right to personal freedom under Article 114, 'as a defensive measure against communist acts of violence endangering the State'.[2] Starting with Prussia, the *Länder* now used these new emergency powers to authorize their police forces to take people into 'protective custody' (*Schutzhaft*). The wave of mass arrests began a few days later, once the national elections of 5 March had given the Nazis further authority to launch their monopolization of political power across Germany.

In the next two months some 40,000 to 50,000 people were detained without trial as *Schutzhäftlinge* throughout Germany. These were the people Krack described as 'police prisoners': almost all men, mostly members of the KPD, most of them likely to be held for periods ranging from a few days to several months.[3] On a longer view, in Prussia alone around 30,000 to 40,000 people were arrested between February 1933 and August 1934, while the total for Germany as a whole may have reached six figures.[4] These are cumulative totals that hide a continuous cycle of arrests and releases. Still, not long after Krack wrote his report, around 27,000 men and women remained in detention as *Schutzhäftlinge*, according to a national survey conducted by the Reich interior ministry at the end of July. By far the largest number (nearly 15,000) were being held in Prussia, along with 4,500 in Saxony, over 4,000 in Bavaria, and smaller numbers in Germany's other *Länder*.[5] The figures are evidence of the scale of political repression undertaken by Germany's new masters— their commitment to smash the potential for organized communist resistance and to intimidate into submission anyone else contemplating opposition. The NSDAP's undertaking in August 1932 that once in power it would carry out 'the immediate arrest and conviction of all communist and social democratic officials [and] the relegation of suspect persons and subversive intellectuals to concentration camps', echoed in public and private declarations by Hitler, Göring and Frick in March 1933, was thus amply fulfilled in spirit, if not precisely to the letter.[6]

However, it was one thing to announce a policy of mass arrests, but another thing to enact it. The passive voices of the normal narrative account—so many arrested, so many held, so many murdered, so many released—silence both each person's experience of terror, and also the institutional solution to an enormous logistical problem. For a state whose ordinary prison population numbered about 63,000 at the end of 1932,[7] these were staggering numbers of new detainees for whom secure accommodation had to be found. Where were they to be held? Who would guard them? Under what conditions? For how long? Who, for that matter, was even to carry out arrests on such a huge scale? These questions were to be answered, in the words of Wolfgang Sofsky, 'under the signs of improvisation, rivalry, arbitrariness and revenge':[8] the arbitrariness and revenge exhibited by the squads of Nazi paramilitaries who picked up and held many of the detainees in their own murderous hideouts, the improvisation and rivalry by the authorities who worked to institutionalize detention without trial. Through 1933–34, these activities resulted in the establishment of about seventy concentration camps and thirty *Schutzhaft* sections in regular prisons and jails, together with the sixty more short-lived 'torture chambers' controlled by SA and SS detachments.[9]

How these first camps were established, how they mutated into the very different camp system established in 1936, and how to discern the continuities and discontinuities that run through this period are the themes of this essay. To explore them, I will draw on the considerable research into the history of the Nazi concentration camps that has accumulated since the mid-1980s. The recovery of this history has been a discontinuous process. The very first historians of the concentration camps were their own liberated inmates, whose memoirs were published in both East and West Germany in the 1940s and 1950s but then fell into relative oblivion, at least in the West.[10] Among these, Eugen Kogon's *Der SS-Staat* (1946),[11] an unusual synthesis of memoir and history, was not rivalled until the appearance twenty years later of *Anatomie des SS-Staates*, a collection of expert reports commissioned for the 1963–65 Auschwitz trial in Frankfurt.[12] A number of other studies appeared in the next twenty years, but even in 1990 Gudrun Schwarz, summing up the state of knowledge on the Nazi camp system as a whole, could deplore the fact that 'only a few pieces of research into a small number of camp types have appeared up till now', so that 'the entanglement of the camp system in the totality of political and social life has been ignored and the "campification [*Lagerisierung*] of public life" has not been integrated in the analysis of National Socialism.'[13]

Schwarz's complaint reminds us—if we need to be reminded—of the scale and complexity of the Nazi camp system. Not only was there more than one 'camp type' (the concentration camps proper were only those camps administered after 1934 by the SS *Inspektion der Konzentrationslager* (IKL) and its successor the *Wirtschaftsverwaltungs-hauptamt* (WVHA)), but the history of incarceration in the Third Reich is just one element in the extensive repertoire of National Socialist terror, which extended beyond the security and police state to encompass the judicial and penal system, forced labour and the economy, social policy, eugenics and biopolitics, the conduct of imperialist war, and genocide. Though shrouded in veils of lies and sometimes wilful ignorance, the concentration camps formed a grim backdrop to virtually every department of public life in Nazi Germany. And as the reach of the Third Reich expanded after 1939, so did its camps fill with hundreds of thousands of inmates, their numbers replenished even as the war was drawing to its close.[14] It is in this sense that Hannah Arendt was correct in placing the concentration camp at the heart of her analysis of National Socialism as a form of totalitarianism. And yet her specific characterization of the camps as sites of aimless, irrational violence, of the sheer exercise of power, is precisely what recent research has questioned.[15]

Thanks to the work of new generations of German historians, a body of research has now accumulated which has not only unpacked the iconic term 'concentration camp' but also transformed our understanding of the Nazi security state as a whole. As well as academic historians, contributors to this include the authors of numerous local histories and commemorative research projects that have uncovered the existence of dozens of barely remembered camps and shed new light on those already known.[16] In place of a somewhat undifferentiated image of terror, this new literature emphasizes the shifting (though also overlapping) functions of the concentration camps, from political repression to social exclusion to economic exploitation. From this perspective, Wolfgang Sofsky's 1993 study of 'the' concentration camp as a perverse ideal type begins to look more like a last flourish of the Arendtian model, which is now being overtaken by detailed research into the history of individual camps and searching analyses of camp regimes and functions.

Most of this new research has been published in German, however, with the result that among non-German-speaking readers its findings are little known outside specialist circles. There have been a number of important new studies by British and US historians, notably interpretations of the Gestapo and racial terror by Robert Gellately and Eric Johnson and now Nikolaus Wachsmann's pioneering study of the regular prison system.[17] Otherwise, the contemporary English-language literature is rich in studies of genocide and biopolitics, but sparser in its coverage of the police system, and very limited as far as the camps are concerned. Moreover, beyond a few pages in Michael Burleigh's survey history of the Third Reich, virtually the only English-language work that integrates recent German research is Gellately's *Backing Hitler*. Even for a survey of the historiography one has no choice but to look to German publications.[18]

The most familiar institutional expressions of Nazi repression remain the wartime camps, which have compelled attention precisely because of their unprecedented combination of vast scale, unbelievable brutality and exterminatory intent. Whatever else we know about the Third Reich is shadowed by this dominating, bewildering fact, which has come to stand in for the whole partly by its sheer monstrosity, partly by virtue of repetition. Relatively less familiar is the history of the pre-war camps, the institutions that, so to speak, preceded the unprecedented. To put the matter starkly: in January 1933, the core institutions of the Nazi police state—detention without trial, concentration camps, an independent secret police—did not exist. Yet within two months all these things had come into being, if in an embryonic and unco-ordinated shape, and by the end of the year they had acquired a systematic though still unfinished structure.

Where did these new institutions come from—how were they conceived, established, received? The short answer is that there are no *ex nihilo* creations in complex bureaucratic states. Some threads, however frayed, tie even the most radical innovations to the past. This was true even of the Nazi seizure of power, when established bureaucracies collaborated with their new political masters to wrap the nakedness of Nazi power in a palliative clothing of legality and precedent. If Nazi leaders and local activists had their own immediate and longer-term objectives, the other actors in the spring of 1933, the ministerial bureaucrats and the local officials, largely looked to what they knew to meet the challenge of stabilizing the new regime in an unpredictable political environment, and to exploit the fresh opportunities it offered. The overriding political objective was to neutralize potential opposition while the Nazis took over effective power throughout Germany. The means was to take activist opponents, especially communists, into custody and thereby decapitate any burgeoning resistance movement; in practice this meant the creative exploitation and expansion of existing powers and institutions, before their transmutation into novel forms. It was this process of brutal political agenda-setting and improvised enactment that generated the most durable institutions of Nazi power, the triangular structure of detention, political police and camps. Because the history of the political police has been told relatively more often,[19] I will concentrate in this essay on the two flanking institutions: the powers of detention which allowed the police to take political opponents into 'protective custody', and the concentration camps to which they were first consigned.

II

Before the Nazi seizure of power, powers of police arrest and custody were in principle defined and limited in law. Like the nineteenth-century

Prussian and imperial constitutions, article 114 of the Weimar Constitution guaranteed personal freedom, meaning that it could be limited only by judicial process or constitutional amendment. Yet there was also a history of exceptions to this rule. In the context of the 1840s political upheavals, Prussian law had established the concept of 'police detention' (*Polizeihaft*), giving the police the right to detain a person 'for their own protection (*Schutz*)' or in the interests of public order and safety.[20] In its earliest form, this provision acknowledged the principle of personal freedom by requiring the arrested person to be brought before a court by the day following his or her arrest. However, within a few years, Prussia's law on the declaration of a state of siege (the *Belagerungszustandsgesetz* of 1851) created the concept of 'military security detention' (*militärische Sicherungshaft*), empowering district military authorities to temporarily suspend the constitutional provisions on personal freedom and to detain persons without trial and with no effective time-limit. These powers were used to repress political opposition in the 1870s and 1880s, and were applied more widely during the First World War against political protesters and strikers. In December 1916, following protests by the Social Democratic party (SPD), the Reichstag passed a revised national version of the siege law which upheld the basic power of detention without trial but somewhat ameliorated its terms; it was also at this time that the term 'protective custody' (*Schutzhaft*) came into general use. The last application of this law came in early 1919, when the provisional republican government used it to detain hundreds of communists during the revolution.

The imperial siege law was rescinded by the Weimar Constitution, which replaced 'the state of siege...by the state of emergency'.[21] Under Article 48(2), the president was empowered to temporarily suspend constitutional basic rights, including the right of personal freedom, 'in the interests of public safety and order', and president Ebert invoked these powers several times between 1920 and 1923 to suppress communist insurgency in a number of *Länder*. Less well known is the fact that during these emergencies thousands of persons, again mainly communists, were taken into protective custody by the military authorities. At the height of the disorders in 1923, many of these detainees were held in disused POW and military camps, identified in the contemporary polemics as 'concentration camps'.[22] Once the state of emergency was terminated, however, all detainees not charged with any offence were released.

After 1924 the emergency powers of Article 48 were not invoked until the economic and political crisis of the Depression deepened and Brüning began to rule by emergency decree in 1930. But up to February 1933, the only further suspension of Article 114 came during Papen's takeover of the Prussian state government in July 1932, when the suspension remained in force for no more than a week.[23] Otherwise, police powers in relation to arrestable offences were limited by §§112 ff of the code of criminal procedure (*Strafprozessordnung*). A form of *Schutzhaft* was retained in the Prussian code of police procedure (*Polizeiverwaltungsgesetz*) adopted in 1931, but in narrowly restricted circumstances and with the continuing proviso that the arrested person must be brought before a court (i.e. charged) or released by the following day.[24] However, even while the legal restrictions remained, the Prussian police expanded their confidential information-gathering on communists, accumulating a trove of names and dossiers that was exploited as soon as the legal restrictions on arrest were lifted in 1933.

When the Reichstag Fire Decree established a new state of emergency on 28 February 1933, the power of detention that it authorized was thus not entirely unprecedented, nor was the fact that its ostensible legitimation was the prevention of 'communist acts of violence'.[25] Yet in both intention and practice, the decree was the foundation stone of a new extra-constitutional order that used the lingering authority of legal phraseology to wholly undermine the rule of law. Under its umbrella authority, the *Länder* governments were left to issue their own decrees empowering their police forces to order detention without trial.[26] In Prussia, where Göring now controlled the largest and most important police force in Germany, these powers were deliberately given not to the local and more autonomous police forces, but to the 600 state police offices at *Kreis* level, and at the same time the restrictive provisions of the 1931 code of police procedure were expressly set aside.[27] By this time the political crackdown was already under way, including official bans on political rallies by opposition parties, especially communists and socialists; violent and intimidatory activity by SA and SS men, again mainly against leftists; and Göring's infamous decree on 15 February indemnifying the Prussian police for any use of armed force, as well as his appointment of thousands of Nazi and right-wing paramilitaries as auxiliary policemen on 22 February.[28] After the elections on 5 March any need for restraint had disappeared, and the campaign of mass arrests began. Throughout Germany, the police and their auxiliaries now basically had *carte blanche* to summarily arrest their political opponents and deal with them as they wished. Their primary targets were communist leaders and activists (about 90 per cent of the early detainees), along with smaller numbers of socialists and trade unionists, and then, as the remaining political parties dissolved in the early summer, dissident members of the middle-class parties. These men and women were now exposed, without the protection of the courts, to their triumphant new political masters.

III

With police jails and prisons becoming rapidly overwhelmed by the numbers of political prisoners after 5 March, the authorities were faced with an urgent problem of finding secure detention facilities. It is now clear that state agencies were involved in virtually all of the camps and detention centres established in Germany from March 1933 onwards, and that many were explicit collaborations between organs of the state and the Nazi paramilitaries. It is true that the absence of clear central directives and controls at the beginning of March left the SA and other paramilitary formations free to set up temporary holding places in their own head-quarters and other requisitioned buildings, and the sadistic and vengeful violence meted out in these places to captive political enemies can scarcely be exaggerated. However, the idea that the SA established a network of 'wild' concentration camps that were gradually taken under more restrained state control has largely been discredited. The concept of the 'wild' camp goes back to the disingenuous claim made after the war by Rudolf Diels, the first head of the Prussian Gestapo, that 'there were no orders and no instructions to establish the first concentration camps; they were not founded, they simply appeared one day.'[29] In fact, if we look at Diels's Prussia as an example, what happened was that the problem of mass sites of detention was largely solved by the state, but at the local rather than central level—in other words, where the arrests were actually taking place. Prussia's district administrators (*Regierungspräsidenten*) were left to take the initiative; it was their piecemeal solutions that the central authorities then developed into a more co-ordinated detention policy in the late spring and summer of 1933.[30]

Disagreeable as it may be to adopt the perspective of these local offi-cials, let us consider the situation in March 1933 from their position. By mid-March, the police authorities in Hanover, for example, had over 130 *Schutzhäftlinge* in custody, and by the end of March almost three times that number—far in excess of the holding capacity of local jails.[31] At this point no one knew how many more people would be arrested, how long any of them would be held and who would pay for the costs of their deten-tion. It was a headache that the police turned to the *Regierungspräsident* to help them solve, proposing the establishment of a 'collection camp' (*Sammellager*) somewhere in the district. Obviously the first step was to investigate available facilities, and in response to enquiries circulated by the *Regierungspräsident* it emerged that the workhouse in Moringen had empty accommodation available. After speedy negotiations, a formal agreement was reached on 5 April between the state and local authorities that the Moringen workhouse would become a concentration camp for about three hundred *Schutzhäftlinge*, paid for by daily capitation allowances. They were to be held in segregated accommodation and guarded by units of police and SA and SS auxiliaries; but overall institutional authority would remain in the hands of the civilian workhouse director, Hugo Krack, whom we met at the beginning of this essay.

Similar makeshift solutions to the problem were being found throughout Germany at the same time. Not surprisingly, the authorities were on the look-out for existing sites that could be made sufficiently secure to serve as detention centres and quickly put into operation. As well as speed another significant consideration was cost. The Depression had squeezed state and local budgets to crisis point since 1930; it was important to hold these new costs to the minimum, especially before the Reich interior ministry agreed in May to help defray them.[32] For the authorities handling the issue as a logistical problem, the exploitation of existing facilities with surplus accommodation was an obvious solution, and a cheap one at that. As one police official commented in August, recommending the use of the Breitenau workhouse, 'the prisoners there not only cost the state 30 Pf. less than in the police jail, but on top of that they also do productive work for the province.'[33] For a workhouse director like Krack, a source of new inmates for his half-empty buildings was likely to be seen as a godsend, a guarantee of continuing employment at a time when the workhouse as such seemed to be falling into disuse. The total population of the capacious Prussian workhouse network was no more than a thousand in 1932: Krack's own Moringen facility could accommodate around eight hundred men and women, but was housing fewer than a hundred.[34] Not surprisingly, then, in Prussia about one in three concentration camps were sited in workhouses, and in Germany as a whole about one in eight.[35] As well as workhouses, public facilities pressed into service as concentration camps in March and April included abandoned prison cellblocks, welfare homes, camps of the voluntary labour service and similar work camps, and disused military barracks and exercise grounds, along with miscellaneous publicly owned properties and some requisitioned private buildings.[36]

The exploitation of workhouses and labour camps deserves particular notice for two other reasons. First, as Wolfgang Benz and Barbara Distel have pointed out, '"protective custody" was widely seen as a response by the normative state to exceptional circumstances, and enforcing it in workhouses, judicial prisons and labour service camps seemed equally normal.'[37] The conversion of the familiar into something new—this was how the 'permanent state of emergency' envisaged by the Reichstag Fire Decree and the Enabling Act was secured for the longer term. It was not something that happened by fiat, or only abstractly and distantly in Berlin. Thus the political detention of communist 'subversives' was enacted into legitimacy through the regular transactions of regional and local officials. It was enforced by the local police and paramilitary guards who staffed the camps, and was no doubt welcomed by many ordinary Germans who looked on communists as subversives and rabble-rousers who deserved what they got. Blurring the boundaries between the normal and the abnormal, making the exceptional into a new norm by responding to immediate practical pressures: this was the product of numerous quotidian bureaucratic acts carried out by police and civil administrators in the earliest months of 1933, whether sympathetic to the new regime or not. The overlap between older practices and new, ostensibly legal policies was enough legitimation, especially if it was clothed in comfortingly euphemistic language that belied the radically new standards of political repression; and the hope of saving sparse public funds—perhaps even boosting a depressed local economy by siting a camp in the vicinity—provided enough additional motivation to overcome residual reservations.

Second, although only a minority of *Schutzhäftlinge* were held in workhouses and labour camps, the issue of labour preoccupied the authorities and provided one of the principal public legitimations for the camps in general. It built on an old association between 'work' and 'order' and on the inherent relationship between penal and welfare strategies, which it is worth pausing to consider.[38] In contrast to the British system of indoor relief, outdoor relief for paupers was the rule in nineteenth-century Germany,[39] and the primary role of the workhouse had been to discipline men and women regarded as disorderly, unsettled, feckless or workshy. Germany's 1871 penal code gave the police the power to consign certain convicted vagrants and prostitutes to up to two years of 'correctional' workhouse labour (known as *Korrektionshaft* or *Nachhaft*). Prussian legislation of 1912 (the so-called *Arbeitsscheuengesetz* or Workshy Law) created similar powers in respect of welfare recipients who failed to meet their civil obligation to maintain their dependents. During the war, the siege law had also been used by military authorities to detain vagrants in custody.[40] In the 1920s some efforts had been made to shift the emphasis of social policy from penal to welfare principles, but under the 1924 social welfare law (*Reichsfürsorgepflichtverordnung*) relief remained dependent in principle on compulsory labour.[41] At the same time both progressive and conservative circles were attracted by the possibility of using long-term court-ordered detention (*Bewahrung*) as a disciplinary, deterrent and preventive tool in the fight against the socially disruptive and inadequate. Numerous attempts were made before 1933 to get such powers adopted into law; nothing came of them, but the idea did not go away.[42]

From 1930, however, the whole field of welfare social policy was thrown into crisis by the fiscal effects of the Depression. Soaring unemployment burst the reserves of the new 1927 insurance system, while falling tax revenues stretched the capacity of state and local authorities to fund their welfare systems. Although it was hardly plausible any longer to treat the millions of workless as 'workshy' rather than 'unemployed', the belief that benefits should be linked to work did not disappear. Creating work projects in the Depression was a problem in itself, but some local authorities tried to do this for largely deterrent purposes. In addition, Brüning's June 1931 emergency order announced a Voluntary Labour Service (*Freiwillige Arbeitsdienst*—FAD) in which recipients of unemployment benefit would be supported for up to twenty weeks' labour on projects of public utility.[43] The scheme would fund public bodies (municipalities, churches, foundations and so on) to sponsor public works projects, the labour for which would be provided through organizations such as the trade unions, church and youth groups, and political groups like the *Stahlhelm* and the *Reichsbanner*.

The FAD had prominent moral and social as well as fiscal intentions. For one thing, it was addressed especially to the disproportionate numbers of unemployed youth, who were feared to be on the road to demoralization, desocialization and loss of a work ethic (many of them were literally on the road as well, either in search of work or because they had given up looking). For another, some FAD land reclamation projects were explicitly tied to the idea of settling the unemployed or landless on newly cultivable land. In this the FAD looked back to late nineteenth-century labour colonies which had both penal and social objectives, like the benchmark Wilhelmsdorf colony established in 1882. It also converged with other private projects for rural settlement on depopulated estates, many of them run by right-wing groups with explicitly *völkisch* agendas. Among these (though in some disarray by 1931) was the *Bund Artam*, founded in 1924, which, not irrelevantly in the present context, counted Heinrich Himmler and the Nazis' agricultural spokesman Walther Darré among its early members. Finally, the municipalities, which had the residual financial responsibility for supporting the unemployed, were keen to kill two fiscal birds with one FAD stone: to get useful local improvements carried out, and to spare their own strapped budgets. Some even disregarded the voluntary principle by making benefits payments to young people contingent on their enrolling in FAD projects.

At its maximum extent in November 1932, the FAD was occupying some 285,000 young people (mainly men, and out of about 1.5 million registered unemployed youth) in projects like afforestation, road-building, land reclamation and smaller construction jobs like sports fields and playgrounds.[44] But the point here is less the total scale of the projects than the fact that FAD camps, run by a great variety of political and civic organizations, were visibly scattered across the German countryside, and that a public debate about the scope of labour service and the voluntary vs. compulsory principle was in full swing. In the depth and intensity of the economic crisis of capitalism, labour service modelled new ways of understanding productive work beyond the principle of mere economic rationality. To their proponents, the camps seemed to embody the principle of collaboration across the political spectrum and collective work for the public good, while also offering a practical means to combat political radicalization and social disorder. In practice, though, they may also have acted as sites of politicization. This was certainly one motive for the NSDAP leadership's official decision to participate in the programme in 1932, despite opposition to the voluntary principle: here were state funds that could be used to support unemployed SA men, to compete with rival political groups, and to prevent defections from the ranks of the Nazis into the FAD movement.

Looking back across all these developments, we can readily see that the term 'work' bore mixed and complex values in the history of social welfare as well as the prison. It was simultaneously understood, in different contexts, as a means of redemption and a means of breaking the spirit, as community-building activity and as degrading individual punishment. After 1933 the Nazis resolved these inherited antinomies rhetorically in their own way, putting compulsory labour at the axis of their racialized concept of the 'People's Community' (*Volksgemeinschaft*).[45] 'Arbeit adelt', Work Ennobles, as the *Reichsarbeitsdienst* slogan put it—but only conditionally. In an inversion, indeed a rejection of the liberal hierarchy of individual and social value, the overriding value in the Nazi new order was not the individual but the communal good, with individuals meaningful only as atoms or cells in the organic whole. Racist ideology excluded some groups entirely from the community and its values, including work—thus for Jews work was never understood to be honourable, only as parasitic or punitive. But for virtually everyone else, however tenuous or compromised their links to the community, Nazi pronouncements trumpeted work as the ostensible means of reconciliation and redemption; and the harder the case for redemption, the harder the burden of labour. In the mendacious language of Nazi rhetoric, labour service and the concentration camp joined the prison and the workhouse as mirror-image sites where different groups of people would literally work out their different relationships to the community. Though specious, this linkage of disciplined work and ideological re-education became a staple of Nazi propaganda. It established the terms in which the camps were represented to the German public, and masked the vicious and systematic regimes of harsh and often economically useless labour, brutal mistreatment and deliberate humiliation to which inmates were in reality subjected.[46]

The convergence of these threads and their significance for the transition to Nazi rule can be seen at its most blatant in the case of the Eutin concentration camp described by Lawrence Stokes.[47] When a Nazi government first took office in Oldenburg in May 1932, the new *Regierungspräsident* in Eutin, the SA leader, Heinrich Böhmcker, not only promoted the establishment of FAD camps in his district, but also used FAD funds to support the appointment of fifty SA men as an auxiliary police force dedicated to the aggressive pursuit of political opponents. The latter use of state funds was quickly countermanded by the Reich government, but some ten FAD camps continued, run by civic groups as well as by the *Reichsbanner* and SA. Once the Nazis came to power nationally Böhmcker was back in business, recalling his auxiliary police, establishing a concentration camp for *Schutzhäftlinge* in a segregrated section of the local jail in Eutin and staffing it with unemployed Nazis. Because the jail was needed for normal uses, the Eutin camp lasted only until October, when its inmates were removed to other nearby sites. One of these was an FAD youth camp located in a disused factory building in the village of Ahrensbök, which had been established by the social democratic *Reichsbanner* in November 1932. The *Reichsbanner* had already been chased out in February by the SA, who used the camp to support their own unemployed members. When the FAD was closed down nationally in October 1933, in preparation for the Nazis' own *Reichsarbeitsdienst*, the SA work camp in Ahrensbök gave way to a concentration camp for the Eutin *Schutzhäftlinge*. These facilities were also able to accommodate seventeen vagrants who had been taken into custody locally in the course of the mass arrest campaign against beggars launched across Germany in August.[48] Stokes describes not only how the Eutin and Ahrensbök detainees simply took over the land reclamation, road-building and forestry projects originally set up by the FAD, but also how the local paper referred to the Eutin camp as a 'work camp' (*Arbeitslager*), the *Schutzhäftlinge* trudging from their accommodation to their work-sites as a 'work column' (*Arbeitskolonne*), and their work as 'labour service' (*Arbeitsdienst*).[49] And this camp, like most others, provided another kind of work experience that was not entirely unlike labour service. Its guards were unemployed SA men and Nazi party members who worked in return for board and lodging, a little pocket-money—and, more often than not, the chance for brutally settling political and personal accounts with their opponents without risk of retribution.

   A similarly striking example of continuity was the concentration camp in Kuhlen in Holstein, through which some two hundred *Schutzhäftlinge* passed between July and October 1933.[50] This camp was a bundle of contradictions. It was established on the site of an FAD camp run since 1932 by a church organization, the diocesan *Landesverein für Innere Mission*, which had numbered some SA men among its workers. Now, as a concentration camp, its commandant was a longtime NSDAP member who had longstanding connections with the *Innere Mission* and also the

Artamanen. The *Innere Mission* remained responsible for provisioning the detainees and conducting the camp accounts, while the detainees continued the estate works that the FAD camp had originally been conducting. SA men already had used the facilities to detain their political opponents illegally before the camp was officially established in July; thereafter arrests were regularly reported in the local press. As the local paper reported in a full-page article on the opening of the camp,

> The concentration camp. . . offers space for sixty as well as modest fare and ample opportunity for work. We will get these saboteurs of reconstruction used to doing useful work for the national economy. And so that the intellect doesn't waste away, a longstanding party member will pass on National Socialist ideology for free.[51]

Another *Innere Mission* camp pressed into service in 1933 was in Ankenbuck (Baden), which had originally been established in 1884 as a workers' colony intended to discipline and retrain the socially marginal (vagrants, ex-convicts and the like). As voluntary admissions fell in the 1920s, the *Innere Mission* had made a temporary agreement with the Baden judicial authorities to take in some serving convicts, and it evidently regarded their request in March 1933 for the camp to accommodate *Schutzhäftlinge* as a renewal of this earlier arrangement.[52]

While Eutin/Ahrensbök, Kuhlen and Ankenbuck may have been unusual in some respects, they were also typical of the generally hybrid character of political detention at this time. Although *Schutzhäftlinge* were supposed to be segregated from the workhouse sections, the daily regime of accommodation, diet and privileges was usually broadly the same for both groups, and they were normally tasked with the same kinds of work (agricultural work, mat-making, straw-plaiting and the like). This was true of inmates in the workhouses of Glückstadt, Brauweiler, Kislau and Moringen (in both of its phases as a camp for men and then for women).[53] The discipline of work was also integrated in both of the two planned models of concentration camp that emerged in the course of 1933, though with a more blatantly punitive purpose.

In Prussia, where the confusions of the spring yielded to a more centrally organized system by the end of the summer, the interior ministry had devised what Johannes Tuchel has called the 'Prussian' or penal camp model. Linked more directly with the traditions of militarized prison discipline and convict labour, this model provided barracked workcamps run by an SS commandant and guard units, but supervised by a civilian governor under ministry authority: a recipe for incoherence as well as violence.[54] In October, the ministry directed that all protective custody was to be served in the network of state concentration camps, and that non-state camps were to be closed (in practice this latter command was more easily issued than followed). The structure controlled by the ministry now linked three large purpose-built labour camps in the Emsland (Esterwegen, Börgermoor and Neusüstrum) with smaller transit camps located in disused prisons (Sonnenburg, Brandenburg and Lichtenburg) and regional collection camps placed in workhouses (Glückstadt, Moringen, Benninghausen, Brauweiler, Gollnow and Quednau). A ministry draft for a statement by Göring in September described the ideal of the Emsland camps at the apex: 'The economic value of these camps resides in the fact that in them thousands of people have been removed from their activities of inciting and poisoning the populace, and are at work creating new living space for the German race by making extensive areas of wasteland into cultivable soil.'[55] The Emsland camps were in fact established in a moorland region where projects of land reclamation by both civilian and convict labour had been carried out fitfully in previous years. But the new camps were immediately notorious for the atrocious treatment of their inmates; they were places of violent and humiliating repression, and could claim neither rehabilitative nor economic functions. After the demise of the Prussian camp system the sites were taken into the control of the judicial authorities, and remained brutally exploitative prison labour camps.[56]

The complex reasons for the failure of the Prussian model and its takeover by Himmler's *Inspektion der Konzentrationslager* in the second half of 1934 have been explored in detail by Tuchel.[57] Essentially, they boil down to dissension within the Prussian government about the character and control of the political police (Gestapa), vacillations in enforcing the penal model of camp organization, and the energy of Himmler's alternative and more radical vision for the police and the camps. A climactic step in Himmler's monopolization and centralization of Germany's police forces was his April 1934 take-over of the Prussian Gestapa, which coincided with the issue of the first national regulations on protective custody, giving the political police sole power to order detentions.[58] Although Prussian detention policy was not yet entirely in Himmler's hands, his power to set the future agenda was becoming unassailable.[59] It was now Himmler's model, derived from the Dachau camp established on his authority as Bavarian police commissioner in March 1933, that became the matrix for the Nazi concentration camp system. Dachau and the system that derived from it has become all too familiar as the archetype of 'the' concentration camp: an appalling combination of organized brutality, extreme discipline and punitive, often pointless labour.[60] Yet even Dachau too had originally been 'domesticated' in public representation as a potential economic boon to a depressed town, and as a place where, as the local paper put it, 'members of the *Volk* who fall victim to foreign seducers. . . are being educated to become useful member of the National Socialist state by the healing effects of productive work and tight discipline.'[61] Although this was theoretically a Bavarian state camp (it was housed in a disused munitions factory owned by the state), it was taken over by Himmler's SS less than a month after its establishment, and it was through the SS that Himmler pursued his objective of an integrated national police force and detention system: a terroristic police state in the fullest sense of the term.

For Himmler, protective custody was not an emergency device to be rethought once the immediate political risks to the regime had been negotiated, but a crucial permanent mechanism for the foundation and maintenance of the Nazi *Volksgemeinschaft*.[62] The difference between Himmler's vision for Germany as a whole and that of his main rivals for control over the police, detention and the camps, i.e. Göring in Prussia and the Reich interior minister Frick, became increasingly obvious as the number of *Schutzhäftlinge* in Germany as a whole fell to no more than 3,000 in 1934. Many detainees had been handed over to the courts, including newly established special courts (*Sondergerichte*) for political offences, for trial and sentencing under the more repressive laws against treason, subversion and rumour-mongering promulgated in March and April 1933.[63] Others had been released, either one by one or in the big amnesty granted in August 1934 on the occasion of Hindenburg's death. The remarkable overall reduction since the highpoint of detention in 1933 accompanied the Reich interior ministry's attempts to establish its own control over the use of protective custody, and indicates Frick's intention to replace emergency police powers with permanent judicial sanctions: in other words to enact into legal norms the new standards of repression established in the course of the seizure of power. Troubling to Himmler's rivals for political authority were therefore not only his expanding powers over the German police, but also the fact that his SS camp in Dachau was holding on to greatly disproportionate numbers of detainees: about 1,600 of the 3,000 total.[64] However, when Frick insisted that Himmler explain the high number of Bavarian *Schutzhäftlinge* in January 1935, Himmler instead obtained Hitler's approval for keeping 'his' detainees in custody, effectively undermining Frick's entire strategy. Six months later Hitler finally negated Frick's plans and endorsed Himmler's alternative vision by sanctioning a massive expansion of the SS, to include an extended and permanent system of concentration camps funded by the state and administered and staffed by Himmler's SS.[65]

Hitler's decision sealed the transition from the early state concentration camp system to its successor, the SS system. Where the 1933–35 camp system had aimed to throttle political opposition within Germany, the SS system folded the camps into larger programmes for neutralizing *all* of

Germany's so-called internal enemies, political, racial and 'social', and for terrorizing the European peoples to be conquered by Germany in its forthcoming war of expansion. The new camp system was indeed integral to the linked aims of active planning for war and the vision of a new Germany.[66] Himmler shared Hitler's organic concept of the German national community and the fantasy that it was engaged in a perpetual struggle against destructive and subversive forces that menaced the *Volk* from within and without its borders. Only an equally permanent and ruthless system of military and police self-defence, equipped with unlimited preventive as well as repressive powers, could resist these infections. In Himmler's vision, the police needed unfettered executive power to define and arrest whoever they considered to be Germany's internal and external enemies, unconstrained by any legal or constitutional norms.[67] The concentration camps would be the sites where the unreformable majority among the German detainees would be permanently excluded from the community, the salvageable minority made docile by work, and subject peoples brought to heel. This extra-legal system of policing and detention had been under construction by Himmler since 1933, through his progressive acquisition of authority over all German police forces between 1933 and 1935, through his establishment of the IKL in June 1934 (nominally as part of the Prussian Gestapa over which Himmler had just taken control) and through the elimination of the SA as a rival force in July.[68] From this commanding position, the remaining building-blocks were put in place with Hitler's sanction in 1935/36, viz. a permanent, extra-judicial and state-financed concentration camp system, the formal exemption of the Gestapo from any residual administrative and judicial oversight, and the merger of the SS and police leadership under Himmler's command.[69] Under the new dispensation, the Gestapo controlled the arrest and release of political detainees, while their detention in the concentration camps rested in the hands of the IKL.[70]

Between 1936 and 1939 a network of six purpose-built concentration camps, constructed as economically as possible by inmate labour and staffed exclusively by the SS, replaced the scattered smaller camps inherited from the Prussian authorities by the IKL. The network comprised Sachsenhausen (financed by the sale of Esterwegen to the judicial authorities, and opened in the summer of 1936), Buchenwald (financed by a Reich loan; opened summer 1937), the expanded camp at Dachau (1937/38), the two quarry camps at Flossenbürg (May 1938) and Mauthausen (August 1938) and the women's camp at Ravensbrück (May 1939). From 1937/38, the financing of the camps was absorbed into the Reich budget, and camp labour was being integrated into the SS's own economic planning.[71] The IKL scheme envisaged a camp system capable of holding up to 50,000 inmates. On the eve of the war, 21,000 men and women were in custody in the camps: seven times the number when Himmler had gained control of the camps in 1934/35.[72]

The expansion of the camps was accompanied by a marked shift in the composition of the inmate population, as Himmler's strategy of preventive 'social' policing filled them with persons defined as criminal, socially marginal or deviant, rather than politically suspect. The Nazi regime had linked political and social discipline from its inception: already in 1933 the police in many parts of Germany had begun to arrest tramps, beggars and the homeless on an unprecedented scale, using the existing vagrancy laws.[73] In the first co-ordinated arrest campaign in September 1933, which was accompanied by an equally co-ordinated propaganda campaign, some ten thousand such people were taken in police custody across Germany. In the absence of long-term facilities for their detention most were quickly released, but not before some had been put into makeshift camps, and press publicity depicted them undertaking 'useful' agricultural labour and public works. Some victims of this and later police campaigns were sent as correctional inmates (*Korrigenden*) into workhouses, including many of the workhouses now accommodating political detainees. These new correctional inmates were not always segregated from the political detainees, and the overlap between inmate categories was unmistakable. Non-political inmates of the Rebdorf workhouse were transferred on several occasions to Dachau between 1933 and 1935, to relieve overcrowding in the workhouse and to provide needed workers for the camp's labour force.[74] In the Fuhlsbüttel police camp near Hamburg, the arrival of the first 'asocial' detainees in the autumn of 1933 disrupted the solidarity that the political prisoners had developed, foreshadowing the policy of deliberately fostered conflict among inmate groups that was to be put into practice in the later 1930s.[75]

The blurring of political and social repression thus began almost immediately. However, until 1937/38, workhouses and prisons remained the primary destination for those arrested both under the existing vagrancy laws and under the first significant Nazi amendments to the vagrancy and penal laws. Among its other provisions, the Habitual Criminals Law of 24 November 1933 went some way to establishing the powers of indefinite preventive detention (*Bewahrung*) that had been under discussion since the 1920s. It created the category of indefinite 'security detention' (*Sicherungsverwahrung*): this could be imposed by the courts on certain categories of 'dangerous' repeat offenders and was served in the regular prisons. The law also shifted responsibility for ordering correctional workhouse detention from the police to the courts, and allowed indefinite detention as well.[76] But meanwhile a number of other important enactments, notably in Prussia, enhanced *police* powers of surveillance and preventive detention too, enabling the arrest of two thousand so-called habitual and hereditary criminals in the 'special action' ordered by the criminal police authorities on 9 March 1937. For the first time the victims were sent en masse straight to the concentration camps, and indeed the arrest campaign may have been authorized precisely in order to provide labour power for the construction of the new camps at Sachsenhausen and Buchenwald.[77] Finally, in December 1937 the interior ministry issued the first national regulations 'on combating crime by preventive police measures'.[78] Alongside the existing provisions for court-ordered 'security detention', this decree now gave the police new and broad powers to designate persons as habitual or hereditary criminals or as 'asocials', to detain them without trial for the protection of the community, and to assign them to indefinite 'preventive detention' (*Vorbeugungshaft*) in 'secure rehabilitation and work camps'.

Although Himmler never achieved his objective of a uniform national preventive detention law, and although the concentration camps never secured a monopoly of political or social repression in Nazi Germany, his secret police and criminal police now each had permanent and largely discretionary powers of detention without trial, which they used to the fullest extent. Their coexistence and the blurring of categories was signalled in the two major arrest campaigns of 1938. In the first of these, the Gestapo's April 1938 'National Action against the Workshy' (*Aktion Arbeitsscheue Reich*) sent some two thousand able-bodied men into protective custody (*Schutzhaft*) in Buchenwald; while the second, the June action by the criminal police, dispatched over ten thousand so-called 'asocials' into preventive detention (*Vorbeugungshaft*) in Sachsenhausen, Buchenwald and Dachau. By November 1938, two-thirds of all concentration camp inmates were non-political detainees: the police were hauling them into custody as criminals, vagrants, alcoholics, prostitutes or social misfits of all descriptions, and the SS assigned them to backbreaking labours in an utterly specious programme of 'rehabilitation' through work. In effect, in the restored conditions of more or less full employment in the German economy, the 'workshy' had been reconceptualized as the 'asocial'. Those who refused to work were now by definition excluded from the national community, and the twentieth-century concentration camp had taken over from the nineteenth-century workhouse as the means of social discipline enforced by the police.[79]

IV

Making use of the recent accumulation of German research into the pre-war concentration camps, this essay has aimed to show how closely the early camps were inflected with existing institutions of confinement and practices of social discipline through labour. The immediate silencing of alternative and oppositional voices was also crucial for hammering home the new lessons in national order and dissembling their radical intentions and real effects. The point is not that workhouses as such were incipient concentration camps; nor was the Nazi takeover of power in 1933 anything less than a horrifying and cynical assault on democratic proce- dures and the rule of law. But existing practices of extra-judicial detention and involuntary labour, together with emergency responses to the social crisis of the Depression, provided ostensible precedents and institutional locations that disguised the brutal and ruthless character of Nazi repres- sion, and eased its official and popular acceptance. This was clearest in Prussia, where the proposed penal camp model developed in 1933/34 rested on a recognizable tripartite structure of labour camp, prison and workhouse. But even the viciously novel regime that prevailed in Dachau was publicly sold as a strenuous but fair process of re-education through work which was supposed to reintegrate those labelled as political dissi- dents and social marginals back into the 'people's community'. The same was true of the SA camp in the town of Oranienburg (1933–34), which combined an almost unparalleled record of assault and murder with an astonishingly transparent local publicity campaign designed to present it as a 'harsh but correct' remedial institution for the politically wayward.[80] Conceivably, the Prussian state camps might have been reintegrated into the judicial and penal structure, though one that was already premised on massive violations of the rule of law.[81] Himmler's project, however, was premised on a new system of totally extra-judicial terror: the virtually limit- less expansion of police powers of detention without trial, and the establishment of an autonomous, large-scale and permanent concentra- tion camp system that set new punitive standards for the entire apparatus of detention. And here labour was to be made the means not just of punish- ment, but of extermination.

My grateful thanks to Robert Moeller and Nikolaus Wachsmann for their comments on an earlier draft of this essay, and to Neil Gregor for his forbear- ance as editor, and to the Center for Advanced Holocaust Studies at the United States Holocaust Memorial Museum in Washington, DC, for support during the final stages of writing.

3

Working-Class Identities in
the Third Reich

Dick Geary

Recent research has not only demonstrated that the Nazis gained significant support from substantial sections of the German working class before 1933, but has also increasingly questioned the extent to which workers remained resistant to National Socialist propaganda between 1933 and 1945, and to its attempts to create a 'People's Community' (*Volksgemeinschaft*) in which class divisions had been overcome.[1] As Geoff Eley points out in a review of the literature,

> the immunity against Nazi influences previously ascribed to the working class has definitively gone. Whether colluding in the exploitation of coerced foreign labour during the war, or wearing the uniforms of the genocidal army on the eastern front, or generally participating in the "good times" of the Nazi era from the mid 1930s to 1942–43, it was now accepted, German workers could no more withdraw themselves from the consequences of Nazi rule than any other group, whether those consequences were structural (like the radicalized labor market and its rewards), social (as in the new patterns of discriminatory sociality) or cultural (in the new public mores and their sanctions).[2]

Thus Inge Marßolek and René Ott have demonstrated enthusiastic support for the regime on the part of workers in the aircraft and automobile plants of Bremen, whilst Klaus-Michael Mallmann and Gerhard Paul have shown that discontent on the part of labour in the Saarland never went beyond what they describe as 'loyal antipathy' to the Third Reich.[3] Similarly, Ulrich Herbert's research into foreign workers in Germany between 1933 and 1945 demonstrates that their German counterparts were generally indifferent to their fate and sometimes displayed brutality towards them, whilst Alf Lüdtke's study of letters sent home from the front by soldiers who in civilian life had been workers in Leipzig (a social demo-cratic stronghold before 1933), finds that this correspondence often reproduces Nazi racial stereotypes and gives not a hint of class identity. He writes that the letters 'dismantle notions both of the homogeneous workers' consciousness and of social class as the primary focus of people's efforts to place themselves in society and history' and goes on to claim that 'for the most part workers did not keep their distance from the cheering masses. They joined them, for example, at the Nazi May Day of "national labour", or when Hitler's voice was heard on the radio, or in the newsreel celebrating another "great day" in the nation's history'.[4]

Robert Gellately and Eric Johnson have argued more generally that the Third Reich rested largely on a general consensus (in the first case) or at least accommodation with the regime (in the second case), which included the German working class.[5] The oral history projects of Lutz Niethammer and Alex von Plato concerning the post-war period further demonstrate how deeply workers and labour leaders were influenced by their partici-pation in the Hitler Youth and Nazi sports organizations.[6] As a result Mark Roseman, in a generally circumspect analysis of the social consequences of the Third Reich, nonetheless claims that, whatever reservations they may have had, workers did internalize the view that there was a *Volks-gemeinschaft* and that they had a place in it. He writes, 'Nazi Germany did seriously disrupt the transmission of an older culture and. . . facilitate the integration into a national political culture both of regional subcultures and, crucially, of the working class.'[7] In the words of Mallmann and Paul there was a 'revolution in ways of looking at the world. . . a brown cultural revolution of the mind [*der Köpfe*]'.[8] In this view, therefore, the Nazis did succeed in creating a class-less community, just as David Schoenbaum had argued in the mid-1960s.[9]

A number of mechanisms are reckoned to have produced this outcome. The first of these was a substantial improvement in the living standards of German workers in the Third Reich. It is not difficult to believe that those who had suffered the experience of unemployment welcomed its removal. Moreover, by 1939 real hourly wages were up 7 per cent and real weekly wages up 23 per cent on the values of 1932. These manifest material improvements, according to Michael Prinz and Rainer Zitel-mann, engendered an incipient consumerist revolution, characterized by the advent of mass tourism through the Strength through Joy (*Kraft durch Freude*—KdF) leisure organization, as well as the production of the People's Radio (*Volksempfänger*) and the People's Car (*Volkswagen*). Workers now got a second paid day's leave at Easter, and often had their first experience of a holiday away from home through the initiatives of the

KdF organization. Established under the leadership of Robert Ley, this supervised and provided facilities for athletics, gymnastics, boxing, water sports, winter sports and sailing, as well as the factory sports programme. More famously it laid on vacation journeys, short trips, hikes and even cruises to Madeira and Scandinavia. In 1934 these various activities catered for 2.3 million and in 1938 over ten million German citizens.

The Nazis also sought to satisfy what Alf Lüdtke has called the 'representational needs' of labour through the deployment of a worker-friendly discourse. Playing on the traditional pride of skilled workers in their trades, the regime paid homage to the 'dignity of labour' (*Ehre der Arbeit*) and 'German craftsmanship' (*deutsche Qualitätsarbeit*), and organized a national skills competition, which proved very popular with younger workers. The Beauty of Work (*Schönheit der Arbeit*) organization, also established as part of the German Labour Front (DAF) in November 1933 under Ley's auspices, sought to improve working conditions by making the factory shop floor lighter and brighter, by providing washing and changing facilities, canteens and restrooms, as well as lawns and sports facilities. May Day was renamed the 'Day of National Labour' and made a public holiday.

Moreover, leading figures in the regime, including Hitler on 1 May 1933, went out of their way to portray themselves as men of the people and to praise the contribution of manual labour to the nation's greatness. Ley, the leader of the DAF, not only made a point of visiting factories throughout the Reich and speaking to their employees, but also issued a proclamation in May 1933 which stated that

> the entire German nation has sung the praises of the working man with a strength and enthusiasm without precedent and has thus done honour to itself and the creative spirit... [National Socialism] puts the worker and the peasant, the artisan and the employee, in short all working people, at the centre of its thought and action and therewith at the centre of the State... For without the German worker there is no German nation.[10]

To quote Lüdtke once again, 'the government and in particular the *Deutsche Arbeitsfront* (DAF) implemented programmes that offered both material benefits and the satisfaction of representational needs' to the German working class.[11]

So the Third Reich presided over a rise in the living standards of the working class and made direct appeals to its sense of honour and workmanship. It also witnessed a re-structuring of that class, which, according to some accounts, destroyed class solidarity. First of all national and regional collective wage agreements which had been achieved by labour in the Weimar Republic were abandoned in favour of the 'performance principle' (*Leistungsprinzip*), which entailed an individualization of pay packets. This system of wage calculation (so-called *Refa-Verfahren*), which was partly modelled on Fordist/Taylorist concepts of scientific management, together with increased supervision on the shop floor, reduced the ability of workers to slow down production and arguably destroyed the loose networks of solidarity that had previously character-ized factory labour, though it also favoured energetic and skilled younger workers. Moreover medical aid and welfare support—at least in the case of large firms—were increasingly delivered by the individual factory rather than external agencies. This tied workers to their place of employment and reduced their independence. It has also been argued that the exten-sive rationalization of production, encouraged by the DAF, further reduced the power of skilled workers by facilitating the employment of less skilled and female employees.[12]

A second factor which altered the structure of the German working class was the geographical uprooting of millions of Germans as a result of enemy bombing and the wartime evacuation of women and children from industrial centres. This may have destroyed the residential networks which had previously formed the basis of socialist and communist mobilization. Moreover, the development of new centres of industrial production, such as aircraft manufacture in Bremen and the *Reichswerke Hermann Göring* in Salzgitter, saw the recruitment of a new labour force from different parts of the Reich. This new labour force was not only segmented by the new methods of payment described above but also lacked the traditions of solidarity and communication upon which a large and previously powerful labour movement had rested. As a report from Berlin to the Social Democratic Party (SPD) in exile of April 1936 stated, 'new plants in particular, which do not have an old established permanent workforce, lack any sense of solidarity.'[13]

Furthermore, in the course of the Second World War, the German labour force was restructured along racial lines. The conscription of millions of Germans into the armed forces during the five years of war, combined with Hitler's initial resistance to the full economic mobilization of women, created a crisis for German industry by massively depleting the pool of labour available for the war economy. This situation, as well as a disregard for 'inferior races', led the government of the Reich to import huge numbers of foreign workers from the whole of occupied Europe. By 1944 there were between seven and eight million foreign workers within the Reich. The Italian, French, Belgian and Dutch workers amongst these were rewarded at rates roughly equivalent to their German counterparts, though with greater reductions from their wage packets and compulsory residence in labour camps. Russians and Poles, on the other hand, who constituted the majority of this workforce, essentially performed forced labour, in many cases received starvation wages and were sometimes treated with great brutality.

However, those German workers who had not been drafted into the military came to occupy supervisory positions over the foreign workers. In these positions they often displayed indifference to the plight of their 'racially inferior' co-workers and sometimes treated them brutally. How German workers treated their alien underlings seems to have varied from place to place and factory to factory, though in general they were less hostile to and more supportive of their foreign workmates where processes of production generated mutual dependencies. Nonetheless, the war resulted in increased mobility prospects for 'Aryan' workers at the expense of their 'racially inferior' workmates and produced a racial hierarchy within the working class. This constituted one more nail in the coffin of class identity and solidarity, as did the fact that shared experiences in the war (e.g. the experience of enemy bombing or the struggle for survival against the Reich's enemies) united Germans of different backgrounds and cut across divisions of class.[14]

It is not my intention here to deny the significance of these developments. Nor do I wish to claim that no workers supported the Nazi regime. On some issues, especially foreign policy successes before the war and the removal of unemployment, for example, there was almost universal approval. Some fragmentation of class identity certainly took place, whilst the emergence of new solidarities is indisputable. However, claims concerning the destruction of class identity can be exaggerated and in certain respects rest on false assumptions. I wish to argue that the story told above falsely describes working-class living standards in the Third Reich, which in any case have rarely been the fundament of class identity and solidarity. Moreover, evidence about working-class attitudes, in so far as we have it, is difficult to read at the best of times and its typicality questionable. How one reads it for a society in which civil liberties and independent organizations have been destroyed is infinitely more complicated. I will argue that working-class behaviour in Germany between 1933 and 1945 cannot be understood without reference to the specific context and that in any case it has never been appropriate to generalize about 'the German working class'. In fact working-class identity in Germany had always been fragmented and had become more so as a consequence of mass and long-term unemployment before the Nazi seizure of power. Even before the advent of the Third Reich, therefore, the commitment to a politics of class had characterized only some groups of German workers. Furthermore, certain developments after the end of the war raise questions about the extent to which the Nazis had really succeeded in transforming social relations and obliterating class divisions in their entirety.

First we will examine working-class living standards in the Third Reich. Most of the rise in real wages described above can be explained by an increase in the number of working hours. Moreover, using 1932 as a base for comparison exaggerates the extent of improvement, given the low wages and short-time working which characterized this year. In fact, it was only in 1941 that real wage levels reached those of 1929, which in turn were little higher than those of 1913. An SPD report from Central Germany in September 1938 states that even workers who had previously been unemployed for some time complained about the fact 'they earn much less now than in say 1929.'[15] In any case, as Jeremy Noakes points out, rising real wages were to some extent offset by shortages of some foodstuffs and by a deterioration in the quality of both food and consumer goods.[16] It may be true that the individualization of pay packets benefited young, energetic and skilled workers; however, as Tilla Siegel shows, it was not to the liking of all workers, some of whom described working practices in the Third Reich as 'Stakhanovite'.[17]

Certainly the defeat of unemployment removed a great burden; but it took longer than is sometimes realized and was for some quite painful. In the winter of 1935–36 there were still two million unemployed, despite the removal of various cohorts from the unemployment statistics as a result of conscription into the armed forces from 1935 and the draft of some 240,000 young men into the Labour Service. Moreover, in the early days of the regime, various measures were put in place to encourage women to leave the labour force. Additionally those who lost their jobs in the purge of the civil service in April 1933 were not allowed on to the unemployment register. At the same time the welfare agencies of the regime adopted strategies to remove their unemployed clients from entitlement to benefits (and hence from the unemployment register). One contemporary reported that welfare officials were now able to 'reject the unworthy' and 'use coercion against the "asocial"'. In his view the Nazi regime made it possible to get rid of 'cheats'. Furthermore, compulsory labour (*Pflicht-arbeit*) became the necessary condition for the receipt of unemployment and welfare benefits, and those who refused to perform such labour also disappeared from the register of unemployed. In several German towns in 1934 single male benefit applicants were obliged to work in camps outside city boundaries, and in some of these camps the regime was penal. At one work camp outside Bremen, for example, the inmates were forced to wear institutional clothing and supervisors were armed. Any complaint about these conditions from an inmate might result in his categorization as 'asocial' and render him liable to much greater persecution. The purpose of this policy towards welfare clients was, of course, quite transparent: to get rid of claimants. In this it succeeded.[18]

The removal of unemployment, which in itself could be used as a weapon to control labour, went hand in hand with the introduction of an increasing number of controls over the German work force. From 1935 all German workers had to carry an *Arbeitsbuch*, which detailed their training and employment history. In June 1938 a Decree on the Duty of Service issued by Göring attempted further to restrict labour mobility and authorized the compulsory direction of workers to jobs deemed important to the state. Additional regulations in the February of the following year established that workers could be conscripted for an indefinite period, and in fact infringements of industrial discipline were criminalized. As a result absenteeism or shirking at work could result in fines or imprisonment. In 1939 one worker was actually hanged for persistent absenteeism. These measures generated such discontent amongst German labour that the regime had to back down, and in November 1939 Hitler made clear that workers should be employed in their hometowns to quell the unrest. Additionally the organization of the factory in a 'works community' (*Betriebsgemeinschaft*) was meant to mirror that of the 'people's community' (*Volksgemeinschaft*), in so far as the orders of the boss (*Betriebsführer*) were just as much to be obeyed as those of Germany's Führer. In fact the 'retinue' (*Gefolgschaft* = work force) were obliged to swear an oath of allegiance to their employer and disloyalty resulted in penalties. Despite the rhetoric, which claimed the new arrangements were based upon mutual trust and mutual obligations between employers and their workers, the reality was that they strengthened the power of capital over labour—in a sense restoring pre-Weimar conditions. With the onset of war in 1939, of course, labour was subjected to even more controls. In 1944 no fewer than 2,000 workers a month were being arrested for breaches of labour discipline.[19]

Under these circumstances it is difficult to see the Third Reich as a modern, consumerist society. Even if Michael Prinz and Rainer Zitelmann are correct in their hotly disputed contention that such a society was the aim of Hitler and the DAF, the real trajectory of Nazi economic policy made it highly unlikely. In Germany in the 1930s private consumption and the output of consumer goods responded only slowly to the economic upturn. The product of German economic growth, especially after 1936, was redistributed to profits, which rose significantly faster than wages, and to the German state rather than to private consumers (unlike the contemporaneous evolution of the British and US economies). Moreover, the massive falls in world food prices in the 1930s were not passed on to the German consumer. In 1936 the per capita consumption of major foodstuffs apart from fish in Germany was still lower than it had been in 1926, and working-class consumption in 1937 was lower than it had been in 1927. No German worker ever got a *Volkswagen*: only 250 models were ever built, despite the fact that 336,000 employees paid through deductions from their pay packets for a future purchase. Moreover, even the offerings of the KdF organization are easily exaggerated. Some 85 per cent of KdF holidays were short trips (enjoyed by 6,811,266 Germans in 1938) rather than the much-vaunted Baltic cruises (which benefited 131,623 of the Reich's citizens in the same year). Furthermore, only 15 per cent of the beneficiaries of KdF schemes were blue-collar workers (1 per cent of the manual labour force). Most were salaried employees and SS and Nazi Party members, a fact which generated complaints from some workers.[20]

So the Third Reich in peacetime (and even more obviously after 1942) witnessed only a limited improvement in working-class living standards. In any case, even if the regime had brought about a greater improvement in the material lot of the German working class, it does not necessarily follow that such an improvement would have undermined class identity. The whole history of European labour before 1950 saw working-class offensives mounted not by the most impoverished employees but those with (often rising) resources and expectations, bred by the skills and the experience of apprenticeship. Such skilled workers also constituted the bulk of the leadership and rank and file of both trade-union and socialist organizations. What this means is that those workers who subscribed to a politics of class did not usually do so for reasons of abject poverty.[21] However, the fact that labour organization and class politics were principally the creation of workers with bargaining power and expectations does have some relevance for those historians who argue that the Third Reich witnessed a fundamental reorganization of the labour process which eroded the strength and cohesion of skilled workers. This position is summarized by Mary Nolan, when she writes that 'skill hierarchies and the sexual division of labour in industry were reshaped.'[22] Here she is following the work of Carola Sachse, Rüdiger Hachtmann, Tilla Siegel and Thomas von Freyberg, who have argued that industrial rationalization and new systems of payment increased the power of capital over labour and divided workers at the point of production.[23]

Now this may well have been true of the giant companies, such as Siemens, and of the automobile and aircraft plants that have been the focus of most of this recent research; but there is a real problem for those who wish to argue that this constituted a restructuring of German labour as a whole. As Alf Lüdtke suspects and Günther Morsch demonstrates, such rationalization was not characteristic of German industry in general. This becomes even clearer in the work of economic historians like Harold James and Richard Overy, and in Volker Berghahn's account of the Americanization of industrial production in Germany. James shows that German consumer industries in the Third Reich were sustained not by investment in capital equipment but by lowering the quality of their products. Overy points out that increases in productivity in the Third Reich, which should have been pronounced had industrial rationalization taken place on a major scale, were modest in comparison with many other states in the interwar period and especially so in comparison with German economic growth after 1950. In fact, the performance of the German economy under the Nazis only looks exceptional in comparison with the poor performance of the Weimar Republic and the disastrous years of the Depression. What Germany was doing between 1933 and 1939 was making good the lag—in comparison with other nations—of the 1920s and early 1930s. It was not until the 1950s, as Volker Berghahn points out, that the 'Americanization' of German industry really took place. Therefore, the extent to which older shop floor hierarchies were replaced in German industry generally—as distinct from what happened in Siemens or other large firms—can be doubted. If anything, moderniza-tion in some sectors increased the difference between new enterprises, for example in automobile and aircraft manufacture, where serial techniques of production and new technology might be deployed, and older concerns, which were much more difficult to reorganize according to Taylorist precepts. Here older buildings and older machines were the rule and the 'beauty of work' meant little, whilst the standards applied in the manu-facture of machine tools remained largely unchanged, even in the German aircraft industry.[24]

Equally contentious (*pace* Nolan) is the belief that gender hierarchies within the labour force were transformed. It is true that, despite Nazi ideology, there was an increase in the number of females employed outside home from five million in 1933 to 7.14 million in 1939. The war years, of course, then saw a further significant increase in female wage labour, though Hitler's resistance prevented the full mobilization of the potential female labour force until 1943. However, even then part of the increase in female employment could be attributed to an increase in the number of women employed as domestic servants; by far the greatest rise in the number of women workers was made up of imported foreign females, of whom there were 1.7 million by May 1944. There is little evidence that women conquered supervisory or skilled roles within industrial enterprises on any significant scale.[25]

In any case, even if shop floor hierarchies had been generally and signif-icantly altered between 1933 and 1945, the impact that this would have had on the class identity of German labour is far from clear. Labour histo-rians have become increasingly insistent over the last twenty years or so that class (as distinct from local or occupational) solidarities are rarely formed on the shop floor, where differential systems of skill and reward have always had the potential to divide rather than unite interests. Rather it is factors exogenous to the labour process—the attitudes of other social groups, the prescriptions of law, residential structures, marriage patterns, popular culture, the role of trade unions and political parties—which explain why some workers form bonds across factory and local divides and why others do not.[26] This takes us into the single most important reason for doubting that the identity of the German working class was unequivocally transformed by economic or any other developments between 1933 and 1939. There never was a single, monolithic German working class. Different groups of workers had very different histories and identities; and many of these identities—religious, ethnic, political, gender—cut across or undermined the solidarity of class long before 1933.[27] Moreover, a substantial number of workers had expressed support for Nazism even before Hitler became Chancellor. A united working class, conscious of a single class identity, was thus always a chimera. Moreover, the experience of mass and long-term unemployment in the Weimar Republic had already done a great deal to fracture, demobilize and demoralize large sections of the German working class before the Nazi seizure of power.[28]

This insight can be carried into our understanding of what happened to German workers between 1933 and 1945. Where class loyalties had never been strong, as in the Saarland, or where labour forces were new, as in the aircraft industry of Bremen, or where workers had possessed strongly nationalist identities, as in the Krupp works in Essen, it is not surprising that evidence of class identity is difficult to find. It was always so. That letters of Leipzig workers from the front repeat racial stereotypes and are concerned with war experiences tells us little about the presence or absence of class identity, for we have long known that multiple and even apparently contradictory identities, such as those of nation and class, can co-exist simultaneously. It is scarcely surprising, given the context of the murderous struggle on Germany's Eastern Front, that those therein engaged were more concerned with national and racial identity than issues of class. In any case, heterophobic prejudices and nationalist values were not new to the German working class between 1939 and 1945. Ulrich Herbert also makes the interesting point that the racial preferences of German workers did not slavishly follow the official Nazi line; for many it was their Italian co-workers (seen as lazy and overly amorous), whom they detested most.[29] The existence of different views within the German labour force was reflected in chronological changes in the popularity of the regime, charted by Ian Kershaw's seminal work on public opinion in the Third Reich: views were more positive in the economic boom of 1936–38 than in the economic crisis of the winter of 1935–36, for example.[30] The complexity of working-class attitudes towards the regime is also reflected in Tilla Siegel's summary of research on workers' attitudes and Alf Lüdtke's statement that 'the shift from non-compliance to compliance and to active, if not enthusiastic support, was no linear change. . . many zig-zagged back and forth.'[31]

Perhaps most crucially, class identity has never been easy to forge across skill, occupational, generational and gender divisions. Indeed, it was the crossing of these sectional divides to which the socialist parties and their activities were dedicated. In this context, therefore, the destruction of the institutions of the German labour movement and the incarceration or murder of its leaders by the Nazis were crucial. The dissolution of independent social, as well as economic and political, organizations in the Third Reich, combined with the absence of civil liberties and legal protection against the agencies of the Nazi Party and state, requires the utmost attention and is crucial to any understanding of action (or inaction) and identity in Germany between 1933 and 1945. The ability of individuals to defend themselves and take collective action has always depended upon the possibility of joining together in organizations and the existence of a social space free of interference. The Third Reich destroyed both. The creation of bonds between workers in different jobs and localities, the creation of solidarity across lines of gender, generation, skill, occupation and region, has never been an automatic function of economic interest but has required agencies of a supra-local and supra-occupational dimension. Class identity has to be created and has always been brittle. Its creation in liberal/pluralist societies has been the aim and function of the institutions of the labour movement: the press, leisure and cultural organizations, pressure groups and above all political parties. To destroy these agencies, as the Third Reich did, was to produce a privatization of existence and ambition within the confines offered by Nazism.

In such a context a retreat into private life or even collusion with the regime (as in the case of joining Nazi party organizations or denouncing fellow citizens) is arguably better construed as survival strategies than 'consent'. For consent can only be measured in situations in which individuals can choose between real alternatives. To get on in life, to maximize earnings in the Third Reich, it might make sense to join the Nazi party, and the rush to join the party after January 1933 may be better understood as 'opportunism' than as the result of ideological affinity with the regime. Moreover, we know that relatively few (about 25 per cent) denunciations of fellow citizens to the Gestapo were inspired by ideological considerations and that most stemmed from much baser and more mundane motives, in particular the settling of personal grudges. In this context it is also worth noting that Eric Johnson's sample of denouncers in Cologne finds workers under-represented and even more significant that no underground social democratic or communist cell was ever broken up as a result of denunciations from the general public. In this case the Gestapo had to rely on paid informers.[32]

What this demonstrates to my mind is, first, that it is difficult to generalize about the behaviour and identity of the German working classes under Nazism. Reports to the SPD in exile, for example, demonstrate—in the words of Jeremy Noakes—'the variety and complexity of working class attitudes to the regime'. Thus we have in one and the same report from Berlin in April 1936 evidence of working-class solidarity in a large armaments factory in Berlin *and* of an absence of solidarity in a new metal plant in the Tegel district of the same city.[33] Secondly, working-class behaviour in Germany between 1933 and 1945 can only be understood in the context of the absence of independent organizations, the removal of civil liberties and the fact that at least 150,000 social democrats and communists were imprisoned or thrown into camps between 1933 and 1945. Moreover, recent studies, which have tended to downplay terror and stress consensus in Germany, have surely gone too far. It is true that there were fewer Gestapo officers than we used to believe. However, if W.S. Allen's evidence from Nordheim is to be believed, then Germans still thought the Gestapo was everywhere.[34] In any case, did it really matter if they were denounced by agents of the regime or by 'ordinary' fellow citizens? The reality of being reported was still there. Moreover, the Gestapo was not the only agency of control in the Third Reich. As Eley points out, the terror unleashed on the streets of Germany in the spring and summer of 1933

> was wielded not by designated police organs alone, but via the collective violence of the SA and party thugs, with a ferocity felt by Communists and Social Democrats above all. Once the political left had been broken, the more modulated institutional surveillance by the Gestapo then became reattached to troublesome clergy and religious sects. . . .'[35]

In fact, as Johnson's study of the Nazi terror shows, the Gestapo did not simply rely on the general public in the prosecution of its major concerns (the war against Jews and the Left), which it continued to pursue viciously at the same time as often ignoring the petty misdemeanours of the general public. To the exemplary terrorism of the attack on social democrats and communists in the early days of the regime were added the destruction of the SA leadership in the 'Night of the Long Knives' in 1934 and the antisemitic pogrom of the 'Night of the Glass' in 1938. These set the context in which Germans had to live and work between 1933 and 1945. This context was further radicalized in the later stages of the Second World War. In the first half of 1943 alone 982 Germans were convicted of treason, of whom 948 were executed. At the same time almost 9,000 Germans were charged with left-wing activity, 8,727 with 'resistance' and just over 11,000 with 'opposition'. A further 10,773 were arrested for fraternizing with foreign workers and prisoners of war.[36]

The significance of context is made even clearer by developments after 1945, when circumstances had obviously changed decisively. Firstly trade-union, social democratic and communist organizations reappeared with remarkable rapidity in Germany after the war ended. Moreover, early 1947 saw strike waves in the Ruhr. Though these can be understood as reactions to hunger and massive food shortage, they were much more than this. Like the strikers of 1920 in the wake of the Kapp Putsch, those of 1947 also demanded the socialization of the mines, the appointment of trade-union representatives to public bodies and the dismissal of reactionaries from public service. Of the fifty-two recorded strikes in North-Rhine Westphalia in 1947, only three were solely about wages, whilst thirty-one sought to increase the powers of factory councils. This resurgence of older ambitions was further reflected in and partly a consequence of the fact that the German Communist Party (KPD) remained robust in the British zone of occupation in the immediate post-war years. In the regional elections of 1947 in North-Rhine Westphalia the KPD won 14 per cent of the popular vote overall and over 20 per cent in the following towns: Duisburg, Oberhausen, Gelsenkirchen, Gladbeck, Recklinghausen, Bochum, Castrop-Rauxel, Dortmund, Herne and Wattenscheid. In some other places (Remscheid, Solingen, Bottrop and Wanne-Eickel) its share of the vote was at least 28 per cent. These values compare well with those of late Weimar elections. The KPD was yet stronger in pit and factory assembly elections. In November 1945 it won 44 per cent of the votes (SPD 28 per cent) from eighty pits and two months later 44.2 per cent (SPD 25 per cent) from a further ninety-six coalmines. In all Ruhr pit elections the results were as follows:

	KPD share of vote
1946	38.8%
1947	31%
1948	33%
1949	27%

Not until 1948 did the SPD share of the vote in such elections overtake that of the KPD. So the Third Reich had not extinguished German Communism. The Cold War was to do that.[37]

There may be an additional possibility, however, and one which is formulated rather well by Mark Roseman. It is also congruent with Ian Kershaw's perceptions that Nazi propaganda was most successful where it did not have to compete with strong historical loyalties. This suggests that the Third Reich was relatively unsuccessful at winning over the former socialists and communists of an older generation but made much more headway with workers either outside the socialist tradition or from the younger generation. In the case of the latter, as Roseman tells us, 'Never had a generation been subjected to such a homogeneous and distinct socialization as the Hitler Youth generation. This would make the transmission of older traditions and values very difficult in post-war years.'[38] The reappearance of strikes and communism immediately after the war might thus be seen as the last fling of an older working-class generation, whilst the social peace of Germany's economic miracle might be regarded as the product of younger, individualist and income-maximising workers socialized under Nazism.

4

Social Outsiders and the Consolidation of Hitler's Dictatorship, 1933–1939

Robert Gellately

Two types of 'social outsiders' were persecuted by the Nazis. One group consisted of individuals or groups who lived on the margins of society because they would not, or could not, follow the dominant social values—hard work, cleanliness and sobriety. By tradition, these would have included criminals, beggars, prostitutes or women of loose morals, habitual drunks, vagabonds, the insane and assorted others. Persons of ill-repute were kept at arm's length, driven out, or confined in some way. Regardless of how well or badly they were treated, these social outsiders never disappeared entirely. Prior to the nineteenth century, with its emphasis on scientific solutions to social problems, no one seriously thought there was or ever could be a 'total cure' for all such problem cases.[1]

Other factors influenced the identity and fate of the Jews, who came to be a separate category of social outsiders in Nazi Germany. Jews had lived in German lands for a thousand years, but until the early nineteenth century small town society subjected them to all sorts of special regulations. Many of these barriers fell away in the German lands by the early nineteenth century. After 1871 the legal emancipation of the Jews was completed and the doors opened to their full participation in social, cultural and political life. Not all Germans were pleased; pockets of anti-semitism grew; there were rare cases of mob violence. By and large, however, the Jews became well integrated and prided themselves on their German nationality.[2]

The atmosphere of toleration was put under strain by the First World War. The years of mass killing had social-psychological after-effects, and the new Weimar Republic was riven by nationalist phobias, class conflict, political instability and economic chaos. On top of all this, the electoral system made it impossible for a single party to form a majority and governments were generally weak. The Great Depression magnified all these problems. On the eve of Hitler's appointment nearly 40 per cent of Germany's blue- and white-collar workers were without jobs. To make matters worse, the state clawed back social welfare benefits and unemployment insurance.[3] The desperation of the last pre-dictatorship years was reflected in elections in which a majority of voters (men and women) supported anti-republican parties.[4] Bands of uniformed men allied with various parties fought in the streets and strained Germany's civic culture to breaking point. There was a broad perception that the country was experiencing a disastrous crime wave and that its cultural and moral values were in terminal decline. This was the context in which Hitler was appointed Chancellor on 30 January 1933. His appointment had obvious implications for everyone in the country, but perhaps none were to be more drastically affected than those now deemed to be outside what the Nazis considered the 'people's community'.

I

The Nazi revolution did not begin with a sweeping onslaught on German society, but moved forward in tune with what the great majority of people wanted or would tolerate. Hitler was convinced that the 'first foundation for forming authority is always popularity.'[5] However, he also wanted an authoritarian regime and was more than prepared to use force. He strove to combine popularity and force and there emerged a hybrid regime best described as a 'consensus dictatorship'.[6]

Given Hitler's slender hold on power even in March 1933, the Nazis were right to be concerned about the working class. A general strike might topple the government, as had happened in 1920. However, in the early 1930s the working class was not solidly anti-Nazi, and in the 1932 elections as much as one-quarter of their vote went to Hitler's party. More workers voted for the Nazi party than for the communists or for the Social Democratic party.[7] That did not make Hitler's a working-class party, but we would be wrong to write it off as merely a protest movement of the lower middle class. Unemployment tore into the strength of organized workers and many began to think that Hitler should be given a chance.

There was next to no resistance to the Nazi take-over. The communists were and remained more persistent opponents than the socialists, and paid a heavier price in terms of brushes with the police. Even so, no more than 150,000 members of the KPD were touched by even the slightest form of persecution during the twelve years of the Third Reich. Even if we assume they were all 'resisting', we are left to conclude that communist resisters, among a population of between sixty and seventy million (over a twelve-year period), represented a small minority. Far fewer members of the SPD were 'persecuted' in any way.[8] There is no question about the coercion used against left-wing opponents, but, for all that, Hans-Ulrich Wehler rightly insists that it is mistaken to characterize Hitler's rule in Germany as simply a 'terror regime' in which a tiny band of desperados subdued the great majority. He observes that such 'explanations' were provided by apologists for many years, in order to avoid having to explain 'the broad consensus basis' that Hitler shared with the 'masses of his Germans'.[9] Moreover, newer research (in contrast to studies from the 1970s and 1980s) shows that there soon developed a 'high level of consensus' even in socialist, communist and in catholic milieus.[10] While some individuals in these milieus indulged in non-conforming behaviour, none of it threatened the regime.

The return to full employment broadened Hitler's social support, and many workers took their place alongside others in the 'pro-National Socialist consensus'.[11] They were impressed that the Nazis took seriously their everyday concerns on the shop floor. By no means did all workers 'keep their distance from the cheering masses' on occasions like the Nazi May Day of 'national labour'. Nor did they fail to tune in when Hitler spoke on the radio. They were especially impressed with his successive achievements on the foreign policy front.[12]

The Nazis used terror selectively from the day Hitler was appointed, but there was nothing like the massive violence associated with the Russian Revolution. Wholesale terror was not needed. Instead, Germany experienced a 'legal revolution', an ambiguous concept that was coined to suggest that the Nazis paid due regard to legal appearances, at the same time as they were tearing up the constitution.[13] Many people saw through the thinly veiled efforts to destroy democracy and rule of law, some were disgusted, but many were won over and others simply looked the other way. There was a latent social consensus waiting to be mobilized, and this made it easier for so many to wait on events or to embrace Nazism. Hans-Ulrich Wehler, who experienced what happened, has written of what he called the enormous 'readiness for consensus' that existed at the time.[14] Golo Mann, meanwhile, recalled that 'it was the feeling that Hitler was historically right which made a large part of the nation ignore the horrors of the Nazi take-over. . . People were ready for it.'[15] Martin Broszat, yet another historian with first-hand experience of the Nazi take-over, said that it all went so smoothly that it was more like a 're-adjustment' than a revolution.[16]

II

The consolidation of the regime was initially not dependent on what the regime did about social outsiders. The most pressing issue was unemployment. A second, related priority was rearmament and the assertion of Germany's place in Europe. However, creating a racial utopia was never far from Hitler's mind. Prior to the vote on the Enabling Law, his government declaration underlined the first two priorities, but also alluded to creating a 'real community of the people' and to the need for 'the moral purification of the body politic'.[17] Hitler despised the liberal world of the Weimar Republic, and like other Nazi leaders, he scorned lenient judges, reviled convicted criminals, and hated those whom he called 'degenerates' and 'parasites'.[18] He wanted to purify the 'body politic' (*Volkskörper*) and to establish a racially based 'people's community'.

Given the importance Hitler attributed to popular opinion, it is not surprising that he began by singling out individuals and groups already hated or feared. The first and most obvious target was the KPD, and actions against its militants were widely applauded by a nation of property owners. The first concentration camps were opened in March 1933 onwards and hailed in the press as places to send communists. They and other 'enemies of the people' would be kept in the military-style camps until they saw the error of their ways. By the end of the year, most of the camps were already gone and there was talk in the press that the rest would soon be closed. No doubt the camps were meant to have a deterrent effect on those who might contemplate resistance. But more was involved. Localities like Dachau welcomed the establishment of such camps and the jobs that came with them. The town boasted of having such an institution: far from being kept secret, the existence of the early camps was widely and systematically publicized.[19]

The social reception of the images that were projected varied enormously, as one would expect. Certainly between 1933 and the war there were many hundreds of stories, some including pictures, of these camps in the newspapers. The images may have had a terrorizing effect on those who were officially stigmatized. However, it would be naïve to assume that the camps were designed to frighten the nation as a whole. 'Good citizens' were more worried about the communists, and they were also weary of lawlessness and disorder. Many wanted a crackdown. Moreover, the camps were never intended for everybody, and the social identity of anyone who might be sent to them was fairly predictable. The prisoners were going to be social outsiders of one kind or another. The camps were presented as educational institutions that would provide a 'correction and a warning' for communists and those described as 'social rabble'—that is: outsiders like habitual criminals, the chronically unemployed, beggars, alcoholics, homosexuals and repeat sex offenders, all of whom would be rehabilitated by military-like camps and, at least, kept off the streets.[20]

The camps were not initially intended for the Jews. Indeed, the first steps against the Jews were surprisingly timid given the amount of energy the Nazis had devoted to the topic over the years. Like many other policies at the beginning of the regime, antisemitism was tailored to win more support than it might lose. During 1933 and 1934, Hitler's public statements on the Jews were notable by their absence.[21] There were approximately 525,000 Jews in Germany at the beginning of the Third Reich, and while some clearly worried about would happen next, the majority did not panic or try to leave the country immediately.[22]

Nazi hotheads out in the provinces carried out unco-ordinated and often violent attacks against the Jews, kept up unofficial boycotts of businesses and so on. German public opinion rejected such behaviour, however, and, to bring some order to the chaos, Hitler opted for a national boycott.[23] The boycott was called for Saturday 1 April 1933, and it was presented as a 'counter-measure' against the 'atrocity propaganda' allegedly spread by Jews abroad. Hitler gave his blessing, but said the action must avoid taking 'undesired forms'.[24] The Nazis themselves quickly decided the boycott was a propaganda failure because of the public's aversion to such methods, and called it off.[25]

The government followed with more 'legal discrimination'. The Jews as a group were singled out in a law (7 April 1933) which purged Jews and others from the civil service. The 'Law for the Restoration of a Professional Civil Service' had enormous implications.[26] It applied to the entire corps of officials all the way down to the village level, including judges, the police, university professors and school teachers. Millions were affected by the notorious questionnaires that were part of the law, and follow-up investigations guaranteed lots of snooping.[27] The process spread word that official antisemitism was now government policy.

The promulgation of the Nuremberg laws in September 1935 gave Hitler the opportunity to appear as the sovereign statesman, and the excesses against the Jews of the previous months briefly subsided.[28] The 'Law for the Protection of German Blood and German Honour' outlawed new marriages between Jews and non-Jews; forbad extra-marital sexual relations between them; made it illegal for Jews to employ non-Jewish women under 45 as servants; and illegal for Jews to raise the German flag. At the last minute, Hitler considered a broader version of these laws, one that would have applied to more people of 'mixed race' (that is, the offspring of Jews and non-Jews). Under these still harsher laws, tens of thousands more would have been subject to persecution. He backtracked, however, when confronted by the reactions of their 'German relatives' and the public who thought the laws too sweeping in their potential applicability.[29] The 'mixed-race' offspring (of relationships between Jews and non-Jews) would nevertheless be subjected to official and non-official discrimination in the years to come.[30]

The Nazis were cautious enough not to dare dissolve the marriages that already existed between Jews and 'German-blooded' people, as the latter were now called, lest they be seen as questioning the sanctity of marriage. These 'mixed marriages' were allowed to continue, but could dissolve in an instant if spouses were unable to tolerate the considerable pressures that were brought on them to divorce. People such as Victor Klemperer—who lived in a 'mixed marriage'—survived in Dresden because of the courage and sacrifice of his wife. As for the Jews in general, Hitler pushed forward, but he still paid due regard to legal appearances. He said that the Jews should develop their 'own ethnic ways of life'. In fact their status had reverted to that of pre-emancipation days.[31]

Historians have reached different conclusions about how Germans reacted to these laws. Israeli historian David Bankier underlines the agreement between the people and the regime.[32] Otto Dov Kulka, another Israeli, suggests that most Germans were probably pleased to see these laws with the hope they would put an end to lawlessness and violence.[33] Victor Klemperer asked non-Jews he met what they thought and he concluded that 'all go back and forth or have contradictory opinions'.[34] In the mid-1930s and even later, most citizens did not endorse lawless excesses aimed at the Jews.[35] Nevertheless, random violence grew, and the underground socialists compared it to a pogrom in places. If the population did not embrace what happened, the events, as the ever optimistic socialists admitted with regret, 'definitely left an impression'.[36] Almost without interruption from 1935 onwards, the Nazis continued to harass the Jews, but that paled in comparison to the pogrom of November 1938. The socialist observers ended their long report on the events with the chilling phrase, that 'the campaign of annihilation of the German Jews is by all appearances entering its final stage'.[37]

Antisemitism was radicalized throughout 1938, but the great push came in the Autumn. The Nazi leadership was in Munich on 9 November 1938 to celebrate the anniversary of the Beer Hall Putsch of 1923 when news arrived that a minor official in Germany's Paris Embassy had died of wounds inflicted by a young Polish Jew.[38] The results for the Jews were catastrophic. In his report to Göring on the pogrom which ensued, Heydrich stated that 20,000 Jews were arrested, 36 killed and 36 seriously injured, and said that 'most' of their businesses were destroyed and their homes were damaged. Historians have set the final figure of those arrested at closer to 30,000 and the number killed was certainly in excess of 100.[39] Some Jews responded by committing suicide: between 300 and 500 of them took this way.[40] Approximately 10,000 male Jews were sent to the camps at Dachau, Buchenwald and Sachsenhausen; most were released within several weeks.[41] These arrests represented the largest single Gestapo 'action' ever carried out inside Nazi Germany.[42]

It is difficult to generalize about the reactions of the German population who vacillated and whose real opinions, at least if they were negative, could not be freely expressed. Bankier suggests that the anti-Jewish riots may have 'aroused disapproval among many who had hitherto endorsed "moderate antisemitic measures"'.[43] The socialists, in their underground report of February 1939, brought up the comparison with the annihilation of the Armenians carried out by the Turks during the last war. They were sure that 'the overwhelming majority' of the people 'abhorred' the excesses of November and the 'continuous pogrom' since then, but they almost certainly underestimated how far antisemitism had spread.[44] Although many Jews had left Germany since 1933, in the census of May 1939, a total of 213,000 persons remained who were classified as 'religious Jews'. In addition to that were 19,716 'non-religious' Jews and 84,674 who were registered as 'mixed race'.[45] Once the war came in September 1939, the opportunities for many of these people to find asylum all but evaporated, and they would be subjected to increasing harassment and persecution. Nazi policies towards all Jews were radicalized by the war, and the majority of Jews still in Germany would not survive. Policies were also stepped up against those of 'mixed race', but a 'final solution' to this question was repeatedly postponed.

III

Stigmatizing other social outsiders ran along a parallel track and interacted with both antisemitism and other forms of racism. A 'Law for the Prevention of Offspring with Hereditary Diseases' of 14 July 1933, which made possible compulsory sterilization, set the direction of future policy. Initially aimed at those suffering mental and physical problems, such as 'congenital feeblemindedness', schizophrenia, inherited blindness, deafness and epilepsy, this law has been called 'the model for all eugenic legislation' in Nazi Germany.[46] Approximately 400,000 women and men were sterilized in the course of the programme, nearly all against their will.[47] Approximately 5,000 people died as a result of the procedures, most of them women, but invariably the experience had devastating psychological effects. Not only medical, but social criteria were used in the decisions. Undesired behaviour, such as severe alcoholism, or even unruliness, could lead to sterilization. The same could happen to women who changed sexual partners too frequently or had more than one illegitimate child.[48]

Far from being secret, the massive sterilization campaign was played up in the press; there were more than 50,000 public meetings and assemblies to discuss genetic and racial hygiene (*Erb- und Rassenpflege*) before 1939; schools introduced the topic in the curriculum; there were endless books, literally millions of pamphlets and articles; even some films were devoted to the topic.[49] Although the Catholic Church had reservations, it did not act on them, and there were no protests from the Church about sterilizations. It is likely that the idea of a sterilization law was considered acceptable by many. During the Weimar years, the social democrats were ardent followers of eugenics, and had proposed a law to sterilize criminals, backed by the Nazis. The law failed to pass, but it would be a mistake to assume that eugenics was a 'marginal science' only pushed by right-wing fanatics.[50]

The new regime also focused on criminals, the least liked of all social outsiders, and even as it appealed for public support, began to implement its agenda. Heinrich Himmler, eventually head of the German police, as well as Kurt Daluege, in charge of uniformed police (Orpo) and Arthur Nebe of the detective branch (Kripo), argued for 'preventive custody' to nip crime in the bud. A Prussian decree (13 November 1933) and a federal law (24 November 1933) dealt with 'dangerous habitual offenders'. The Prussian decree stated that police could place someone in preventive custody if they committed premeditated crimes or misdemeanours and were sentenced to at least six months in prison on three different occasions. The decree set quotas for the 'preventive police arrest' of criminals known to police in each district, more or less on the pattern by which the Gestapo arrested political opponents.[51] Soon the police could detain those with no convictions at all, if they had grounds for concluding such persons had a 'criminal will' and might endanger security in the future.[52]

After 1 January 1934, anyone deemed a 'dangerous habitual criminal', even after serving their full sentence, might not be released, but kept in 'preventive detention'. To enforce the image of the dictatorship, the public was informed that life behind bars was to be unpleasant. Time in prison was not only punishment for a crime, but was to have an educational effect. The Nazis insisted that stiffer penalties and harder punishments would work as a deterrent, and rushed to proclaim their successes to 'good citizens'.[53]

Himmler stated the obvious in newspaper articles and in speeches: that it was difficult and expensive to keep track of repeat offenders. Like Hitler, he wanted to send anyone who committed three or four crimes to a concentration camp for good.[54] Underlying these views was the conviction that 'the born criminal will be and remain a criminal; but numerous people, in whom a certain inclination towards crime exists, can through proper education still become valuable members of the community of the people.'[55] In time, however, more kinds of offenders and 'deviants' were added to the list of people in the vague category of 'the born criminal'. Kurt Daluege told the public that 'preventive detention' would help police to achieve a society 'in which every racial comrade could also walk through lonely streets in the evening with complete security. He [sic!] ought to be able to leave the windows open without having to worry about a break-in and above all ought to be able to sleep peacefully again with the feeling that we are watching out for him.'[56] Other police officials proclaimed the days were over when 'unaccompanied women had to worry about getting home safely at night'.[57]

The November 1933 law in Germany against 'dangerous habitual offenders' gave judges of the regular courts options such as ordering 'preventive detention', and opened the possibility of courts recommending the compulsory sterilization of 'dangerous moral offenders'. Judges were quick to take advantage of their new powers, and in 1934 they ordered the 'preventive detention' of 3,723 'habitual criminals'. The numbers fell slowly after that—until 1938, when they picked up again.[58] The courts also sent 'offenders' to hospitals and prescribed sterilizations. Between 1934 and 1939, judges alone used their new power to incarcerate 26,346 people (without trials).[59]

The Criminal Police (Kripo) was given the power to order the 'preventive custody' of certain criminals, a power based on the Reichstag Fire Decree of 28 February 1933. There was tension and overlap between the Kripo's right to order 'preventive custody' and the power of courts to hold someone in 'preventive detention'. The Ministry of Justice eventually advised judges to place more people in 'preventive detention', so that they would avoid being outdone by police. In March 1938 the Ministry reminded judges that the law against habitual criminals put a powerful weapon in their hands, and they ought to use it 'relentlessly'.[60]

Martin Broszat rightly notes

> that there was a tendency to solve the problem of criminality in the Third Reich in the last analysis in the same way as in dealing with something like hereditary disease, namely with the radical approach of 'neutralization', 'disposal', or 'eradication'. People accused of a crime were no longer regarded as human beings with legal protections, but simply as parasites against whom it made no sense to open legal proceedings, but who were simply neutralized and eliminated.[61]

Essentially the same approach was taken to the 'Gypsies'. Social prejudice and state policy against the 'Gypsies' went back to well before 1933, and both grew more intense during the Nazi era. The Sinti and Roma were a small minority in Germany, where in 1933 there were an estimated 20,000 of them. Hitler himself said little about these people, so that their persecution in Germany and the murder of so many of them in the Third Reich suggests that the inspiration came from elsewhere.

Sinti and Roma were subjected to official harassment initially because they were stereotyped as an outsider racial group and allegedly prone to criminality, unwilling or unable to hold a regular job or establish a fixed abode, thus constituting a social problem. Local and regional (non-Nazi party) authorities sought to use the new order to solve their own 'Gypsy problem'. The common denominator of many suggestions and/or demands for action from 1933 onwards that originated 'below', from mayors, county councillors, welfare officials, as well as the police and others, was that the Sinti and Roma should be confined to some kind of camp.[62]

The initial police approach was to enforce existing measures more vigorously, and a limited number were sent to concentration camps. Between 1935 and 1939 specific camps were created in cities such as Cologne, Düsseldorf, Essen, Frankfurt, Hamburg, Magdeburg and Berlin. The camps were less severe than concentration camps, but life in them was regimented, and soon barbed wire was added. After 1939 Sinti and Roma were interned in such camps until their deportation to the east.[63] The dictatorship centralized the approach to the 'Gypsy problem', and created a 'Reich Central Headquarters to Combat the Gypsy Pest' under the authority of the Kripo in October 1938 with headquarters in Berlin. Precisely how many were sent to concentration camps in various campaigns of 1938 has not been established, but isolated evidence suggests that police took the opportunity to arrest 'Gypsies' when they had the chance.[64]

The main priority by 1938 with regard to 'Gypsy Research' was to register and supervise them more closely. Himmler issued new guidelines on 8 December under the heading, 'Battle Against the Gypsy Plague', a term that harked back to police usages in pre-Nazi Germany. He called for a national approach that would divide the Gypsies into those of 'mixed race' and 'pure-breeds'. The 'eventual solution of the Gypsy question' would entail dealing with each separately.[65] Until that point none of the Nazi racial researchers had considered Gypsies to be a 'race', so that the new guidelines sent a new signal with predictable consequences.[66]

The dictatorship wanted to register all members of this minority and establish their 'racial background'. Kripo headquarters in Berlin—and specifically its new special branch that dealt with Gypsies—was put in charge. The Kripo's 'preventive campaign against crime' led to the confinement of many German and Austrian 'asocial Gypsies'. Local police were ordered to report anyone 'who by their appearance, their morals and habits can be regarded as Gypsies or Gypsies of mixed race, including also others who travel about like Gypsies'. The more numerous Sinti, the smaller number of Roma, and other related groups like the Lalleri in the incorporated areas were registered, and by 1 March 1939 most were forced to undergo racial-biological examinations. In a sign of things to come the Kripo was told in early July that, in the event of war mobilization, 'Gypsies' with no fixed abode were to be sent to a concentration camp, along with the vague category of social outsiders termed 'those considered unworthy of serving in the armed forces'.[67]

IV

The 'asocials' were a loosely defined group that was much discussed in welfare and police circles well before the Nazi era. The concept might be used to describe anyone who did not participate as a good citizen and accept their social responsibilities, but was also used to talk about criminals, sex offenders and others. The Nazis wanted to rid society of all those whose way of life did not conform to the new ideals, nor accord with what the Nazis called 'wholesome popular sentiment'.[68] In a more general sense, the Nazis claimed to be offended by life on the wrong side of the tracks, and in 1933 made noises about chasing away street prostitutes, pimps and abortionists. They threatened anyone who would not take up a regular job, and various authorities harrassed 'Gypsies', the 'work-shy', and tramps (in the instructive phrase from a local ordinance) for 'bothering the population'.[69] By mid-September 1933, the Nazis ordered a nationwide round-up to end what they called the 'plague of the beggars' in the streets. Citizens were asked to co-operate by holding back their funds for proper charities, and reminded that Germany was too poor to afford 'full-time beggars, work-shy, drinkers, and fraud artists'.[70] Supposedly, the round-up would also prevent crime, in that it would eliminate the environment that bred deviance.

Himmler ordered numerous other arrest 'sweeps', such as one that began less than a year after his appointment as Chief of the German Police. Early in 1937 the Kripo was told to prepare lists of 'professional and habitual criminals'. A second note explained that in spite of the reduction of crime, certain criminals remained whose deeds indicated an 'asocial' attitude, and even opposition to the state.[71] Himmler ordered a 'special action' for 9 March 1937 to arrest 2,000 people out of work. The instruction was to send to concentration camps those who '*in the opinion of the Criminal Police*' (emphasis in the original) were professional criminals, repeat offenders, or habitual sex offenders.[72] The enthusiasm of the police was such that they arrested not 2,000, but 2,752 people, only 171 of whom had broken their probation. Police used the event as a pretext to get rid of 'problem cases'. Those arrested were described as break-in specialists (938), thieves (741), sex offenders (495), swindlers (436), robbers (56) and dealers in stolen goods (86). Only eighty-five of them were women. Some Jews were arrested, but the precise number is not known. By the end of the year, only 372 had been released while sixty-eight had died in custody.[73] None were to be released unless there was a genuine prospect they would take up work and keep their job.[74]

Given that the 1937 'action' was carried out by police without any reference to the courts, it constituted another step in the rise of the police at the expense of the rule of law. Authorization for the 'special action' was issued through the Ministry of the Interior without it even being discussed with the Ministry of Justice, whose officials—like other citizens—learned about it a month later in the newspapers.[75]

On 14 December 1937 the Ministry of the Interior issued a 'fundamental decree on the preventive police battle against criminality'. The recent reorganization of the Kripo, it said, made it important to unify preventive arrest practices. The decree was based on the Reichstag Fire Decree that justified the creation of the Gestapo, and permitted the Kripo to deal with criminals to protect the community 'from all parasites'. Two approaches were prescribed. The most radical referred to the arrest of those who, because of their police records, were defined as 'professional or habitual criminals'.[76] At the discretion of the police, such persons could be placed in 'preventive custody'; that mandate could also be extended to the vague category of the 'asocials'. The second approach available was 'police-ordered planned supervision', which made it possible for the Kripo to keep ex-prisoners under surveillance, and entailed much more than simple parole. Nazi police were given complete control over the everyday lives of released prisoners, and, for an indefinite period, could impose twenty different restrictions on them. They could determine place of residence and leisure activities, forbid alcohol consumption, certain social company, and visits to a wide assortment of public places. Ex-prisoners could be kept under house arrest, not allowed to drive, own pets or any weapons. Kripo headquarters wanted to be certain that the police, and not the courts, made the final decision about whether 'dangerous habitual criminals' were released after they served their time and lived up to their probation.[77]

By early 1938 the Kripo moved towards complete independence from the courts, claiming that in so far as they dealt preventively with 'criminal enemies of state' they could claim to be carrying out the mandate of the Führer, and needed no court authorization. The German public was informed about the nature and extent of these new powers, although specific police 'actions' that followed were not publicized.[78] The Kripo even tried to get their hands on asocials with prior convictions who were sitting in regular prisons, to have them sent to concentration camps, instead of their being released when their prison term was up.[79] There was no place for 'loose people' with 'no fixed abode' in the Third Reich.[80]

Himmler's instructions to the Kripo on 4 April 1938 defined the 'asocials' as those 'who demonstrate through behaviour inimical to the community, but not necessarily criminal, that they will not adapt themselves to the community'. The list of the 'asocials' who fitted this vague definition included anyone

> who through minor, but oft-repeated, infractions of the law demonstrate that they will not comply with the social order that is a fundamental condition of a National Socialist state, e.g. beggars, vagrants (Gypsies), prostitutes, drunkards, those with contagious diseases, particularly sexually transmitted diseases, who evade the measures taken by the public health authorities.

Also considered asocial were 'persons, regardless of any previous conviction, who evade the obligation to work and are dependent on the public for their maintenance (e.g. the work-shy, work evaders, drunkards)'. The Kripo was empowered to arrest anyone who fell into these broad categories, and selectively was doing so already. To protect citizens and their property, the Kripo was given still 'greater freedom of action' to deal with all 'lawbreakers and all asocial persons'. The Kripo could extend planned surveillance or order preventive custody, which was defined as the 'sharpest method' against criminals and asocials. 'In the first instance' the decree was aimed at people with no fixed abode. At the discretion of the police, such people could be sent to a concentration camp.[81]

At the same time that the Nazi police, especially the Kripo, claimed new powers, they hatched plans for further 'actions'. On 26 January 1938 Himmler informed the Kripo and Gestapo of his wish for a nation-wide sweep against the 'work-shy', who were more difficult to catch than other problem cases. His definition of 'work-shy' was males medically fit to work, but who (without good reason) refused jobs on two occasions, or left after a short time. He contended that if word leaked out about a police action, such people would find a job, but with no real intention of reforming. Therefore, 'to attain a complete removal' of these elements, Himmler called for a 'one-time, comprehensive and surprise attack'.[82]

Himmler put the Gestapo in charge of the first 'asocial action', which was set for early March 1938 but carried out only at the end of April. The Gestapo were not to define the concept of asocial too narrowly. Those arrested were to be kept in 'protective custody', held for two to three weeks in local police prisons, then sent to Buchenwald for a minimum of three months. Because the Gestapo had few files on the 'work-shy', Himmler

asked labour exchanges, state and Nazi welfare offices to provide information. A recent estimate puts the number arrested at around 2,000, all
of whom were sent to Buchenwald.[83]

On 1 June 1938 the Kripo was told to arrest a minimum of 200 unemployed asocials in each police district. Between 13 and 18 June 1938 they
arrested 'asocials' that included tramps, beggars, Gypsies, and pimps.
Anyone who used hostels was investigated to see if they might be 'work-
shy', and such checks continued later.[84] The Kripo threw themselves into
the task and exceeded orders. To judge by statistics mentioned by a
member of Himmler's personal staff, the Kripo seized more than 8,000
people and sent them to concentration camps. At the beginning of 1939,
'well over 10,000' of those taken into custody were still in the camps.[85]
Contrary to orders, the Kripo even arrested men who were no longer
'work-shy' at all, but gainfully employed.[86]

Another ideological justification for arresting the 'work-shy' and
assorted asocials, and forcing them to work, was that it fitted the mandate
of the police, often mentioned in the press, to cleanse the body politic by
eradicating all criminals. Beyond that, the aim of the police was to discipline and punish anyone who did not fit the image of the hard-working
citizen and committed racial comrade. Some mayors got into the spirit
and asked the Kripo to arrest well-known drinkers as 'asocials', in order
to get rid of them; the mayors were told this was the job of welfare organizations, not the police.[87]

Economic considerations also played a role in the large number of
arrests in 1938, when Germany was preparing for war and suffering a
labour shortage. Once social misfits were sent to concentration camps,
often referred to in official directives as work camps, their labour could
be put to use. While in detention, they were exploited to finance the
burgeoning SS empire.[88]

Any persons found to be 'work-shy' during the war, at least if they had
a previous conviction, were sent to a concentration camp.[89] Even before
the war, however, concentration camps increasingly confined social
outsiders. To take Buchenwald as an example: by the end of October 1938
its 10,188 prisoners included 1,007 'professional criminals' and 4,341
picked up as 'asocials'. Together they constituted over half the camp
population and outnumbered those held under the Gestapo's 'protective
custody' orders (3,982). Even the Gestapo arrested many kinds of
'offenders', including 'asocials', so it is unlikely that all the Gestapo prisoners in the camp were 'politicals'.[90]

Buchenwald, therefore, incarcerated as many or more social outsiders
as it did communists. The same is true of Sachsenhausen. The total camp
population between June 1938 and September 1939 fluctuated between
a low of just under 6,000 to a high of around 9,000. The main exception

was December 1938 when the number of prisoners was reported at 12,622, which included many Jews sent there as part of the November pogrom.[91] The figures show that more than half the prisoners at any one time in this period were 'asocials'. No complete figures have survived for all of Germany of those who were held in preventive detention in subsequent 'actions'. A partial reconstruction shows that there were 12,921 at the end of 1938; 12,221 at the end of 1939; and 13,354 at the end of 1940.[92]

V

A racist regime inevitably devotes an enormous amount of its resources to regulating sex. In the first instance, the 'wrong' kind of sex had to be hindered. Hitler and the Nazis were particularly keen to outlaw sexual relations between Jews, other race 'enemies', and Germans. The eugenic basis of the Third Reich virtually guaranteed that considerable efforts would be made to deal with prostitution, for Hitler long regarded it and the associated diseases as typical symptoms of decay and degeneration. One of the first steps the new regime took was to issue orders for police to use measures on the books (such as laws on spreading venereal diseases) to eliminate street prostitution, to take control of brothels and to charge prostitutes if and when they publicly offered their services in a conspicuous way.[93] Local police enforcement of these measures varied greatly, but there were round-ups in many cities during 1933, and thousands of arrests in some places.[94] The full extent of prostitution remains hidden, because much of it was carried out on an 'occasional' basis to supplement incomes.[95] Not only the police, but health, welfare and youth officials became involved in the campaign to deal with this group of 'asocials'. One trend was to seek the sterilization of repeat offenders.[96] In 1933, the Health Offices in Germany had 20,000 women on their books accused of 'frequently changing their sexual partners'. The war complicated the official stance on prostitution, which henceforth varied between wishing to stamp out prostitution altogether and tolerating or even creating better-controlled brothels.

Homosexuals were also regarded as threats to the body politic by Hitler and many Nazi leaders, and those sentiments were not unpopular in Germany at the time. Although lesbianism also offended what the Nazis called 'wholesome popular sentiment', there was no systematic campaign, partly because lesbianism was not regarded as a serious 'danger to the nation's survival'.[97] Hitler apparently believed, even before 1914, that homosexuality should be fought 'by any means possible', and he said he turned 'against this and other sexual perversions in the big city [Vienna] with nausea and disgust'.[98] Beginning in 1933 the police stepped up enforcement of laws (on the books since the nineteenth century) that criminalized homosexuality. The Nazi police also outlawed trashy publications and pornography. Local police created special branches to arrest traders in obscene literature or pictures.

At the end of October 1934 a special branch to fight homosexuality was created at Gestapo headquarters in Berlin to co-ordinate activities against gay men. On 28 June 1935 the regime sharpened the criminal code.[99] Himmler encouraged Gestapo and Kripo to participate, and in 1936 a new 'Reich Central Office for Combating of Homosexuality and Abortion' was created to register all homosexuals investigated by police. The persecution of homosexuals was reflected in court verdicts on men convicted for breaking the provisions of the criminal code. In 1933, there was a small increase in the number of gay men who were convicted in comparison to the last Weimar years (853 convictions, up from 801 in 1932). Arrests rose in each of the following years as follows: 1934 (948); 1935 (2,106); 1936 (5,320); 1937 (8,271); 1938 (8,562). Amnesties had the effect of underestimating the extent of all crimes, and the one at the beginning of the war reduced convictions for 1939—which fell to 7,614.[100]

It was a particularly fearful time for homosexuals, since the Nazis criminalized mere expressions of sexual interest, not just consummated homosexual acts, and thus opened the door for denunciations from the public. The motivation behind these denunciations, in so far as they can be identified at all, varied from gestures of support for official policies on homosexuality, to the desire to take personal advantage of the situation.[101]

The Kripo also dealt with homosexuality, and because of competition with the Gestapo, officials working for both seemed to double their efforts. In the years after 1935, the Kripo arrested large numbers of gays. For example, between April and December 1936, the Kripo alone investigated 6,260 men on suspicion of homosexual activities, and in the same period a year later, the number rose to 12,356. In order to appreciate the fear behind the statistics, we have to recall that Germany had a system of 'police justice', and any brush with the police could have disastrous consequences because there was no guarantee of even an appearance before a judge.

Kripo investigations show an upward trend until statistics stopped in the early war period. Some of the increase resulted because the Gestapo vacated the territory of harassing the homosexuals and the Kripo filled the vacuum. Kripo enforcement methods, like those of the Gestapo, ranged from entrapment to planting evidence. If the accused also happened to be Jewish and/or was considered objectionable for other reasons, then persecution might not relent until the man was sent to a concentration camp and hounded to death.[102]

There remained an important difference between the police persecution of homosexuals (and most criminals), and what happened to 'race
enemies' like the Jews. When it came to homosexuals, as well as most
others deemed criminals, the object was not so much their physical annihilation, but instead, as far as possible, to rehabilitate and re-educate
them.[103] In principle, nothing could rescue Jews. Nevertheless, many gays
ended up in a concentration camp, and a shockingly high number, estimated at somewhere between 5,000 and 15,000, died there.[104]

VI

The persecution of this wide array of social outsiders played a significant
part in the consolidation of Hitler's dictatorship, and has to be seen in the
context of the regime's larger 'accomplishments' during the peacetime
years. Solving unemployment and securing one victory after the next on
the foreign policy front paid great dividends and helped to foster social
consensus. No doubt there were die-hard opponents who hated the Third
Reich from beginning to end. By 1939 and certainly after the victory over
France in 1940, these opponents were reduced to a small minority swimming against a tide of adulation for Hitler.

In 1933 the Nazis did not find a country dominated by antisemitism,
but as Christopher Browning and others have concluded, down to 1939
the regime convinced more people that there was a 'Jewish question'. By
that time 'most Germans' had come to the conclusion that it would be best
to limit or end 'the role of Jews in German society' and for Jews to leave
the country.[105] Thus turning Jews into social outsiders did not hurt the
dictatorship, but won many over to Nazi racism. This does not mean that
the majority of Germans wanted the physical destruction of the Jews.
Rather, it suggests that the regime was well on the way to helping Germans
to exclude Jews from their moral universe.

The persecution of other social outsiders contributed more directly to
the consolidation of the dictatorship. Detlev Peukert concludes that the
German population generally agreed with the more radical approach
taken to all crime.[106] Jeremy Noakes goes further and suggests that 'a
crucial element in popular consent to the regime was the fact that Nazism
embodied, albeit in an extreme form, many of the basic attitudes of a very
large section of the German population.'[107] We can endorse Jeremy
Noakes's broader point that many people

> also approved of the regime's hostility towards unpopular minori-
> ties, not just the Jews but also Gypsies, and of its harsh attitudes
> towards deviant groups—homosexuals, tramps, habitual crimi-

nals, the so-called asocials and the work-shy. They welcomed the
fact that such people were now being locked up in concentration
camps, just as they welcomed the strict line being taken towards
youth. . . In short, the regime confirmed and enforced the values
and prejudices of a substantial section of the population, giving
them official status as 'sound popular feelings'.[108]

Hans-Ulrich Wehler underlines how the effort to create the 'people's
community' found such positive social resonance. He adds that 'it was not
only a skilfully manipulated plebiscitary acclamation, let alone the violence
of terror, that brought the dictatorship so much applause. The agreement
of supporters resulted far more from positive, freedom-affirming, life
experiences that expressed themselves in an utterly serious proclamation
of will.'[109] This point is well illustrated by Alison Owings's fascinating oral
history of the Third Reich. The women she interviewed retain to this day
their remarkably positive attitudes and recall fondly how 'law and order'
was restored, how women could walk in the streets at night without fear.
The interviews, conducted over fifty years after the end of Hitler and the
Third Reich, also make clear that Nazi ideology, including antisemitism,
had made considerable inroads into their ways of thinking.[110]
  The terror inside Germany fell disproportionately on social outsiders
in a quantitative and qualitative sense. This category of people was expan-
sive, as is shown by the consideration given to a law that circulated in the
war years on what were called 'aliens of the community'.[111] Nevertheless,
social outsiders would always remain a minority. For the rest of the
Volksgenossen—members in the 'people's community' and racially fit—
terror was mostly what happened to 'others'. Thus the terror was not
random, but largely predictable. One could read plenty about its many
sides in the press, but it would be seriously mistaken to conclude that the
nation as a whole was supposed to be scared or 'deterred' by media stories
about crime and punishment and the concentration camps. There is no
doubt that some worried about what was happening, and perhaps most
would have preferred a crackdown on 'law and order' that did not ignore
the rule of law. Nevertheless, few good citizens really wanted to look too
closely, particularly at what went on inside prisons or other such institutions. During the war, the harshest sides of the terror—from the actions
of Gestapo, to the growing number of death sentences handed down by
the People's Court—fell on the millions of foreigners brought to the
country. Of the hundreds of thousands who suffered and died in the
concentration camps, or other kinds of punishment camps, most were
non-Germans.
  We cannot, of course, overlook the many completely innocent citizens
who suffered at the hands of Hitler's dictatorship, and we have to consider

that there were numerous structural obstacles that hindered resistance. I have discussed that side of the story on many occasions. Amongst other things, many volunteer denouncers came forward to inform the authorities. It was not necessary for Germany to become a 'nation of denouncers'. On the contrary, all that was needed was for a small, active minority to participate by acting as the proverbial 'eyes and ears' of the police. They helped to narrow the social space in which resistance might have formed. However, the greatest obstacle to resistance was Hitler's undoubted popularity and the not inconsiderable support for so much of the theory and practice of National Socialism.[112]

This essay has shown on a case-by-case basis how social outsiders were identified, ostracized, and even eliminated. It has suggested the extent to which many ordinary people seemed to agree with these actions, were won over positively by them, and supported them in numerous ways. Some people never accepted what was happening, and with inner courage persisted in firm convictions. Others left the country. For all that, many who lived through the period were positively impressed—not just by the festivals, the promises of the future, and the intoxicating display—but precisely by the ruthless efforts to crack down on social outsiders. What they did not like, they overlooked, shrugged their shoulders at, or blamed on the 'little Hitlers'. It is fair to conclude that the consolidation of the dictatorship was immensely facilitated by the Draconian approaches taken to social outsiders. The silent and not-so-silent majority backed the regime and a large number of people, including the great majority in the professions and in the educated elite, were very enthusiastic. To draw any other conclusion would be to deny the massive evidence we have.

5

'Soldiers of the Home Front'

Jurists and Legal Terror during the Second World War

Nikolaus Wachsmann

The SS and the police dominate our picture of Nazi terror. Led by Hitler's right-hand man Heinrich Himmler, they stood at the centre of the Third Reich during the Second World War. All key aspects of terror—arrest, interrogation, imprisonment, deportation and murder—involved the police or the SS, and research into these two related agencies has been indispensable for our knowledge of the Nazi dictatorship. However, the spotlight on the police and SS apparatus (evident in terms such as 'SS State' or 'Police State') has resulted in something of a blind spot regarding other agencies involved in Nazi repression. As far as the Holocaust is concerned, for example, recent research has highlighted the involvement of the *Wehrmacht* and the civil administration in occupied Eastern Europe. And, looking at punishment, one of the most important agencies was the regular legal apparatus, which existed side-by-side with the police and SS. In Hitler's Germany, the police were not alone in persecuting those who had fallen foul of Nazi ideology—judges also punished alleged offenders. And SS concentration camps were not the only site of mass incarceration—regular prisons locked up those convicted by the courts. But there is relatively little awareness, both in the academic literature and in public memory, of the part played by the legal apparatus in Nazi terror. A few studies aside, not much is known outside the small and insular world of legal history about law and order in the Third Reich. Nazi legal terror has been widely neglected.[1]

In many ways, this lack of interest is rather surprising. For even cursory examination shows that the legal system was an integral part of Nazi repression, at least inside Germany. If one looks at the war years, the rise of legal terror is nowhere more obvious than in the application of the death penalty. Capital punishment had expanded in Germany as soon as the

Nazis came to power. After the virtual abolition of executions in the last years of the Weimar Republic, the executioners were soon back at work. Between 1933 and 1938, an average of almost ninety men and women were executed each year, following a judicial death sentence. But this was nothing compared to the war years, when an ever-growing list of offences was made punishable by death - no less than forty-six by 1943–44. Judges unleashed a murderous fury. When the war finally came to an end in 1945, they had passed around 16,000 death sentences. Of course, there was much more to legal terror than capital punishment. As more and more individuals were dragged before the courts, the prison population grew rapidly in size. Inmate numbers almost doubled during the war, from 108,685 on 30 June 1939 to 196,700 five years later. For the first three years of the war, state prisons held more inmates than the SS concentration camps. Tens of thousands of prison inmates died before they had served their sentences. Clearly, Nazi legal terror cannot be ignored.[2]

A comprehensive history of law and terror in the Third Reich remains to be written. This essay aims to give a few pointers in that direction, sketching the development during the Second World War by looking at sentencing, imprisonment and the relationship between legal authorities and the regime. Did the legal apparatus undergo a steady radicalization or were there different stages of escalation? In answering this question, it is crucial to investigate the targets of legal terror. The focus will be on two groups in particular, 'racial aliens' and 'ordinary' Germans. Historical scholarship in recent years has rightly placed racism at the very core of the Third Reich. However, little work has been done on the contribution of the legal apparatus. As we shall see, the courts and prisons under the authority of the Ministry of Justice in Berlin were very much involved in transforming Germany into a 'racial state'.[3] As for 'ordinary' Germans (that is, those normally regarded by the authorities as part of the 'people's community'), the latest research on Nazi terror has stressed that they were only really hit towards the very end of the war. Given that this research predominantly deals with the actions of the police, it is important to evaluate whether the same conclusion also holds true for legal terror.[4]

I

Right from the start of the Second World War, legal officials wanted to contribute to a German victory. Most of the administrators, judges, prosecutors and prison officials were not long-standing Nazi fanatics; while they sympathised with the aims of the Nazi state, there were relatively few 'old fighters' among them. But this made them no less determined to win the war than the Nazi leadership. Many officials, from the national-

conservative Minister of Justice Franz Gürtner down to local judges, saw
this as the opportunity to avenge the 'national humiliation' of 1918, the
defeat in the First World War which a large number of them had experienced first-hand as soldiers. They believed in the myth that the defeat had
been caused by the collapse of the home front, which had allowed revolutionaries to betray the German army. Legal officials, just like the Nazi
leaders, were determined that there would never be another 'stab in the
back'. The Second World War was not yet two weeks old when the
Ministry of Justice announced that judges should now act as 'soldiers of
the home front'.[5]

To ensure that the courts would fulfil this mission, judges were given
many new weapons. The first months after the outbreak of war saw an
avalanche of new decrees, with further measures following in 1940 and
1941, laying the foundation for brutal wartime terror. The new legislation
allowed for the harsher punishment of a wide variety of non-conformist
behaviour, ranging from property crime and contacts with POWs to criticism of the regime. What was particularly striking about this legislation,
apart from its vast scope, was its vagueness, with judges encouraged to
punish defendants they regarded as 'national pests', or to crack down on
behaviour that offended 'healthy popular feelings'.[6] Such loose terminology had already spread through legal regulations before 1939, but the
extent of arbitrariness now entered a new dimension. There can be little
doubt that this was a deliberate strategy by the men at the top of the Nazi
state. Firstly, they knew that vague terminology was likely to result in more
radical sentencing, with individual judges eager to surpass each other in
the harsh interpretation of the law. Second, the use of loose terminology
had a deterrent function, as members of the public could not always be
sure which actions, exactly, would be labelled as deviant by the authorities. As a result, many tried to make sure that they were seen to toe the
party line, in order to minimize the risk of persecution.

German courts made ample use of their new powers, and punishment
did become harder in the first phase of the war, between September 1939
and the end of 1941. This is evident in the sharp rise of death penalties
passed by the courts inside Germany, up from 85 (1938) to 1,292 (1941).
Courts also resorted more frequently to lengthy sentences of imprisonment, with the total number of prison inmates reaching 144,142 by 30
June 1941. In part, this rise in legal terror was linked to the growing
involvement of courts only recently set up in the Third Reich. In addition
to the existing regional and local courts, so-called special courts had operated since 1933 in each of the then 26 judicial districts. Initially, they had
mostly focused on punishing dissent against the Nazi regime. But, from
the late 1930s, the special courts greatly extended their scope, and many
more defendants ended up in front of them. The number of sentences by

the Hamburg special court, for example, rose from 203 (1937) to 382 (1941). For the defendants, the greater involvement of the special courts often meant harsher sentences, not least because their rights were much reduced compared to other civilian courts.[7] The same was true for those defendants unlucky to be tried by the People's Court in Berlin, the most feared of all the German courts. Set up in 1934 to deal with political cases regarded as particularly serious, this court was staffed with handpicked professional judges as well as lay judges loyal to the regime. The People's Court, too, extended its reach in the war years, sentencing more defendants and punishing them more severely than before.[8]

The rise in legal terror did not hit all those living under Nazi rule in the same way. Punishment was selective. German defendants continued to make up the majority of those taken before the courts and held inside prisons. But it was not 'ordinary' Germans who bore the brunt of legal punishment. Rather, particularly harsh sanctions were reserved for those groups of German defendants who had already been singled out before 1939. This included, for example, members of different resistance movements, above all on the political Left. Most important, arguably, was the escalation of legal terror against so-called 'habitual criminals'. As soon as the Nazis had come to power, harsher penalties had been introduced against multiple recidivists, many of whom were small-time petty criminals—bicycle thieves and shoplifters, for example—written off by criminologists as 'incorrigible'. Punishment of these offenders became even harsher in the early war years. Rather than sending 'incorrigible' criminals to lengthy imprisonment, some were now sentenced to death, on the basis of the new wartime legislation. Those serving prison sentences were also worse off. In 1933, the regime had introduced indefinite judicial confinement for 'dangerous habitual criminals'. Until the late 1930s, these inmates still had a chance to be released, but this now became virtually impossible. The inmates were stuck inside prisons, suffering from poor conditions and hard labour.[9]

Above all, legal terror in the early war years focused on foreigners who had recently come under the German justice system. Many of them were accused of political resistance against the Nazi occupation. For example, judges were involved in the suppression of the Czech population, which was subjected by Germany between September 1938 and March 1939. The focus was on opposition in the so-called Protectorate, where the vast majority of Czechs lived. Here, resistance had started early, involving larger nationalist and communist groups, as well as clandestine local organizations. The German authorities uncovered many activists, and generally those who ended up in front of judges were strictly punished. Defendants accused of high treason were not tried in the Protectorate itself, but dragged before the People's Court in Berlin. In 1940, some 579

Czechs were sentenced here—more than half of all the defendants before the People's Court in that year. The number would have been higher still had the Nazi regime not decided to temporarily halt larger trials against the Czech resistance—a tactical move, aimed at pacifying the opposition. The same consideration influenced sentencing, with the judges at the People's Court passing no death sentences against the Czech resistance in the first two years of the war. All this changed once Himmler's lieutenant Reinhard Heydrich was appointed as Deputy Reich Protector in September 1941. There followed a dramatic escalation of Nazi terror against the population in the Protectorate, which also involved the legal authorities. The number of Czechs before the People's Court increased further and, crucially, the judges now frequently sentenced them to death, contributing to a sharp rise in capital punishment: by November 1941, well over 20 per cent of cases brought before the People's Court ended with a death sentence. Numbers were soon to rise further.[10]

It was Polish citizens who made up the largest group of foreign defendants before German courts. True, most of the terror against the Polish population was in the hands of the police. Already in the first months following the German invasion on 1 September 1939, police officials executed several tens of thousands of Poles, including Jews, aristocrats, priests and intellectuals.[11] But courts also cracked down on the population in the Polish territory annexed by Germany. Just as with Czech defendants, many Poles were labelled as serious political threats. Judges and prosecutors could construe even the most harmless remark as a terrorist attack. However, the terror against Poles cannot be reduced to political motives alone: legal repression was also driven by a virulent racism, which lay at the heart of Nazi occupation policy in Eastern Europe, bent on German domination through ethnic cleansing. Of course, enforcing racial discrimination was not a new experience for German jurists: with antisemitism becoming state policy after the Nazi 'seizure of power', judges became key players in the campaign against German Jews. In the case of Jews, inequality before the courts—be it in employment law, property law, family law or criminal law—had become the norm in the minds of many judges. From late 1939, this principle of legal discrimination was applied to Poles as well, even if it meant bending or breaking the letter of the law.[12]

The judicial authorities were so keen to contribute to the 'ethnic struggle' in Poland that special courts were set up in the conquered territory even before the campaign itself was over. Among the first was the special court in Bromberg. Judges had arrived just days after the city had been occupied, passing their first death sentences on 11 September 1939. In the following months, the Bromberg court established itself as the most bloody special court in the whole of annexed Poland. The reason behind the ruthlessness of the Bromberg judges can be found in events that had taken place in the first days of the war with Poland. In the brief period between the German attack and the occupation of the city, there had been fights between local Poles and ethnic Germans in the area, which had left around 700 Germans in and around Bromberg dead. The Nazi authorities were determined to exploit these incidents to whip up anti-Polish sentiment, grossly exaggerating the 'September crimes'. The Bromberg special court played an important part in this propaganda campaign, with trials supposed to highlight the 'underlying pathology in the Polish racial character', as the State Secretary for Justice Roland Freisler put it. The officials showed little concern for procedural rules or legal norms. The fact that many of the accused had not actually killed anybody did not stop the judges from passing the death penalty for murder. Starting from a position of collective guilt of the local Polish population, the judges saw even the singing of patriotic songs as sufficient to convict defendants as 'accomplices'. In their haste to execute the condemned, the jurists broke further conventions. State Secretary Freisler, a committed National Socialist, ordered that the Bromberg officials could go ahead even without the customary confirmation of death sentences from the Ministry of Justice. The condemned were simply lined up inside the local jail and shot.[13]

In terms of its sentencing policy, the Bromberg special court was an extreme case. Other courts in annexed Poland operated in a less lethal fashion. However, they, too, brutally discriminated against Poles. This was true, above all, for the other newly established special courts. Top legal officials encouraged the pervasive racial abuse of Polish defendants. The President of the Higher State Court in Posen advised the Ministry of Justice in July 1940 that only judges who 'possess the harshness indispensable for the ethnic struggle' should be allowed to operate permanently in the East. Individual local judges were commended for their 'utmost severity against the Polish offender'.[14] Nowhere else were German judges as ready to resort to the death penalty as in annexed Poland. Despite the relatively small size of the territory, judges handed down a great proportion of all death sentences passed by German courts. In the last four months of 1939, the special courts in annexed Poland passed some 156 death penalties (including one hundred by the Bromberg court alone)—almost as many the 173 death sentences passed by courts inside the old German borders in all of 1939.[15] The use of the death penalty became even more pervasive in the following years. But the punishment of choice of German courts was the prison sentence and prisons in annexed Poland were soon bursting with inmates. By the end of June 1941, no less than 21,373 prisoners were held here—a very large figure accounting for most of the rise in prisoner numbers in the first years of the war.

Racial discrimination against Polish defendants did not stop at the pre-war German border. Poles inside the old German territory were also singled out. During the war, the Nazi regime increasingly relied on foreign workers to keep the economy going and Poles made up a large proportion of these workers, who were brutally exploited. Infractions of the various rules designed to ensure their submission and inferiority—regulating everything from work duties to the relationship with the German population—were harshly punished, both by the police and by the courts. This was one of the key reasons behind the general rise of legal terror inside the old German borders, evident in the slow increase of prisoner numbers. In some areas, by 1940 Poles already made up a significant proportion of the local prisoner population.[16]

But there were still some limits to racial legal terror in these early years of the war. Not all prosecutors, judges and prison officials used the law as a weapon of racial warfare. Some judges made no distinction between German and Polish defendants. Others, lacking clear instructions from above, were unsure how far they could or should go in the racial application of the law. Any resulting 'lenient' judgements often provoked criticism by the police and SS authorities, complaining that the legal authorities were failing in their duties in the 'ethnic struggle'. Of course, there was more to such criticism than meets the eye. The police and SS not only wanted to enforce Nazi ideology, they also had another motive: the justification of the extension of their own repressive powers at the expense of the legal apparatus, by interfering with court judgements or failing to hand over offenders to the legal authorities. In order to counter complaints and disruptions by the police and SS, the Ministry of Justice in turn pushed for a further escalation of legal terror. If only the treatment of Poles was severe enough, the officials thought, any outside criticism would be silenced. But directing sentencing from above proved difficult. Given that judges were nominally independent, the leading civil servants largely restricted themselves to 'steering' judges and prosecutors, by criticizing 'lenient' officials and reminding them to show no mercy to Polish offenders—especially those accused of supposedly serious offences.[17]

Summing up, Nazi legal terror intensified in the early war years. Above all, this was a result of the repression of foreigners, driven in particular by racial policy. Poles, for example, were far more likely than Germans to be sentenced to death. As far as 'ordinary' Germans were concerned, they were not yet in much greater danger than prior to the outbreak of war. Given the rather buoyant popular mood following the swift victories of the German army in 1939 and 1940, the authorities clearly felt that the home front was pretty stable and saw little need to step up repression across the board. To be sure, there were some harsh sentences, primarily aimed at deterrence. But, more often, 'national comrades' escaped harsh sanctions, even if they broke the law. This is obvious in the application of the new wartime legislation. For example, listening to enemy radio broadcasts had been strictly outlawed almost as soon as war broke out. The ban was widely disregarded: contemporary documents and post-war memoirs show that many Germans—including party members—secretly listened to the BBC and other foreign stations. The authorities were well aware of this and did little about it, at least in the early war years. Comparatively few Germans were arrested and taken before the courts. Punishing Germans for such transgressions was apparently not high up on the list of priorities of the authorities, as long as public morale and belief in the Führer remained high.[18] Only when this changed, as the war turned against Germany, did legal terror turn more sharply against 'national comrades' as well.

II

In 1942, Nazi legal terror entered a new phase. Once more, the death penalty is a clear indicator of this development, as the number of defendants guillotined, hanged or shot reached new heights. In the space of only one year, the total number of death sentences jumped from 1,292 (1941) to 4,457 (1942). Still, most of the accused escaped the death penalty. With the exception of the People's Court, German courts continued to hand down far more sentences of imprisonment. This led to a further increase in prisoner numbers, reaching over 180,000 by the summer of 1942, with inmates facing rapidly deteriorating conditions. Forced labour was hard and rations were minimal, while overcrowding, illness and abuse were rampant. For many thousands of inmates, a prison sentence quickly turned into a death sentence.

Looking more closely at the general shift in legal terror, it becomes clear that it occurred around spring 1942. In May 1942, the People's Court for the first time applied the death penalty to more than 40 per cent of all cases—more than double the proportion in the previous month.[19] Other courts saw a similar escalation in the spring of 1942. In all, German courts passed around three times as many death sentences in June/July 1942 than in January/February of the same year. This trend towards stricter punishment is also evident inside prisons: in only three months, between late March and late June 1942, prisoner numbers inside the old German borders increased by over 7 per cent—a rise not seen since 1933.

How can we account for this intensification of legal terror in the spring of 1942? Broader developments in the Nazi state clearly played their part. This period saw a further escalation of murderous racial madness, with the co-ordination and extension of the Holocaust. At the same time, the public mood inside Germany deteriorated from late 1941 onwards. The general optimism of the early war years started to give way to uncertainty and doubts. The failure of the Blitzkrieg in the Soviet Union, the US entry into the war, Allied bombing of German cities and falling living standards—all this brought home to the German people that the war would not be as swift and relatively painless (for them) as they had hoped. Confidential reports about the public mood in spring 1942 show how widespread disillusionment had become. Arguably the greatest focal point for concern was the sharp cut in rations, which was said to have caused 'disquiet' and 'deep despondency', especially among the working class. Many Germans were already comparing the fall in food provision to the catastrophic conditions towards the end of the First World War in 1917–18.[20] Clearly, this was a cause for concern for the Nazi elite. References to 1918, in particular, would have set alarm bells ringing. As we have seen, decision-makers were determined to maintain strict discipline on the home front. Aware of the shift in the popular mood in spring 1942, legal officials were ready to step up repression to prevent the situation from deteriorating.

There was, however, more behind the rise in legal terror. Legal officials also saw harsher punishment as a way out of the perceived 'crisis of the judiciary'. For several years, and especially since the outbreak of war, they had felt on the defensive, with their influence and authority undermined by the growth of police and SS power. The lingering sense of crisis among jurists became acute in the spring of 1942, as a result of an open intervention by Hitler. In his private circle Hitler had never made a secret of his profound dislike for lawyers and judges. In the evening of 29 March 1942, for example, he raged that legal theories were incomprehensible and dangerous, and that legal officials were mentally defective.[21] But in the Third Reich, Hitler had never spoken with such candour in public, leaving jurists to cling on to the belief that Hitler ultimately respected their work. This illusion was shattered with his Reichstag speech of 26 April 1942. Speaking for about an hour, he gave a long account of the war, before he launched a short but sweeping attack on judges, criticizing them for clinging to formal rules rather than the political interests of the Nazi state. Those judges who failed to see the light, Hitler threatened, would be sacked by him personally. However brief the attack, its impact was considerable. Its significance lay not so much in the new powers Hitler claimed for himself (which he apparently never used), but rather in the reaction of the German jurists.[22] At first, they were shocked and depressed. But, in some cases, this gave way to a resolve to better fulfil Hitler's expectations in future. The Braunschweig general state prosecutor, for example, noted in late May 1942 that those judges who had previously not punished strictly enough were changing their approach, following Hitler's speech. This was a typical example of 'working towards the Führer': individual legal officials applied the law increasingly harshly in their desire to satisfy what they took to be Hitler's wishes.[23] Some judges soon saw a good opportunity to demonstrate their new resolve. Following the assassination of Reinhard Heydrich in Prague on 27 May 1942, they stepped up the terror against Czech defendants. As the judges of the People's Court noted in a case just two weeks later, the 'political incorrigibility of certain sections of the Czech people' from now on required 'the deterrence of the revolutionaries through heaviest punishment'. This was more than mere rhetoric, as the flood of death sentences that followed proved all too clearly.[24]

Legal terror did not ease up after the summer of 1942. In the following months and years, the transformation of the justice apparatus into an apparatus of injustice continued. Capital punishment, for example, reached its climax in 1943, with a staggering 5,336 death sentences. One important step in this on-going process of radicalization was Hitler's appointment on 20 August 1942 of Otto-Georg Thierack as the new Minister of Justice. Previously, the ministry had been in the hands of experienced civil servants with a national-conservative outlook, first Franz Gürtner, and, after his death in 1941, Franz Schlegelberger. By contrast, Otto-Georg Thierack, the former president of the People's Court, was a Nazi believer through and through, and he was set on improving the standing of the legal system in the Nazi state. To this end, he inaugurated a new era of co-operation with the police. He also increased the pressure on individual judges, sending out so-called judge's letters (*Richterbriefe*), which were supposed to 'guide' judges towards a National Socialist interpretation of the law by highlighting 'wrong' and 'right' judgements.

However, it would be short-sighted to describe Thierack's reign as a turning point for the legal system in the Third Reich. The perversion of the law in Nazi Germany had started way back in 1933, and had intensified during the war. Crucially, as we have seen, the most radical phase of Nazi legal terror had already begun in the spring of 1942, several months before Thierack's appointment. It was during the stewardship of the ageing career civil servant Franz Schlegelberger, who had worked in the Ministry of Justice since 1921, that the justice apparatus started its descent into the last circle of legal terror.

Turning to the victims of legal repression, there was initially no major shift in the focus of the authorities. At first, many of the same groups were hit who had been singled out for brutal punishment earlier. Looking at German offenders, the authorities continued to push for harsh penalties against political resistance. So-called 'habitual criminals' were also punished more harshly than ever. Even some of those officially sentenced to imprisonment were now murdered, after the legal authorities agreed to hand them over to SS concentration camps. Thus, around 10,000 prisoners in indefinite judicial confinement were transferred between 1942 and 1944 to the SS for 'annihilation through labour' as part of Thierack's rapprochement with Himmler.[25] At the same time, legal terror against foreigners and 'racial aliens' also escalated in 1942–43. As far as political resistance by foreigners was concerned, the legal authorities were now also involved in the brutal repression of civilians across Western Europe. From 1942 onwards, suspected opponents were arrested in France, Holland, Belgium and Norway, and secretly—in 'Night and Fog'—taken to Germany. Thousands were tried and locked up in German prisons, isolated from all other inmates.[26]

Just as in the early war years, Poles continued to make up the largest group of foreigners held by the legal apparatus. Their racial discrimination was now fully enshrined in law, with the Decree on Penal Law for Poles and Jews (in operation since 1 January 1942). The decree was extraordinarily brutal, threatening defendants with

> death, or, in less serious cases. . . imprisonment, for expressing anti-German sentiment by means of malicious or seditious activities, in particular for anti-German statements or the removal or defacement of public notices by German authorities or offices, or for disparaging or damaging the good name or the welfare of the German Reich or the German people by any other actions.

In other words, any behaviour that displeased the judges could now be punished with death. In their desire to ensure the lethal punishment of 'racial aliens', the legal authorities had made the law completely arbitrary. The defendants were essentially helpless, not least because basic rights such as legal representation, access to translators or the ability to call witnesses had also been curtailed over time.[27]

The lethal legislation against Poles was often applied with gusto by the judges. In the first six months of 1942, close to half of all death sentences by German courts were handed down against Poles. Even the police and SS acknowledged that sentencing had become stricter.[28] Poles faced capital punishment for a vast range of alleged offences, including 'insubordination against German masters'. What this involved can be illustrated by the case of the 29-year-old Pole Jan Owczarek, a forced labourer on a farm near Munich. In the summer of 1942, he lodged a police complaint against his employer, who was also the local Nazi peasant leader. According to the labourer, the farmer had forced him to perform hard work without lunch. When Owczarek had complained about this, the two men got into an argument, which descended into a brawl during which the Pole was severely injured by the farmer's wife with a pitchfork. But in the eyes of the authorities, it was the Pole who deserved punishment, not the German couple. The police turned him over to the Munich special court, which tried the case on 7 August 1942. Even though the judges acknowledged that the farmer had not really been hurt, they still sentenced Owczarek to death—'also in the interest of deterrence', as they put it.[29]

Despite the continual rise in death sentences, Polish defendants were still far more likely to be sentenced to imprisonment. Inmate numbers shot up as a result. By the end of September 1942, some 32,332 prisoners were held in the annexed Polish territory—almost 10,000 more than during the previous year. Polish prisoners everywhere faced catastrophic shortages in food, clothing and medicine. Abuse took many different forms, from physical attacks to further cuts in the already minuscule rations. Discrimination was encouraged from above with new prison rules for Polish prisoners in 1942. Poles could now be forced to perform especially hard and often dangerous forced labour, for up to fourteen hours per day—more than any other prisoners except Jews. Poles also faced stricter disciplinary punishment if they broke any of the countless prison rules governing every movement. Among the most feared sanctions was detention in a dark cell for up to two weeks, without bed, fresh air or exercise, and no more than a piece of bread and a jug of water each day. The brutal reality of incarceration took its toll, and many Polish prisoners were weak and ill. But sickness offered no escape from racial abuse. For example, while selected German prisoners suffering from tuberculosis could still qualify for some minimal treatment, Polish (and Czech) prisoners were officially excluded and left to die in a specially designated prison. All this helps to explain why Polish prisoners were much more likely than Germans to die in captivity.[30]

The legal authorities also did their best to crack down on any surviving Jews in Germany and occupied Poland. Judges continued to enforce the ever-expanding catalogue of racial regulations, encouraged by the Ministry of Justice. On 1 October 1942, it used the very first of its judges' letter to emphasize that Jews were 'racially inferior' and deserved the harshest penalty: 'The Jew is the enemy of the German people, who has provoked, stoked and prolonged this war. In this way, he has brought unspeakable harm to our people.'[31] Among the harshest sanctions were those meted out for so-called 'race defilement'. According to the 1935 Nuremberg Laws, sexual contact between unmarried Jews and non-Jews was punishable with imprisonment, and no more. But by the early 1940s, some judges were sentencing Jews to death, applying unrelated legislation to ensure that the defendants were killed. Thus, in March 1942, the Nuremberg Special Court sentenced the former head of the local Jewish community to death as a 'national pest', alleging that he had exploited wartime circumstances—such as black-outs—to carry on an affair. Three months later, the Cologne special court sentenced a 32-year-old Jewish barman, accused of having had sex with several non-Jewish women, to death as a 'dangerous habitual criminal'.[32]

By the time these murderous sentences were passed, the extermination of Jews in Europe was already under way. Top legal officials had detailed knowledge of the Holocaust, with State Secretary Freisler personally attending the notorious Wannsee conference on 20 January 1942. Many local judges and prison officials were also aware that Jews were being murdered in Eastern Europe. This did not stop the legal authorities from contributing to the smooth running of the genocide. This involvement was particularly obvious in the area covered by the *Generalgouvernement*, where most of the death camps were located. As early as 15 October 1941, courts here were ordered to sentence Jews to death who 'had left their designated district without permission'. Members of the population who hid escaped Jews were also sentenced to death. Courts in the annexed Polish territory and the Czech Protectorate also sent individuals to their deaths for trying to save Jews.[33] Meanwhile, courts inside Germany punished those who dared to talk openly about the extermination of the Jews, trying to enforce the public silence about the Holocaust. Rumours about shootings and gassings were punished by judges as 'malicious attacks' or 'undermining the home front'. In May 1943, the special court in Würzburg sentenced the wife of a train driver to six months imprisonment because she had cried when she witnessed the deportation of Jews from the local railway station, explaining her tears with the words: 'she who has no heart, is no German woman.'[34]

The legal authorities were even involved directly in the deportation of Jews. As early as spring 1942, the Ministry of Justice agreed to leave Jewish prison inmates to the police, if the police wanted to deport them before their sentences had ended. Hundreds of Jews were taken out of prisons as a result, and sent to their certain deaths. This policy of aiding and abetting the SS murder of 'racial aliens' was intensified under Minister of Justice Thierack, who decided to withdraw the legal apparatus from attacks on 'racial aliens' altogether. This was Thierack's way of dealing with the external criticism of 'lenient' jurists. His predecessors had reacted to interference from the police and SS by stepping up legal repression. Thierack believed that this approach was destined to fail, as the legal authorities could never be as radical as the police and SS. In his view the legal system 'could only contribute on a small scale to the extermination' of Poles and Jews, as well as Russians, Sinti and Roma. Leaving them to the police instead, he wrote, 'would produce much better results'. Therefore, Thierack agreed in a meeting with Himmler on 18 September

1942 that, in future, the punishment of offences by such 'racial aliens' would be left to Himmler's apparatus. Many of those already serving judicial sentences would be taken from prisons to concentration camps for 'annihilation through labour'. While this agreement was never put into practice in its entirety (Poles, for example, continued to be sentenced by courts until 1945), it did cement the police supremacy over 'racial aliens'. Fewer cases reached the judges, and inmate numbers inside prisons started to fall—linked to the fact that between late 1942 and mid-1943 the prison authorities handed over more than 6,000 Polish and 1,000 Jewish inmates to the SS, as well as around 700 Russians and Sinti and Roma.[35] After its peak in 1942–43, the wave of legal terror against 'racial aliens' started to subside.

Instead, from 1943, the courts turned back toward the German population. Selected German offenders, as we have seen, had been on the receiving end of brutal punishment for many years. What happened in the later stages of the war was that the authorities drew the circle of 'dangerous' German offenders wider than before. More Germans were locked up, contributing to a further rise in prisoner numbers. The peak was reached in the summer and autumn of 1944, with almost 200,000 inmates—more than ever before in German history. The shift of legal terror to Germans was particularly marked in the People's Court. For the first time since 1939, judges in 1944 again sentenced a majority of German defendants. In all, some 2,120 Germans were sentenced in that year alone, compared to 291 in 1941. An increasing number of Germans who had never been in conflict with the law before—among them many women and youths—now came before the courts. The authorities were reacting to two developments in particular. First of all, the growing dissent among the German population increasingly worried them. To be sure, grumbling—about work, provisions or the party—had been a fixture of life in the Third Reich from the beginning. But as the war turned against Germany, such criticism became more intense and widespread, until even Hitler was no longer excluded. In turn, dissent was now punished more strictly than ever. Nervously invoking the supposed lessons of 1918, legal officials were determined to nip any supposed threat to the home front in the bud. Ironic remarks about Nazi leaders or doubts about the German ability to win the war were often punished as 'undermining the war effort', resulting in lengthy sentences of imprisonment or even death. This offence alone accounted for almost 40 per cent of all the Germans sentenced by the People's Court after February 1944.[36]

In addition, there was a sharp rise in property crime among the German population from 1943 onwards, reflecting the changing wartime circumstances. These offences tended to increase, in particular, immediately after air raids: the chaos and destruction made thefts and break-ins much easier, while the dislocation and loss suffered by many increased their willingness to break the law. But such thefts—among the most serious offences in the eyes of many legal officials—were only the tip of the iceberg. In response to the deteriorating living conditions inside Germany, with growing food shortages and rationing, many Germans disregarded aspects of the strict economic wartime restrictions. Among the most common offences were illegal barter of foodstuffs, the unauthorized slaughter of animals, and the misuse or theft of ration cards. Underlying all this was a burgeoning black market economy. Here, all goods—however scarce—could still be purchased, at a price. In early 1944, for example, the going rate in the Hamburg area for a goose was around three bottles of cognac.[37] The German authorities were exasperated by the fact that large sections of the population regarded the breach of the economic regulations as perfectly acceptable. Those who lived by the rulebook, it was widely believed among the public, were just plain stupid. Even some legal officials had sympathy for this attitude, regarding the offenders as essentially 'good' people who had become victims of wartime circumstances. The Ministry of Justice railed against this view, reminding officials that punishment was necessary for reasons of deterrence—otherwise the economy and the war effort would suffer. Deterrence was to be guaranteed by publicizing sentences in newspapers and on posters. To give just one example, when Erich Schönegge was executed in Halle on 13 July 1943 for the theft of around 100 chicken and ducks, the Ministry of Justice issued a press release detailing his punishment. Other lethal sentences against property offenders were announced on posters. However, the courts sentenced a large number of Germans for a variety of economic offences, there was no consistency. The Ministry of Justice reprimanded some legal officials for being too lenient, others for being too hard. Thus, the officials in Berlin were critical of a case involving a 23-year-old mechanic who, having stolen a radio and a woollen blanket more than three months *after* an air raid, was sentenced to death as a 'plunderer'. But it is doubtful whether attempts by the Ministry of Justice to 'guide' judges had much effect. Trying to uphold the difference between truly 'dangerous' offenders, and those who had merely 'slipped up', the Ministry got muddled, hiding behind nebulous terms such as 'healthy popular feeling'. The result was mounting arbitrariness, confusion and insecurity about the law.[38]

III

By early 1945, most Germans knew that the war was lost. Yet even as the 'Thousand-Year-Reich' was collapsing all around them, jurists continued to advance legal terror. Death sentences were carried out until the very end: in the Brandenburg-Goerden prison, the last mass execution of some thirty-three inmates took place on 20 April 1945, only one week before it was liberated.[39] There can be no doubting the severity of legal punishment in the last months of the war. Some judges resorted to their harshest penalties yet. The Hanover special court, for example, sentenced around 12 per cent of all defendants to death in 1945—up from between 7 and 8 per cent in 1943–44.[40] Special courts were not alone in their quest for harsh punishment. As the war was coming to a close, even more brutal tribunals started to get involved. On 15 February, in a last throw of the dice, Minister of Justice Thierack announced the setting-up of so-called drum-head courts martial (*Standgerichte*), on Hitler's orders, staffed by a presiding judge and two officials from the party, police, army or SS. These courts—effectively mobile death squads—soon roamed the country, instructed to sentence to death individuals who 'jeopardize German combat strength or determination'.[41]

The mass of prison inmates also suffered greatly in the last months of Nazi rule. Cells were filthy and hopelessly overcrowded, and inmates were starving and disease-ridden. In the quite small Ebrach prison in Bavaria, some sixty-one inmates died in 1945 before the war was over—as many as had died in the previous five years taken together. Many other prisoners lost their lives during prison evacuations. As the Allies closed in on Germany, the authorities were determined that no inmate should fall into foreign hands. Inmates judged 'harmless' were released early. The others, both Germans and foreigners, faced an uncertain fate. Most of them were forced on exhausting marches to other prisons, walking long distances, with very little food. The conditions were particularly appalling in the East, where many inmates succumbed to the freezing temperatures. Some of the prisoners never even made it on the transports. The Ministry of Justice ordered that 'particularly asocial subversive prisoners' could be killed, if they could not be moved in time. As a result, several thousands of prison inmates were executed, including Poles, foreign political prisoners and small-time German criminals. The largest such massacre took place in the night of 30 January 1945 in the Sonnenburg penitentiary, where about 800 prisoners were shot dead, some of them in their beds.[42]

But legal terror in the final months of the Nazi regime has to be put into perspective. For, despite the inhumanity and brutality, there were two trends working against a further intensification of legal terror. First of all, not all the legal officials were immune to the defeatism that gripped wide sections of the population. To be sure, some officials remained fanatic supporters of the regime, redoubling their efforts to root out 'subversion'. Others, however, realized that the time of Nazi rule was up. Keen to have no more blood on their hands, some judges now used more lenient punishment. A few judges even found ways of avoiding service on the courts martial altogether. Had German jurists showed such scruples earlier, thousands more men and women may well have escaped from the ruins of the Third Reich alive.[43] Secondly, the German courts in 1945 dealt with fewer cases than in previous years. The legal apparatus had been disrupted for years, with court buildings damaged and legal officials called up to the army. But the system had continued to function. Only towards the end of the war did it slowly collapse into chaos: the Allies overran one court building after the other and countless documents were left behind or destroyed. The breakdown of the legal apparatus was symbolized by the partial destruction of the People's Court in Berlin, during a bombing raid on 3 February 1945, which also killed the president of the Court, the former State Secretary Roland Freisler. Not surprisingly, the remaining judges at the People's Court only sentenced some 345 individuals in 1945—ten times less than in the previous year. Another reason for the decline in cases brought before the German courts lies in the unrestrained police terror in this period. Rather than handing suspects over to the legal authorities, the police killed many of them on the spot.[44] In short, while conditions inside prisons reached a nadir towards the end of the war, fewer individuals were now sentenced to imprisonment. Also, proportionally fewer death sentences were passed. In a sample of three special courts operating inside Germany, the number of death sentences declined from 111 (1944) to 28 (1945).[45] As far as sentencing was concerned, Nazi legal terror apparently climaxed between 1942 and 1944, not in the last months of the war.

IV

One can distinguish at least three periods of Nazi legal terror during the war. The first lasted from the outbreak of war in 1939 until late 1941, and saw a sharp rise in repression: legislation became tougher, punishment stricter and the death penalty shot up. Repression in these early years was itself soon overshadowed by the wave of terror that hit Germany in the second phase, between 1942 and 1944, when legal terror reached its brutal climax. Prisons were completely packed and executioners were busier then ever, moving from one prison to the next to put thousands of condemned individuals to death. Also, the co-operation between legal authorities and the police was stepped up, symbolized by the transfer of thousands of prison inmates to the SS for 'annihilation through labour'. The causes of the intensification of legal terror were complex. Outside pressure played an important part. But judges were more than puppets who had their strings pulled from above. They still held considerable power in their own hands and had their own reasons for stepping up repression, driven not least by the determination to enforce discipline on the home front. In the last months of the war, legal terror entered its final phase, which is most difficult to characterize. In many ways, repression showed no sign of abating. Courts still passed brutal sentences and prospects for the prisoners were worse than ever. This development was counteracted, at least in part, however, by the growing wartime chaos and also by the opportunistic manoeuvres of judges already thinking about the time after the Third Reich.

Looking at the targets of Nazi terror, it seems that legal terror against 'ordinary Germans' did not culminate in the final months of the regime, as may have been expected. Rather, the height of terror was apparently reached in 1943 and 1944. In this period, judges dealt with an increasing number of Germans who had previously not been singled out for punishment. They were not 'habitual criminals' or members of the organized resistance, who had already been punished severely in previous years. Rather, they were socially integrated members of the community, often persecuted for offences against the wartime economic regulations or dissent. Of course, there were limits to this development. Only a small proportion of the population was actually hit directly by legal terror, as many offences were never reported to the authorities in the first place. And by no means all of those arrested received harsh punishment: many cases were dismissed before they came to court, and, during trials, judges often continued to count unblemished political or criminal records as mitigating factors. Having said this, one should be careful not to underestimate the impact of legal repression, especially as it became more difficult to predict. Widely publicized in Nazi Germany, it certainly caused anxiety among the population. This was one of the reasons why there were so few serious challenges to Nazi authority in the final years of the Third Reich. As the war turned against Germany, the 'people's community' was increasingly held together by distrust, fear and terror, rather than support for the regime.[46]

Finally, jurists participated fully in the Nazi struggle against 'racial aliens'. Legal officials helped to make sure that racism remained at the core of the Third Reich. By the time the war broke out, legal officials could look back on years of discrimination against German Jews. Now, from September 1939, the terror against 'racial aliens' was stepped up before courts and in prisons. For these defendants, there was no equality before the law. Of course, the regime often set the pace here. But most legal officials were in agreement with the official policy of racial abuse. They were responsible for the deaths of many thousands of 'racial aliens', who were executed or died under dreadful conditions in the prisons. The involvement of the legal authorities in the Nazi racial state was clearly recognized by the Allies in the immediate post-war period. In 1947, US judges in Nuremberg found former leading legal officials guilty of having pursued a 'program of racial extermination under the guise of law'.[47] Too few historians have built on these conclusions, however, and further research is needed to bring more light into what is one of the darkest corners of German legal history.

6

Germans, Slavs and the Burden of Work in Rural Southern Germany during the Second World War

Jill Stephenson

The spoils of war have long included human as well as material resources, which have been exploited in various ways to satisfy the needs and desires of the victors. There was therefore nothing new about belligerent countries in the Second World War putting prisoners-of-war (POWs) to work. In Britain, for example, both German and Italian POWs were deployed in agriculture. Nazi Germany, along with Japan, was, however, a particularly ruthless and rapacious exponent of human exploitation, with men and women from vanquished countries transported to Germany in their millions to fuel Hitler's war effort. Many of them were abused and maltreated in flagrant violation of the Geneva Convention. While the racist foundations of Nazism required that foreigners of allegedly 'inferior' racial origin serve as helots of the 'Aryan' race, the immense scale of the transportations was a response to Germany's acute labour shortage, especially when compared with the resources at its adversaries' disposal from 1941, once the USSR and then the USA had entered the war. The shortages affected both industry and agriculture. On the land, as the conscription of able-bodied men took effect, farmers' sons and labourers, and perhaps the proprietor himself, were called up, leaving the running of a farm to the women of the family along with elderly men and children.

Yet, from an ideological point of view, an influx of foreigners was highly unwelcome to the regime. While POWs and volunteer or coerced civilians from vanquished western European countries such as Norway, Denmark, Holland and Flemish Belgium were regarded as 'racially valuable', French and Walloons were not. Even these latter were, however, accorded a significantly higher status in the racial hierarchy than the over-whelming majority of eastern Europeans who, nevertheless, accounted for the greatest numbers of foreigners in Germany during the war.[1] The Nazi regime therefore inflicted on itself a problem which it was incapable of solving: the war which it unleashed necessitated the removal from every German community of German men, to serve in the armed forces and in the occupied territories. To replace, if only partially, the labour which was thus lost to the German economy, the regime imported millions of mostly unwilling foreigners who overwhelmingly were classed as 'racial inferiors', and it deployed them in virtually every kind of productive concern and in the vast majority of German communes, the commune being the smallest unit of local government.

The consequence was that 'Aryan' Germans were brought face to face with 'enemy aliens' in ways which were entirely at odds with the inten-tions of a regime which had endeavoured, from 1933, to purge the 'people's community' (*Volksgemeinschaft*) of 'aliens', especially Jews. Regulating and policing POWs and coerced civilian workers who were forced to make a major contribution to the German war effort, frequently under stringent discipline and in primitive and inhospitable conditions, became a major preoccupation of both the German civilian authorities and the NSDAP at regional and local level. While the controls imposed on the foreigners were partly geared to preventing them from escaping and perhaps returning home, there were even greater fears about the possibility of foreigners sabotaging the concerns in which they were employed, and thus damaging the German war effort. Above all, the Nazi authorities were determined to minimize contact between foreigners and Germans. This was particularly the case because it quickly became apparent that many German civilians, especially those in rural areas, did not subscribe to Nazi theories of 'superior' and 'inferior' races. Their conduct towards foreigners tended to be governed by other priorities, which were often pragmatic and sometimes humani-tarian. In south German farming communities, this confirmed beyond doubt that Nazi functionaries had failed in the peacetime years to implant the fundamental precepts of Nazi ideology, those concerned with racial characteristics and the racial hierarchy. Even the concept of the *Volksgemeinschaft* was not one with which peasants could easily identify. Their allegiances were stubbornly local, as a police report of 26 January 1941 from Aufsess in Bavaria explained: 'One can't talk about a *Volksgemeinschaft*. . . For the farmer, his own property is his only father-land'.[2] The ramifications of this became apparent when, after the defeat of Poland in September 1939, foreigners were deployed as labourers in south German agriculture.

Estimates of the total numbers of foreigners brought to Germany vary, but the most recent detailed study puts the figure for POWs and civilian labourers from both eastern and western Europe at thirteen million.[3] Some of these died in Germany—either as a result of maltreatment or as casualties of Allied bombing—while others were able to make the journey home during the war and did not return to Germany. In the case of women, up to autumn 1943 this was often because they were pregnant.[4] There was therefore a somewhat variable population of foreigners, although many were in Germany for years at a time. They included French POWs who worked on farms in Württemberg 'for fifty-eight months', from June 1940 until April 1945.[5] Ulrich Herbert has estimated that probably the largest single total of foreign workers was 7.6 million, in August 1944, of whom almost 1.7 million were from Poland and almost 2.8 million were Russians, Ukrainians and Belorussians from the USSR, those known in Germany disparagingly as '*Ostarbeiter*' ('eastern workers'). There were smaller numbers from other eastern European nationalities, including Czechs, Slovaks, Croats and Serbs. One third of the 5.7 million civilian foreign workers in August 1944 were female, with 87 per cent of these from eastern Europe. As the official charged with the foreigners' recruitment, Fritz Sauckel, admitted, fewer than 200,000 of the civilian workers were genuine volunteers.[6]

At the start, in 1939, it was envisaged that foreigners would be deployed overwhelmingly in agriculture, as a continuation on a large scale of pre-war practice. As much greater numbers of foreigners became available to the Germans through conquest, however, and as Hitler's leadership prosecuted the war across Europe and into the Soviet Union, the conscription of ever-increasing numbers of German men into the *Wehrmacht* made the utilization of foreign labour in industry a practical and irresistible option. This led to a mammoth programme of recruitment for both industry and agriculture, which won some volunteers but overwhelmingly used force of a primitive and brutal nature. By 1941, this sometimes amounted to kidnapping, with teenagers and adults being seized from their homes or on the streets of eastern European towns and villages, sometimes with distraught parents trying to resist the seizure of their children. In some cases, whole families were transported, with children as well as parents put to work on German farms. They were taken in lorries and cattle trucks, effectively as prisoners, normally to a transit camp in the first instance, to be processed by the German authorities. One seventeen-year-old from a Polish farming family later told how, in spring 1942, she had been seized, loaded on to a goods lorry and taken, via Cracow and Vienna, to a transit camp in Salzburg. There, her hair was cut and then she was bathed and examined by a doctor—to ensure that she was carrying no disease or parasites—before being handed over to a Bavarian farmer as a labourer.[7]

Those who tried to resist being requisitioned by the Germans might be hanged. The fear of being snatched by a German recruiting team and sent to work in Germany led some young men in both western and eastern Europe to go into hiding where many joined partisan or resistance forces. Thousands of those who reached Germany, especially if they had been sent from the USSR, died before they could be put to work. The long journey in freezing conditions with little or no food, in overcrowded goods wagons, weakened men and women catastrophically and made them an easy prey to disease. The Nazi view of their allegedly lowly racial status condemned those who survived all of this to starvation rations and arduous work, a policy with which many major German industrial firms willingly complied. Even when, in 1942, with Germany's military position beginning to seem vulnerable, government authorities accepted that the foreigners would be valuable workers only if they were fed, clothed and kept reasonably healthy, this was not necessarily followed through in practice, as German material resources became ever scarcer while at the same time there seemed to be a limitless supply of eastern European labour. By the end of the war, some workers from western European countries such as France and Italy were, along with many of the much larger numbers of eastern Europeans working in industrial concerns, among those who were worked or starved to death.[8]

Industry and extractive concerns such as coal mines were areas where large numbers of foreigners from both western and eastern Europe were deployed. For the most part, they were unskilled workers who were given only rudimentary training, including familiarization with the basic German language terms used in their occupation. They were obliged to work for very long hours and were often treated with appalling brutality. There was also a relatively small number of foreign industrial workers, including French, Belgians and some Soviet workers, who arrived equipped with skills that were much prized by their German overlords. Some western Europeans lived relatively freely, renting rooms from private landlords and patronizing German-owned shops, inns and social facilities. For the most part, however, both for convenience and as a means of segregating foreign labourers from the civilian German population, those employed in industry and mines were accommodated near their place of work in barracks which had their own facilities, including kitchens and brothels, which were also staffed by foreigners.[9] Segregation was an important consideration for the Nazi leadership, partly because it was deemed inappropriate that Germans should fraternize with citizens of enemy countries. More importantly, however, in Nazi Germany, segregation was regarded as being essential to maintain the alleged purity of the 'Aryan' race. The *Tübingen Chronicle* warned in February 1940 that '[a] seeping in of Polish blood must at all costs be prevented, especially given that the Polish nation is probably not entirely free of an eastern European

Jewish taint. Keeping our German blood pure is the first duty of every German citizen.'[10]

In 1940, foreigners accounted for only 3 per cent of the workforce in industry, but by 1944 this figure had risen to 29 per cent. In agriculture, the comparable figures were 6 per cent and 22 per cent, which meant, in absolute terms, 661,000 and 2,402,000 respectively.[11] In the three south German states, Bavaria, Württemberg and Baden, at the turn of the years 1940–41 there were 125,774 POWs and civilian foreign workers in both industry and agriculture, of whom 10,102 were women.[12] Regardless of the initial intention to utilize foreign labour chiefly in agriculture, in practice industry had the pick of the foreigners, and increasingly had priority in terms of their allocation. Nevertheless, significant numbers of them were deployed in Germany's rural areas, on farms and in artisanal businesses such as flour mills, to try to ensure that the domestic food supply for 'Aryans' was maintained. In northern and especially in eastern Germany, this tended to mean that they worked in teams on large arable farms, where there was a long history of utilizing Polish labour, although there were also smaller farming concerns in this area. Ensuring that segregation between natives and foreigners was maintained was more difficult on these farms than in industry, and throughout the war there were varying degrees of fraternization, especially between foreign men and German women.[13] In western and southern Germany, where the small family farm or rural trade was the basic unit of agricultural business, it soon became clear that enforcing segregation would be extremely difficult, if not impossible. This was partly because it was in the nature of family farming that the small number of people on a farm tended to work at close quarters, in arduous manual labour. Consequently they became acquainted with each others' strengths and weaknesses, backgrounds and preferences, problems and aspirations.

Many foreign workers, particularly those from Poland, were themselves from a farming family, and they might therefore have more in common with south German peasants than the latter had with south German urban dwellers, to say nothing of north Germans. This became particularly apparent once urban Germans from the north and west were evacuated from enemy bombing to the safer south. One feature that Poles, in particular, shared with many south German farmers was an allegiance to the Roman Catholic Church, which was itself under increasing pressure in Germany during the war. Uniate Ukrainians, too, had an affinity with the Catholic Church, and some other workers from the USSR regarded the Catholic Church in Germany as an appropriate substitute for the Orthodox Church. There were also smaller numbers of Protestants among the foreign workers, and some of them made contact with co-religionists in southern Germany through attendance at church services.

For the small south German farmer, the most important consideration in dealing with his or—as conscription progressively withdrew men from the farms—her foreign worker was the contribution which he or she made to the continuing viability of the farm or artisanal business. By 1939, with an estimated Reich shortage in agriculture of some three-quarters of a million labourers, many small-scale south German farmers regarded their family businesses as being in crisis, even before successive rounds of wartime conscription had their debilitating effect. The economic upturn from the mid-1930s had seen a resumption of the trend, which had been clearly visible from the later nineteenth century, of migration from the countryside to the towns. The Depression around 1930 had temporarily halted or even reversed this trend, but the Nazi regime's drive for rearmament in the 1930s had resulted in a seemingly insatiable demand by industry for extra labour. Hired labourers and also farmers' sons and even daughters were tempted away from rural to urban areas by the higher wages offered either in industry or in other urban occupations which had been vacated by those transferring into the armaments industry. In Baden, for example, with a population of 2.5 million, there was in 1938 a short-fall of 55,000 agricultural workers for whom compensation of only 6,200 farmhands could be generated, with some 10,000 people providing temporary assistance at harvest time. To meet a labour shortage that was regarded in south German agriculture as catastrophic, migrant workers from several European countries, including Austria, Italy, Yugoslavia and Poland, were recruited. There was nothing new about this: Germany had imported foreign workers both before and during the First World War.[14]

The progressive withdrawal of millions of men from civilian life and into the *Wehrmacht* during the Second World War, therefore, severely aggravated a problem that was already causing concern. Under these conditions, it is hardly surprising that Bavarian farmers welcomed the Polish labourers who were assigned to them in 1939–40 as 'saviours in a time of need'. This sentiment was echoed across southern Germany. In Türkheim, near Ulm, for example, in November 1939 when 'the conscripted proprietors and farm workers were replaced by prisoners-of-war', the relief was palpable.[15] The first priority for a farmer, particularly one whose family had farmed the same fields for generations, was to maintain the viability of his concern, at a time when not only had men been conscripted into the *Wehrmacht* and war industry but, in addition, many farm horses had been requisitioned by the army. Many small south German farmers could not afford labour-saving machines, and those who could found that increasing wartime shortages of fuel and rubber for tyres greatly reduced their ability to use them. Manual labour was the only alternative, with physical strength at a premium. While there were female foreigners deployed on the farms, in small, labour-intensive farming communities foreign men, as latterly virtually the only male workers, played an essential part by performing the heavy work which had previously been undertaken either by men who were now conscripted or by draught animals.

According to Ulrich Herbert, even by the end of 1940, 'German agriculture would no longer have been in a position to maintain food production at the required level without the two million or so foreign men and women working in it'.[16] The position increasingly worsened over the following four and a half years. It was estimated that, from summer 1941, in many of the communes in Baden and Württemberg some 80 per cent of all male farm workers, including proprietors, were absent as a result of the more severe conscription occasioned by the invasion of the USSR. At the same time, in Memmingen district in Bavaria, 150 farms were without their male proprietor.[17] At the end of May 1943, with Germany's fortunes on the wane, the foreigners' value was emphasized by the Stuttgart state prosecutor: 'the conscription of almost all able-bodied men' meant that, apart from 'the females who are still available', farm workers in Württemberg were 'almost exclusively. . . Poles, Serbs and prisoners-of-war'. This became an ever more serious concern. Some farmers' or artisans' wives who had not been allocated a foreign worker closed down their business because they no longer had the resources to operate it.[18] By the later stages of the war, many small farming concerns would not have survived without the assistance of foreign labour.

Soon after the arrival of the first Polish POWs in autumn 1939, local regulations were issued about both the limits to their freedom and the 'strict but correct' treatment which they were to receive from Germans. It soon became clear, however, that, whereas maintaining apartheid between Germans and Slavs in an industrial, urban environment required constant vigilance on the part of the authorities, effecting it in the countryside was fraught with problems. In February 1940 a circular from the Württemberg Ministry of the Interior admitted that 'the influx of Polish male and female farm workers brings with it a number of difficulties which must nevertheless be overcome if the Reich government's aim of affording agriculture tangible assistance is to be realized.' The bureaucrats at the ministry had envisaged maintaining supervision of the Poles by requiring them to report daily to their local police authority, but they now realized that this was 'impracticable' because of the distance of most farms from the nearest police station. The only solution which they could devise was to instruct farmers to ensure that their foreign workers did not leave their commune.[19] Regulations for the entire Reich were issued on 8 March 1940. These amounted to a system of apartheid by which Germans were to avoid any contact with the foreigners which was not necessitated by the latter's working conditions. In particular, there was a prohibition of any social or sexual contact between German 'Aryans' and Polish 'sub-humans'. These proscriptions were subsequently applied to relations between Germans and Polish civilians as well as other Slav forced workers, especially those from the USSR.[20] Yet the implementation of such regulations depended entirely on obedience and co-operation on the part of the German population. It soon became apparent that these were only partially forthcoming.

The regulation of the deployment of coerced foreign labour in south German agriculture, on small family farms, brought with it increased government and party interference in the conduct of rural businesses whose proprietors already resented the additional wartime controls regarding the growth and distribution of their produce which had augmented restrictions imposed on them during the 1930s. Many farmers demonstrated that they were no more inclined to accept official interference and follow official instructions about how to treat their foreign workers than they were prepared to accept interference and instructions concerning the sale or bartering of their produce or the slaughtering of their livestock. For farmers, the foreigners were employees to be treated as well, or as badly, as they had previously treated German labourers. In addition, in the farmers' view, the foreigners' activities in their free time were no concern of theirs, and they were not prepared to spend their own limited free time policing them. It is true that some employers reported their foreign workers to the authorities, which sometimes resulted in punitive action against the foreigners by the Gestapo.[21] In December 1940, the Stuttgart state prosecutor recorded that Polish agricultural labourers were often 'lazy, unwilling and spiteful. Experience shows that, the longer the war lasts, the more reluctantly they work.'[22]

From Bavaria came mixed accounts. As early as December 1939, it was reported from Ebermannstadt district that twenty-three male and fifteen female Polish civilians had been set to work on farms and that their 'attitude. . . so far was good'. In Hollfeld, the farmers were said to be pleased with the work done by the twenty-nine Poles in the commune, with only two complaints. On the other hand, some of the Poles had complained to the police about their treatment at the hands of their Bavarian employers. By the end of 1940, however, in Bavaria as in Württemberg there was some discontent about the attitude of Polish workers, who had clearly become aware of their value to communities which were heavily dependent on their labour.[23] A direct correlation is discernible between a farm's need for labour and the extent to which its foreign labourers were treated favourably rather than brutally, which is particularly obvious in the later stages of the war although it is visible from the start. At the same time, there was a matching correlation between the ever-increasing shortage of labour and the growing self-confidence and assertiveness of at least some foreign workers, as they became aware of their value to farmers and, from 1942, as news of Germany's military reverses reached them.

Nevertheless, while generalized complaints were made, relatively few farmers, artisans or tradesmen were likely to report infringements of official regulations by foreign workers to the police because this might well have resulted in the foreign worker being imprisoned or even sent to a concentration camp, leaving the employer without his labourer, something which most farmers, or farmers' wives, were at pains to avoid at almost any cost. As the Stuttgart state prosecutor reported, 'farmers, through their indifference', seemed to support the foreigners' refusal to adhere to the controls prescribed for them.[24] Thus rural dwellers and their families made choices about their treatment of foreigners which sometimes conflicted with the regime's prescriptions and at least potentially implicated them in activities designated as criminal. In some communes, the foreigners had considerable freedom with not only their employer but sometimes even the local mayor turning a blind eye to their breaking their curfew or visiting co-nationals in another commune, perhaps somehow obtaining a bicycle to facilitate this.[25]

While Polish POWs tended to be housed together and escorted to and from the farms on which they worked under armed guard, it became possible in 1940 for them to opt for civilian status and therefore—like Polish and other forced civilian workers—to live on the farms where they worked. On many farms, they became accepted as members of the household, with the advantages and disadvantages which this entailed. These included working very long hours, possibly being given accommodation in the farmhouse, eating meals communally with the native members of the household, and having their clothes washed—if not very frequently—along with those of the other household members. On some farms, clean clothing was left in a pile, with family members and foreign workers helping themselves to whichever garments came to hand, without any thought of a shirt, for example, 'belonging' to any individual. Sometimes a farmer's wife would provide a foreign worker with clothes belonging to her conscripted, or late, husband.[26] In addition, Polish or Ukrainian workers might accompany a Catholic farming family when they attended church, until this was explicitly banned in March 1940. Any familiarity of these kinds was forbidden by repeated orders from Himmler and his SS subordinates, and Germans were warned that they, and not only the foreign workers, would be punished for violation of them.

In January 1940, the senior SS authorities in Baden and Württemberg ordered that not only should all 'unseemly behaviour' be reported to the SD (*Sicherheitsdienst*—Security Service), but that all instances in which a German 'has not maintained the necessary distance' between himself and a foreigner should also be reported. There was a recognition that, in rural areas, with Poles coming into close contact with the German population,

> there is the danger that far too close and trusting a relationship can develop. . . Each citizen must realize that the Poles belong to an enemy state and to a cultural level far below that of the German rural population. Every farmer and every farmer's wife must take account of this superiority. . .[27]

Some individuals were punished for the simplest acts of kindness towards a foreign worker, such as providing him or her with food or clothing. In January 1944, farmers from Fürstenfeldbruck district were brought before a court for having sent their Polish and Russian workers to Munich with food which they were to exchange for clothing.[28] Apart from anything else, this violated the wartime rationing controls.

The most Draconian punishment for disregard of official warnings about conduct towards foreigners was, however, meted out to women and girls who had sexual relationships with foreigners, including Frenchmen as well as eastern Europeans. Until Hitler banned the practice in November 1941, because of the unfavourable reaction to it of Germany's foreign allies, local NSDAP activists were encouraged by Himmler's SS to stage the ritual public humiliation of women who were guilty of 'racial defilement' ('Rassenschande'). This usually involved cutting off the woman's hair and shaving her head in a public ceremony, after which she might be led around her home commune and the neighbouring district bearing a placard detailing her offence, before being consigned to prison or even a concentration camp. While some ardent Nazis, such as the Esslingen NSDAP district leader, Eugen Hund, regarded this as justice, even some party officials found it distasteful. Ferdinand Dietrich, the Öhringen district NSDAP leader, gave protection to two women who had become pregnant by foreigners, one of them a Pole. There can, however, be little doubt that some Germans derived voyeuristic pleasure from the public humiliation of women who had violated traditional Christian morality, although, at the same time, there was widespread revulsion against such scenes in small south German communes where the women being pilloried were neighbours. Yet the women did not have the worst of it: on Himmler's express instructions, a Polish man found to have a German lover was almost invariably hanged, on the grounds that he had allegedly polluted 'German blood'. This was usually a public event, with the other foreign workers in the locality obliged to attend in order to impress on them the fate which they would suffer if they behaved similarly.

The clear majority of cases of 'Rassenschande' in southern Germany occurred, not surprisingly, in rural areas, where adult German men were increasingly thin on the ground while forced foreign workers often lived on the farms where they worked. In Friedrichshafen district, for example, there were several instances of 'forbidden relations', but not a single one in the town of Friedrichshafen itself; all occurred in the surrounding rural communes. Sexual relations between German women and foreigners occurred more frequently in Catholic areas of southern Germany, undoubtedly because of the closer relationships which developed with Catholic Poles, in particular. There was no distinction of class or status: women from all levels of rural society were involved. The Stuttgart state prosecutor reported in 1943 that farmers' wives or daughters who became pregnant by a foreign worker and were either denounced to or detected by the authorities frequently argued that they had consented to sex with the foreigner in order to maintain him as a productive worker on the farm. If this was a sign of the desperate straits on some of south Germany's farms, it was also likely to be a plea in mitigation in the hope of avoiding a custodial sentence, the penalty for German women having sexual relations with any POW or eastern European.[29]

By contrast, German men who had sexual relations with foreign women were theoretically punishable with a spell in a concentration camp, but frequently they were not charged with any offence. The foreign woman, however, might well be sent to a concentration camp. Polish or Soviet women workers who became pregnant by other foreigners were at first permitted to return home, but from autumn 1943 this ceased to be the case. The value of their labour was paramount, but, while the authorities approved of abortion in their case, in Catholic areas country doctors would generally refuse to perform a termination. The fate of a foreigner's child, like so much else in her life, depended on the attitude of her employer. If he or she was prepared to treat the new baby as a member of the household, it would be looked after on the farm and would probably survive. Some farmers, however, regarded this as too expensive of food supplies and effort, and insisted that the infant be surrendered to a 'foreign children's care unit', where it was likely that it would be left to starve.[30]

Other forms of fraternization were regarded less implacably but as highly undesirable nevertheless. There was a particular prohibition on Germans' allowing eastern Europeans to share their table at mealtimes. In February 1940, the *Tübingen Chronicle* ran the headline 'Not at the same table as a Pole!'.[31] Yet in farming households the custom was for all members of the household, including labourers and maids who were not family members, to sit around the farmhouse table—normally the only table in the household—and break bread together. Many south German farmers were not to be deterred from this by increasingly hysterical official injunctions. As a former Polish worker in Bavaria explained, the rationale was perfectly simple: 'Within his own four walls, the farmer declared to his assembled household: "Those who work on my farm, eat at my table"'. This meant, on many farms, helping themselves to food from a communal bowl.[32] To do otherwise was, in the view of many farmers, to treat a foreign worker as unworthy, which—while it was precisely what the authorities intended—was felt to be unlikely to increase his enthusiasm for work. It was at least partly for this reason that, as the Ochsenfurt NSDAP district leadership reported in July 1942, 'the foreign workers and prisoners-of-war on the land receive very good provisioning.' A few months later, the NSDAP district leadership in Erlangen reported, 'through gritted teeth', that it was 'self-evident' that farmers shared their table with foreign workers. In this Bavarian district, party functionaries intervened only if they learned that foreigners were sharing sleeping quarters with Germans, something which did occur on some farms.[33]

Common practice of this kind, however, drove a coach and horses through Nazi rationing policy, which was geared to protecting 'Aryan' Germans from privation partly by prescribing much less favourable food rations for foreigners. The result was, as Theresia Bauer has argued, that

> throughout the war, forced workers on peasant farms were better provided with food than both urban forced workers in factories or armaments production and the German urban population—and, lastly, much better than the population in the occupied home territories of the forced workers. Thus the agricultural forced workers broke through a National Socialist 'nutritional hierarchy' which was strictly determined by racist principles and therefore condemned 'less valuable' people to starvation to the benefit of members of the 'higher' race.[34]

This was a constant area of concern to the regime and of envy to those who felt that they were less well placed. Some women evacuees from Germany's devastated towns complained that foreign workers were being fed better than they were, and even went as far as denouncing farmers to the authorities, whose view was that provisions given to enemy 'aliens' were provisions lost to the Volksgemeinschaft. The farmers, however, remained unrepentant. Their simple maxim was that those who worked to maintain their farms—which generally did not include evacuees—in the face of great adversity in wartime, should receive preferential rations.

The evacuees, too, were incomers to south German villages, escaping the terror and destruction of bombing in the towns and cities of northern and western Germany. Their vociferous complaints about the relatively primitive conditions of their south German billets were more than matched by the contemptuous complaints made by their rural hosts about their demeanour and conduct and, in particular, their refusal to lend a

much-needed hand on the farms. This was regarded as especially offensive as conscription claimed ever more of the rural labour force. From
Ebermannstadt it was reported in July 1941 that '[t]he peasant cannot
understand the refusal by these "ladies" [from Hamburg] to give any assistance with farm work.' In Oberschopfheim, a village in Baden, the best
that could be said about evacuees from Rhineland cities was that they were
'unproductive'. The reaction from Württemberg was no more favourable:
'We can understand that they are in a difficult position, but it's not unrea-
sonable to expect that, just a few times during their stay, they might make
the effort to be useful.' It was therefore scarcely surprising that 'enemy
alien' foreign workers were often treated with greater regard and even
affection than fellow members of the *Volksgemeinschaft* who themselves
showed little consciousness of the Nazi ideal of racial solidarity.[35]

By no means all Polish or Soviet forced workers were treated with
humanity by their rural employers. Yet the evidence is that those who were
treated roughly by a farmer, perhaps being beaten by him, had the misfor-
tune to have been allocated to a farm where, before the war, the same
employer had beaten his German farm labourers. Some female foreigners
suffered sexual abuse at the hands of their employer; yet it had not been
unknown before the war for a farmer to expect a German girl who had
been allocated to him, under one of the Nazis' service schemes, to have
sex with him. Above all, on many small farms conditions of life were hard,
and perhaps primitive, for all concerned, not only for the foreign workers.
With farm animals sharing the family's accommodation, the absence of
both electricity and a piped water supply, interior walls that were not plas-
tered and bedrooms that were unheated, some farming families lived in
circumstances that bred a rough and ready approach to individuals'
comfort and well-being. There were also some south German farms which
were more prosperous and had more amenities, to the extent that, for some
foreigners, conditions there were superior to those from which they had
been forcibly removed at home. For foreigners from the poorest backgrounds in eastern Europe, this included the amount and quality of the
food supply.[36]

The natural propensity of the rural population to value those who made
a contribution to their community was in many places enhanced by the
encouragement given to them by members of the clergy to show compas-
sion and charity to co-religionists who found themselves in difficult, even
distressing, circumstances. In southern Germany, it was particularly the
Catholic clergy who took a lead in this. At first, from autumn 1939, Polish
POWs attended services alongside Germans, having been escorted there
under guard from their living quarters. This aroused the ire of the authorities who deplored the common celebration of the mass by Germans and
Poles almost as much as they were outraged by communal meals in the

farmhouse. In some localities, minor Nazi functionaries tried to ensure that those who were not wearing prominently the violet-coloured badge whose 'P' labelled them as Poles were excluded from services. One former Polish coerced worker in Baden attributed this, however, to the need felt by minor functionaries to demonstrate their activism so as not to be relieved of their post and sent to the front.

Particularly inflammatory, as far as Nazi functionaries were concerned, was the way in which German Catholic priests praised the Poles as particularly pious and devout Christians who should serve as a model for emulation by their own congregations. After a Christmas service in Würzburg in 1939, the NSDAP's district leader remarked:

> It is becoming more and more understandable. . . [if] our farmers treat the Poles as their equals; if such clergy, forgetful of all honour, are not ashamed to present the fine, innocent Poles as exalted role models, a source of dangerous[ly] Un-German feeling comes to light.

In March 1940, in a commune near Lahr in Baden, Poles sang their own hymns in Polish at the end of a mass which was also attended by Germans. This kind of experience made a deep impression on rural Germans. For the Catholic clergy, it was important not only to emphasize the devotion of the Poles but also to encourage their congregations to show concern for their fellow worshippers by providing them with necessities which they lacked, for example food and clothing, as well as small luxuries such as tobacco or beer. The result was a ban on Polish POWs attending normal church services and an intensification of SD surveillance of the clergy. '*Ostarbeiter*', too, were explicitly forbidden to attend German services, while Slavs generally were to be excluded from the celebration of festivals such as Christmas. Nevertheless, in some Bavarian villages, Polish workers were exempted by their employers from working on Christian holy days and permitted both to participate in religious processions and to attend family baptisms and weddings.[37]

As the war progressed, with Germany's position weakening and foreign workers becoming ever more aware of their indispensability, they became increasingly assertive and demanded better conditions. In at least some cases, this meant not conditions equal to those of their employers—which they already enjoyed—but conditions that were better than those of their employers. A report from Rodheim in Bavaria, in August 1943, told how, on a farm run by a widowed mother with her daughter and a male Polish worker, the women had consumed less food than they wanted in order to ensure that the Pole had as much as he demanded, including plenty of butter. When the Pole had, nevertheless, struck the daughter, the police had become involved, leading the mother and daughter to intercede urgently on his behalf. The Nazi official who reported this attributed it and other instances of deference to a Polish worker to 'the stupidity of our dear fellow citizens'. Yet he clearly felt acute frustration about the dependence of small farmers on 'racially inferior' labourers and their desperate willingness to make virtually any concession to them in order to keep them working productively on the farm. Those who retained the services of a foreigner, after many foreign workers on farms had been drafted into war industry, tended to appreciate how much of an advantage they had. In many other cases, a farmer's wife or widow, who might have small children to care for, had been left to run a farm without the aid of a foreigner. There was no other assistance to be had. Only those women who had at least three very young children could expect to be allocated a female foreign worker—usually a Ukrainian girl—to help out in the household.[38]

It is clear, then, that rural communities operated on a pragmatic and often rough-and-ready basis which did not accommodate the luxury of an ideological imperative. Contrary to Nazi racial prescriptions, rural south Germans were not impressed by theoretical constructs of 'enemy aliens', but rather judged incomers into a rural community—which lived simply and, in many cases, in harsh economic and social conditions—according to the added value which they could offer the community or one of its households. In wartime, with an acute labour shortage, foreign workers generally made a contribution which was highly significant and sometimes came at a price, as they increasingly realized how valuable that contribution was to their hosts. The assimilation of foreign workers, who were mainly Poles and Ukrainians, along with *Ostarbeiter* and some western Europeans, into farming communities reinforced the household nature of small-scale farming, and challenged Nazi norms in various ways. First, the Nazi regime's demands for change during the war, to meet production and delivery targets, were partially thwarted by farmers' insistence on maintaining not only themselves, but also their foreign workers at a reasonable level of nutrition. If this was mainly for pragmatic reasons, to maintain the strength and productivity of the foreign workers, it was often also a matter of human decency. Second, farmers often ignored the regime's demand that they report any violation of the Draconian restrictions imposed on foreign workers, usually because a worker who was killed or incarcerated was a labourer lost to the farm. Yet it is clear that familiarity sometimes also bred something akin to respect. Thus, third, bringing foreign workers into close contact with the German rural population made the enforcement of ideological, social and sexual norms difficult, especially where the clergy encouraged a compassionate attitude towards the foreigners. It would be a mistake to imagine that the conditions experienced by foreigners on small south German farms were *good*, especially by twenty-first-century standards. Nevertheless, at its most basic, when compared with the conditions experienced by many coerced foreign workers in German industry, especially in terms of food supply, those working on a farm had an infinitely better chance of survival. At its most favourable, they might enjoy a surrogate family life in partial compensation for the one from which they had been torn.

7

Did Hitler Miss his Chance in 1940?

Ian Kershaw

I

On 6 July 1940, Hitler returned in triumph to Berlin to celebrate before a vast, adoring public the grandiose victory over France and the conclusion of the astonishing western campaign. It was his greatest ever homecoming. To the hundreds of thousands who had waited for hours along the flower-strewn streets of the Reich capital, it seemed as if the end of the war was close at hand. Only Great Britain now appeared to stand in the way of final victory. Few among the cheering crowds imagined that she would pose much of a lasting obstacle to the mighty *Wehrmacht*. But even in the full flush of the crushing defeat of the French, Hitler's military advisers—and even the dictator himself—were less than sure that Britain's resistance would be swiftly overcome. And behind Britain was the shadow, if still indistinct, of the United States. Though as yet the sentiment was seldom spoken out loud, the lingering fear was there nonetheless: should the United States mobilize her colossal might and wealth to enter the war, as in 1917, the chances of German total victory would rapidly recede. The twin problem: how to *get* Britain out, and how to *keep* America out of the war, loomed large, therefore, in the thoughts of Hitler and the German military leadership during the imme-diate weeks following the capitulation of France. The outright priority was to persuade Britain to negotiate a settlement (or, failing that, compel her to do so through military force).[1] Removing Britain from the war would both deter America from engagement in Europe and free Germany's rear to allow Hitler to engage upon the war he had wanted to fight since the 1920s: the war to destroy 'Jewish-Bolshevism' (as he called it) and gain an enormous eastern empire at the expense of the Soviet Union.

But within an hour of Hitler's speech to the Reichstag on 19 July, the first press reports were telling him of Britain's icy response to his 'appeal to reason' to come to terms with Germany and avoid the destruction of her empire.[2] On 22 July, a broadcast speech by the British Foreign Secretary, Lord Halifax, made public what Hitler already knew, that Britain would not entertain the possibility of a negotiated settlement and was determined to fight on.[3] Even before Halifax's speech, Hitler had acknowledged the categorical rejection of his 'appeal' and on 21 July raised with his commanders-in-chief the prospect of invading the Soviet Union that very autumn.[4]

His underlying reasons were ideological, as they had been for almost two decades. Through an attack on the Soviet Union he would destroy the power of the Jews, embodied in his world-view by the Bolshevik regime, and at the same time gain 'living space' for German settlement. Victory would make Germany masters of Europe and provide the base for a racially purified empire which would be equipped eventually to challenge the United States for world domination. But the urgency implicit in the startling suggestion that the Soviet Union should be attacked that autumn was not ideological but military-strategic. And that was how Hitler presented it to his commanders-in-chief.

It was now obvious that the war to destroy Bolshevism would not be fought as he had envisaged it, with Britain's support (or at least tolerance). Britain was holding on, he declared, in the hope of help coming from America. He had already asked the navy to prepare for an invasion of England. But he saw this as very hazardous, and a last option. The way to force the issue, in his view, was to destroy the Soviet Union. He was ready, therefore, to plunge Germany for a short time (he thought) into war in the east with the war in the west still not conclusively won, raising the spectre of the war on two fronts, dreaded by military strategists and the general public alike. Hitler justified the war as necessary to remove Britain's last possible major ally on the Continent. With Russia out of the equation, Britain, he thought, would have to sue for peace. At the same time, victory over the USSR would free Japan to undertake its ambitious southern expansion without fear of Soviet power in the rear, with the combined effect of tying down the United States in the Pacific and deterring its involvement in the Atlantic and in Europe. The projected short eastern campaign offered, therefore, the prospect of overall final victory in the war. After that, at some indeterminate future date, would come the showdown with the USA. There was no contradiction between ideology and military-strategic considerations in Hitler's thoughts of invading the Soviet Union. They went hand in hand. But in the actual decision-making, the latter dominated.

When the prospect of attacking the Soviet Union that autumn was rapidly ruled out as impractical, he postponed it until May 1941. This was the date he announced to a gathering of military leaders at his alpine residence near Berchtesgaden on 31 July 1940. He expected military victory over the Soviet Union within five months. 'With Russia smashed, England's last hope would be removed', was how he justified the move.[5] It was a momentous decision—perhaps the most momentous of the entire war. And it was freely taken. That is, it was not taken under any other than self-imposed constraints. It was not taken in order to head off an immediate threat of attack by the Soviet Union. There was no suggestion at this time—the justificatory claim would come later—of the need for a pre-emptive strike. Hitler himself had acknowledged ten days earlier that the Russians did not want war with Germany.[6] Nor was the decision taken in response to pressure from the military, or from any other lobby within the power-echelons of the regime. In fact, even on 30 July, the day before Hitler's pronouncement, the Commander-in-Chief of the Army, Field-Marshal von Brauchitsch, and the Chief of the General Staff of the Army, Colonel-General Halder, agreed that 'it would be better to be on terms of friendship with Russia.' They preferred to concentrate the military effort on the possibilities of attacking British positions in the Mediterranean (particularly Gibraltar) and the Middle East, saw no danger in Russian engagement in the Balkans and Persian Gulf, and envisaged helping the Italians create a Mediterranean empire and even co-operating with the Russians to consolidate the German Reich in northern and western Europe, from which basis a lengthy war against Britain could be contemplated with equanimity.[7]

The only pressure upon Hitler was subjective: it lay in his sense that no time could be lost before striking at the Soviet Union if the overall initiative in the war, based on the balance of power and armed might, were not to drain away from Germany towards Britain and, ultimately, the USA. Whatever the misgivings of some generals about the venture, Hitler's decision was neither opposed nor contested. In fact, sensing what was coming, the army's General Staff had already begun to prepare feasibility studies weeks before Hitler announced his intention to attack the Soviet Union.[8] His military leaders were as aware as he was of the strategic position. They put forward no alternative strategy for attaining final victory, if Britain could not be invaded or bombed into submission. Moreover, like Hitler, they greatly underestimated the Red Army. And they shared his detestation of Bolshevism, some of them even his identification of the Soviet regime with the power of the Jews. But it is doubtful in the extreme whether they would have of themselves come to recommend a decision, within a few weeks of the defeat of France, to prepare urgently for an invasion of the USSR. That decision was Hitler's, and his alone.

The immensity of the catastrophe which he thereby invited would unfold ever more plainly from the autumn of 1941 onwards once the German advance on Moscow stalled as the terrible Russian winter closed in. But the question at issue here relates not to the attack itself, but to the decision to launch it, taken the previous year. Did Hitler, even as the logistics for what would come to be known as 'Operation Barbarossa' were being worked out, have options which might have given him a better chance of ending (or even curtailing) the threat to Germany posed by Britain's continuation of the war and America's presumed eventual entry? Germany's navy leadership thought so. And, for a while, so did the Foreign Ministry.

The decision, effectively taken on 31 July 1940, to attack the Soviet Union the following spring was not turned into a war directive until 18 December. Even that directive, of course, did not mean in itself that an invasion had to be launched. But in December the points were switched irreversibly on to the track that led to that invasion. In the four months that intervened between July and December 1940, by contrast, Hitler seemed in matters determining German strategy strangely vacillating—unsure which way to turn, hesitant, weak even, while at the height of his power in his external dealings with lesser dictators (Mussolini and Franco) and the puppet leader of defeated France (Marshal Pétain). He appeared at times to entertain military and foreign-policy suggestions which stood in contradiction to the war in the east. But by the late autumn it was clear that he had returned to the chosen path from which he had never seriously wandered: attacking the Soviet Union at the earliest opportunity with the strategic aim of attaining final victory in the war, as some put it, by conquering London via Moscow. Had he by then, in his single-minded determination to attack the Soviet Union, missed his chance? Was the German catastrophe determined not in the Russian snows of autumn 1941, but in the fateful choice a year earlier when other options seemed open?

That an alternative—militarily far more promising—strategy was available, but was squandered through Hitler's insistence on attacking the Soviet Union, was not infrequently claimed in the postwar years.[9] It offered an exculpatory device for some military leaders, all too keen to look no farther than Hitler himself as the cause of 'the German catastrophe'.[10] Later historical research has usually been far more sceptical—invariably concentrating upon Hitler's ideological imperative for the war in the east.[11] What follows revisits the problem by looking not just at Hitler's subjective preferences, but at the objective constraints on his actions; and by looking at the ways in which his military leaders—especially the navy leadership—advanced their case. If it can be shown that no coherent alternative strategy in fact existed, or at least that none was put to Hitler, then it is difficult to claim that a genuine option lay open. If, however, one was proposed and rejected, then the merits of the alternative warrant evaluation, as do the reasons why it was found wanting.

II

Strategic thinking among the leaders of the German navy—competing in what was usually an uphill struggle with the army and air force for status, influence and resources—had from the outset run along different lines to that of Hitler, though it was no less aggressive and no less ambitious in its vision of territorial expansion and eventual world domination. Where Hitler had wanted to harness British friendship to destroy the Soviet Union, looking to build a huge land empire in eastern Europe and impregnable strength from which at some distant future date Germany could engage in a showdown with the USA, the navy saw the destruction of British world power as the central war-aim. It demanded a big and powerful fleet, capable of taking on and defeating the Royal Navy in a classical naval war. Accompanied by the construction of an enormous German colonial empire, this would provide the basis to challenge and defeat the United States in the contest for world domination. Attacking Bolshevik Russia did not figure prominently in this thinking. Bolshevism was, of course, accepted as an evil to be confronted and destroyed at some point. But it was taken for granted that it could be contained, then smashed at a later date, once German pre-eminence had been established. Naval thinking in the Third Reich was, in essence, an updated and amended variant of that of Tirpitz's time.[12] It drew on one of the two main strands of German imperialism, that of the overseas colonial empire. Hitler's ideas (and those of the Nazi Party) arose from the alternative strand of imperialism, also with deep roots in the Wilhelmine period, that looked to expansion and conquest in eastern Europe.[13] For the army, though not the navy, this latter version, with its inbuilt demands for a large land force to ensure continental mastery, had evident attractions. But the maritime and continental alternatives could easily stand alongside each other in the pre-war years. Though army, navy and air force competed for resources, there was no need to choose between the alternatives. With the decision in 1939 to construct a large surface fleet, envisaged in the Z-Plan, it even appeared for a time as if the navy was getting its way.[14]

But the navy's conception of preparing for a major struggle by the mid 1940s was completely upturned when the Polish crisis led to war between Germany and Great Britain in September 1939. In a remarkable memorandum of 3 September 1939, the very date that Britain and France declared war on Germany, the Commander-in-Chief of the Navy, Grand Admiral Raeder, came close to criticizing Hitler for taking Germany into war prematurely, and admitted that the navy, which according to the Z-Plan was arming for a war 'on the ocean' at the turn of the year 1944–45, was still in autumn 1939 nowhere near sufficiently armed for the 'great struggle with England'.[15]

By the spring and early summer of 1940, however, this initial gloom had given way to unbounded optimism. In the wake of the part played by the navy in the Scandinavian conquests in April, then especially the stirring events during the western campaign in May and June, culminating in the dramatic victory over France, naval leaders had worked out their utopian vision of the future world power of Germany resting on the strength of the navy to protect its overseas possessions.[16] Huge territorial annexation was envisaged. According to a memorandum of 3 June, composed by Counter-Admiral Kurt Fricke, Denmark, Norway, and northern France were to remain as German possessions, safeguarding the Reich's north-western seaboard. A contiguous swathe of territories—mainly to be taken from France and Belgium, added to some returned former German colonies, and others exchanged with Britain and Portugal—would establish a large colonial empire in central Africa. Islands off the African east coast, most notably Madagascar, would offer protective bases.[17] Admiral Rolf Carls, head of naval command in the Baltic and for long seen as Raeder's likely successor, went even further. Parts of Belgium and France (including Normandy and Brittany) would become German protectorates, based on the Czech model. The French colonial empire would be broken up in favour of Germany, Italy and to some extent Spain. South Africa and southern Rhodesia would be removed from the British Empire and become an independent state, while northern Rhodesia would come into German possession as a bridge to link its east- and west-African territories. All British rights in the Persian Gulf, most notably the oil-fields, would pass to Germany. Britain and France were to be excluded from any control over the Suez Canal. British mandates in the Middle East would be taken away. Germany would take over the Shetlands and the Channel Islands. Strategic bases were to be established on the Canary Islands (probably in an exchange of territory with Spain), in Dakar and Senegal on the African west coast (at the expense of France), and on Madagascar, Mauritius and the Seychelles in the Indian Ocean. Carls admitted the vision might seem 'fantastic', though advocated its realization in order to 'secure Germany's claims of its part of the globe once and for all'.[18] Yet another memorandum, dated 11 July, imagined the great battle-fleet necessary to defend a large colonial empire and wage war against the USA after Britain had been totally defeated and its once-mighty Empire had broken up. Coastal defences would be massively extended. Bases on the Azores, the Canaries, and the Cape Verde Islands would offer security against attack from across the Atlantic. Taking possession of New Guinea as well as Madagascar would offer protection against attack in the Indian Ocean. Links between Germany and its colonies could be upheld without difficulty by dominance in the Indian Ocean, Red Sea, and Mediterranean.[19] Once more, it was a breathtakingly grandiose vision.

However, such memoranda fell well short of anything resembling coherent strategic thinking. They remained no more than megalomaniac pipe-dreams composed in the intoxication of seemingly imminent final victory. In fact, without the defeat of Britain, which was their underlying premiss, even the first steps towards their realization were out of the question. And they did nothing to prepare the navy for the strategic choice which, by the summer of 1940, Hitler had effectively made: the invasion of the Soviet Union by spring the following year. The dictator's interest remained, as it had done throughout, focused on the prospects of empire in the east of Europe, not in central Africa. For him, in contrast to the navy, building a colonial empire in Africa would only come *after*, not before, the defeat of Bolshevism and formed part of the inevitable future confrontation with the American continent.[20]

For its own part, the naval leadership, when it descended from utopian dreams to practical planning, was preoccupied with the immediate task which had been thrust upon it only weeks earlier: preparing the operational plans for the invasion of Britain by the autumn, aimed at removing British involvement in the war and freeing Germany's rear for the attack on the Soviet Union.

Though preliminary naval contingency planning for a possible invasion of Britain had been undertaken as early as November 1939,[21] serious operational consideration did not begin until June 1940. On the very day that the French sued for peace, 17 June, General Walter Warlimont, who, as head of the National Defence Department of the *Wehrmacht* Operations Staff, was close to the very centre of military thinking, told Raeder that Hitler had expressed no intention of attempting a landing in England 'since he fully saw the extraordinary difficulties of such an undertaking'. Accordingly, the High Command of the *Wehrmacht* had made no preparations for such a move. Warlimont also indicated the evident divergence in Hitler's thinking from the underlying stragegic preferences of the naval leadership. He confirmed that Hitler did not want totally to destroy Britain's world empire, since this would only be 'to the disadvantage of the white race'. He preferred to reach peace with Britain, following the defeat of France, 'on the condition of return of colonies and renunciation of English influence in Europe'.[22]

Nevertheless, within a fortnight Colonel-General Alfred Jodl, as head of the *Wehrmacht* Operations Staff Warlimont's immediate superior and Hitler's closest military adviser, had devised a strategy for forcing Britain to capitulate, if she could not be persuaded to agree terms. This involved the prospect of a landing, but also 'war on the periphery', aimed at limited military support for those countries—Italy, Spain, Russia, and Japan—which had an interest in benefiting from the undermining of the British Empire. An Italian attack on the Suez Canal and the capture of Gibraltar were specifically mentioned.[23] The 'peripheral strategy' remained under consideration throughout the summer and autumn, and aspects of it coincided with the thinking of the navy leadership.

The idea of an invasion of Britain, on the other hand, had only a brief life-span. Hitler evidently saw this as a last resort and was highly sceptical from the outset about its practicality.[24] He had emphasized German mastery of the skies as the most important prerequisite for a landing. Raeder fully agreed. But the navy leadership was not only dubious that this could be attained, but also by mid-July expressing its extreme anxiety about transport difficulties and, not least, the worry that, even if German troops could be landed on British soil, the intervention of the Royal Navy could preventing further landings and cut them off, leading to the 'extraordinary endangering of the entire deployed army'.[25] Moreover, the intended completion of preparations for the landing by mid-August rapidly proved illusory.[26] The necessary rescheduling of completion to the middle of the following month meant that only the briefest of opportunities was left before the vagaries of the weather in the English Channel ruled out an attempt before the following spring.[27] And by the end of August it was plain to the navy leadership that preparations for transport could not be completed by the new date set of 15 September.[28] Even before the end of July, the Naval Warfare Executive (*Seekriegsleitung*) had, in fact, been advising against trying to carry out the operation in 1940, and putting it off until May the following year at the earliest. On 31 July, Raeder conveyed the arguments to Hitler, who acknowledged the difficulties, but deferred a final decision until the Luftwaffe had been given the opportunity to bomb England for a full week.[29] The order for the indefinite postponement of 'Operation Sealion' was not actually given until 17 September.[30] But in reality, Hitler had always had cold feet about the prospect of a landing in Britain, and possibly accepted as early as 29–31 July, long before the decisive phase of the 'Battle of Britain' was reached, that it would not be possible to go through with the invasion.[31] The decision to attack Russia had swiftly taken the place of the decision to attack Britain. It was seen as less risky.

Grand Admiral Raeder had already left the gathering of military leaders at the Berghof on 31 July 1940, when Hitler announced his decision to prepare for war against the Soviet Union the following spring.[32] But nothing in the announcement could have been unexpected. Raeder had been present ten days earlier when Hitler had first spoken of a possible attack on the Soviet Union.[33] And three days before the announcement, plainly aware of what was in the air, the Chief of Staff of the Naval Warfare Executive, Counter-Admiral Fricke, composed a memorandum outlining his views on conflict with Russia, which Raeder read the following day, 29 July. Fricke accepted that Bolshevism was 'a chronic danger' which had

to be 'eliminated one way or the other', and posed no objection to the
envisaged German attack, other than acknowledging the sectional disadvantage, since naval interests would take a back seat to those of the army
and Luftwaffe.[34] At the time of the crucial decision by Hitler on 31 July
to prepare for the war against Russia, therefore, the navy not only raised
no objection but had no clearly devised strategic alternative on offer.

Over the following months, however, this was to change. The emergence of a Mediterranean strategy fitted in with the notion of 'war on the
periphery' which Jodl had indicated in his memorandum of 30 June.
Gradually, a military alternative emerged, though one which demanded a
more active diplomacy targeted at Spain, Italy and Vichy France.
Meanwhile, however, the operational planning for the attack on Russia
was taking shape. This was the Sword of Damocles hanging over the
timing of any proposed alternative.

During the late summer and the autumn months, the navy's ideas on
strategy, as they developed, had much—though far from everything—in
common with the thinking in Hitler's headquarters. The rapid fading of
prospects of an invasion of Britain prompted other consideration in the
Wehrmacht High Command of how to break British resistance. For Jodl,
in charge of overall *Wehrmacht* operational planning, the 'peripheral
strategy' he had devised was a crucial concern.[35] But it did not stand in
contradiction to an attack on Russia. Rather, it was aimed ideally at forcing
Britain to agree to terms and freeing Germany's back for the war on
Russia—or, failing that, tying Britain down until victory in the Soviet
Union compelled her to yield. For the naval leadership, on the other hand,
the 'peripheral' (or Mediterranean) strategy was no temporary solution to
facilitate the war in the east. It offered an alternative to that war.

By mid-August, Hitler had agreed plans (which he thought would meet
with Franco's approval) for an operation to take Gibraltar by early 1941
and to support an Italian thrust to the Suez Canal around the same time.[36]
Shortly afterwards, the first serious consideration by the navy to a strategy
focused on the Mediterranean was signalled by an analysis by Admiral
Gerhard Wagner on 29 August of how war against Britain could best be
waged, assuming that 'Operation Sealion' was not to take place.[37]
Bombing raids and the war in the Atlantic to cut off supplies would not,
he took for granted, force a decision over the next months. And by the
following spring, British defensive capacity would have improved,
perhaps with American support. The best way to attack Britain, he
concluded, would be to weaken its Empire through war in the
Mediterranean, in tandem with the Italians. Taking up the thinking in the
Wehrmacht High Command, he pointed out that it would be possible to
capture Gibraltar, with Spanish support, and to block the Suez Canal by
an offensive thrusting from Libya through Egypt. The result would be to

force Britain out of the Mediterranean, which would then be entirely in the hands of the Axis powers. In turn, this would safeguard shipping in the whole of the Mediterranean, ensuring unthreatened imports from north Africa. The position of the Axis powers in the Balkan region would in the process also be greatly strengthened. Turkey would no longer be able to remain neutral, and would fall within their orbit. The raw materials of the Arab countries, Egypt and the Sudan would be available to the Axis. There would be a good platform to weaken British positions in the Indian Ocean through attacks on colonies in east Africa, posing an obvious threat to India itself. The loss of Gibraltar would deprive Britain of one of its most important bases for the war in the Atlantic. Even were Britain to acquire a foothold in the Azores, Madeira, or the Canaries, it would scarcely provide compensation. German mastery in the western Mediterranean would enable pressure to be exerted on French north African colonies and prevent them going over to the Gaullists, and hence to the British side. At the same time, British bases on the west coast of Africa would be endangered. The Italian navy would, as an additional advantage, be freed to support the German war effort outside the Mediterranean, in the Indian Ocean and the Atlantic, while the Italian army and air force could make further advances against the British, above all in east Africa. A final benefit would be the entry of Spain into the war (seen as implicit in the taking of Gibraltar), thereby widening significantly the basis for German naval warfare in the Atlantic. The memorandum concluded

> that the mastery of the Mediterranean will be of decisive strategic significance for the continuation of the war. The operations envisaged for this purpose go well beyond 'interim actions', as they were previously described. Not only will an effective strengthening of the German-Italian war potential and a greatly improved basis for the last decisive struggle against the English Motherland and the sources of strength of the English Empire be attained. [But] since the most sensitive points of the English world empire will be attacked or threatened, there is even the possibility that England will feel compelled to give up further resistence.[38]

This would be all the more likely if American support remained negligible to that point. There was, therefore, no time to be lost. The strategy was in the interests of the navy, Wagner pointed out, ending with the expectation that Raeder would put the proposals to Hitler.

Four days before Raeder could put the case, in his briefing on 6 September, the USA had agreed to provide Great Britain with fifty ageing destroyers—a decision of far greater symbolic than direct military importance, and signalling to the German leadership the increasing likelihood of a British-American coalition in the not too distant future.[39] Following Raeder's highlighting of the danger to the Portuguese and Spanish islands in the Atlantic and to the French colonies in West Africa which would be posed by USA involvement in the war, Hitler gave instructions to prepare for the occupation of the Azores, the Canaries and the Cape Verde Islands to prevent any possible landing by the British and Americans (though naval analysts working on the logistics over the following weeks were not persuaded of the value of such an operation).[40] In the light of the growing 'Problem USA', and asking somewhat disingenuously what Hitler's political and military directives might be in the event of 'Sealion' not taking place, Raeder indeed pressed the argument for a Mediterranean strategy, along the lines of Wagner's memorandum, not as an 'interim' but as a 'main action against England'. He asked for preparations to begin immediately so that they could be implemented before the USA could intervene. Hitler gave orders to that effect. This did not mean, however, that he was signalling approval for a Mediterranean strategy *instead* of the intended strike at the Soviet Union. The proposed Russian campaign—at this time code-named 'Problem S'—came up later in the briefing. And when it did, Raeder raised no objections, merely observing that the most suitable time for the navy would be as the ice melted. He added, a point immediately agreed by Hitler, that 'Sealion' should not be attempted at the same time.[41]

By the time of Raeder's briefing with Hitler on 26 September, the case for the Mediterranean strategy had taken on a new urgency in the light of the attack by British and Free French troops—supporters of General de Gaulle—on Dakar a few days earlier. French Morocco, Algeria and Tunisia were thought to be endangered as the Vichy regime lost ground to the Gaullist movement in French Equatorial Africa. This concentrated German minds. Raeder had asked to speak alone with Hitler—a quite exceptional occurrence—and had begun by expressing his wish to go beyond his specific remit in commenting on the progress of the war. He pressed for a more conciliatory approach to the Vichy regime, wishing to upturn previous relations by incorporating the French as full allies in the war against Britain. Waging war together with the French would, argued Raeder, offer the possibility not only of securing the French possessions and their raw materials, but also of forcing Britain out of central Africa and depriving her of the port of Freetown on the western coast, thus causing significant problems for convoy traffic from the south Atlantic— from Latin America and South Africa. It would constitute a big step towards pushing the British out of the Mediterranean. Even before turning to north-west Africa, Raeder had urged Hitler to concentrate on 'waging the struggle against E[ngland] by all available means and without delay, before America can intervene'. The British, he stated, had always regarded the Mediterranean as the key to their world position. He concluded, therefore, that 'the Mediterranean question must therefore by cleared up over the winter.' Gibraltar had to be taken, and even before that the Canaries secured by the Luftwaffe. German support was necessary to help the Italians take the Suez Canal. From there, he saw an advance through Palestine and Syria—which Hitler said would depend upon the French but ought to be possible—as far as Turkey. 'When we reach that point, Turkey will be in our power. The Russian problem will then appear in a different light. Russia basically fears Germany. It is questionable whether an attack on Russia from the north will then be necessary.'[42]

It would have been difficult for Raeder to have been more explicit about the navy's preferred strategy.[43] The Naval Warfare Executive was keen to establish the fact that Hitler had even indicated his basic agreement with the ideas expressed.[44] Two problems nevertheless surfaced at the briefing—if only implicitly.

The first was the size of the fleet. Raeder pointed out (and Hitler concurred) that the fleet was currently too small for the tasks awaiting it if the Mediterranean strategy were to be implemented—particularly if the war were to acquire a global dimension through the entry of the USA. But shipbuilding capacity could not cater for any extension to existing commitments. Obviously, therefore, a maritime strategy was severely hampered from the outset if the fleet was too small to implement it and resources did not allow for any rapid expansion.

The second was the implication for foreign policy, which Hitler touched upon. He told Raeder that after concluding the Tripartite Pact with Japan (which was to be signed the very next day, 27 September), he would have talks with Mussolini and Franco, and would have to decide whether to go with France or Spain. He thought that France was the more likely choice since Spain demanded a great deal (French Morocco) but offered little in return. Britain and the USA had to be excluded from north-west Africa. That much was clear. But France would have to comply with certain territorial demands of Germany and Italy, before agreement could be reached on the extent of her African colonial possessions. Though Hitler did not stress the point, this plainly weakened the attractiveness to France of any arrangement with Germany. Moreover, Hitler was cool about Raeder's hopes of engaging the French fleet on Germany's side. He was unprepared to move on this without the approval of his Axis partner Mussolini, who was unlikely to be enamoured of any strengthening of Italy's rival, France, in the Mediterranean. Meanwhile, if Spain were to join the war on the Axis side, the Canaries and perhaps also the Azores and the Cape Verde Islands would have to be secured by the Luftwaffe.[45] In effect, therefore, while agreeing to the Mediterranean strategy in principle, Hitler was making its execution dependent upon the outcome of his negotiations with Mussolini, Franco and Pétain. He was well aware that pleasing all of them would be no easy matter.

At the time, in late September, the navy's ideas on directing Germany's war effort at the Mediterranean corresponded quite closely to the notion developed in the Foreign Ministry of a 'continental block' of countries formed into a powerful alliance against Britain.[46] The Foreign Minister, Joachim von Ribbentrop himself, no less, had been keen to build up a powerful world-wide alliance, incorporating both the Soviet Union and Japan, which would be ranged against Britain, at the same time neutralizing the USA.[47] Within this grand concept, a western 'continental bloc' incorporating Vichy France and Spain, alongside Italy, formed a smaller, but vital, component.[48] In military terms, the 'peripheral strategy' as it had developed by early autumn 1940 involved—apart from trying to block British imports—three strands: an Italian-German Middle-East offensive; the taking of Gibraltar; and extension of German control over the African coast and the Atlantic islands.[49] Clearly, as had emerged from the Raeder briefing on 26 September, the military potential of such a strategy rested upon important breakthroughs in diplomacy: quite specifically, upon Hitler's ability to come to satisfactory agreements with the leaders of Spain and Vichy France. And this was precisely where it would founder.

III

As summer turned into autumn, it was still not clear to those close to the hub of power in Germany—including for a while, it seems, Hitler himself—which variant of military strategy should be followed. The setting of different priorities was still possible. That is to say, options were still apparently open.

Hitler's own preference, both ideological and military, was obviously for an early strike on the Soviet Union. That had been plainly established at the end of July. Nothing in the interim indicates that he had changed his mind. But his interest in the 'peripheral strategy' was not simply a ruse. The Russian campaign, which he had initially hoped to launch that autumn, could not take place until spring at the earliest. Meanwhile, however, the worry had deepened that America might join in the war on the British side sooner rather than later.[50] Clearly, Hitler was no less anxious than earlier in the summer to prevent this happening. And the most obvious way was to force Britain out of the war. With 'Sealion' now shelved (and effectively, if not nominally, abandoned), a military and diplomatic focus on the Mediterranean might be seen to offer the best opportunity. Variants of such a strategy were supported, as we have seen, by Jodl (and his deputy Warlimont) in the *Wehrmacht* Operations Staff, by Raeder and the Naval Warfare Executive, and by Ribbentrop, the Foreign Minister. Hitler was prepared for a while to give his backing to the search for a diplomatic opening on the 'periphery' and continued to promote the military planning which would depend upon the success of such a breakthrough. But whereas for Raeder, for Warlimont (if not for Jodl), and even for Ribbentrop the 'peripheral strategy' was viewed as an alternative to the invasion of Russia, for Hitler it did not constitute an alternative, but was merely a prelude to secure Germany's rear before engaging on the showdown with the Soviet Union which was, in his eyes, both inevitable and alone capable of deciding the final outcome of the war. Hitler's heart was never in the 'peripheral' strategy, therefore, as an end in itself. In part at least, this probably explains why his diplomatic effort in the October tour he made to engage in talks with Mussolini, Franco and Pétain proved so unfruitful.

The central purpose of Hitler's meeting with Mussolini on the Brenner on 4 October was—though he came only slowly to the point—to sound out the Duce about the possibility of bringing France and Spain to a 'common line' and in this way to create 'a continental coalition against England'.[51] Mussolini had no objections. But both dictators clearly saw that Spain's territorial demands as a price for entering the war—the gain of Morocco and Oran from France as well as Gibraltar from Britain, only the last posing no problem—would be impossible for the French to meet, and would pave the way to Gaullist success (in turn meaning the penetration of British interests) in the vital area of north Africa. Since Mussolini took the opportunity to remind Hitler of Italian demands for French territorial concessions, it was plain that the potential for finding a diplomatic solution which would satisfy the three Mediterranean powers, Italy, France and Spain, was extremely limited. Moreover, Hitler was clearly going to undertake nothing which might damage relations with his Axis partner. So, though friendly, the talks produced nothing tangible to assist the creation of the 'continental coalition'.[52]

The meeting with Franco at Hendaye on 23 October lacked all promise from the outset.[53] Hitler's bargaining position was weak. He wanted Spain in the war primarily to ease the planned attack on Gibraltar and to bolster the defence of the Atlantic islands off the Iberian coast. But he was not prepared to pay the exorbitant price which he was well aware that Spain would demand: huge supplies of armaments and foodstuffs, and satisfaction of her territorial claims not only on Gibraltar (which was easy to concede) but on Morocco and Oran as well. Hitler's view was probably much the same as the private verdict confided to his diary by Ernst von Weizsäcker, State Secretary in the Foreign Ministry: 'Gibraltar is not worth that much to us.'[54] Germany could not contemplate meeting Franco's material demands. And the territorial concessions, as Hitler had made clear to Mussolini, were out of the question on account of the serious threat they would pose, through the weakening of Vichy France's position, to the hold of the Axis in north Africa. So Hitler had nothing to offer Franco, other than Gibraltar itself. Desirable though the acquisition of Gibraltar was to the Spaniards, it was available only at what, from their point of view, was the high risk of involvement in a war which Franco, despite Hitler's posturing, seriously doubted was as good as won by the Axis. Hitler came away empty-handed.

He fared little better the next day with Pétain, even if the talks were more cordial.[55] Agreement on closer 'co-operation' between France and Germany fell well short of an outright French commitment to join the war against Britain. Discussion remained at the level of generalities. Once again, Hitler's hands were effectively tied, and he had nothing concrete to offer the French. Though Vichy France's entry into the war on Germany's side (and on her terms) made military and strategic sense from the German point of view, it was difficult to make this proposition attractive if mention were made of the mooted tampering with French colonial territory in north Africa in a peace-treaty between the two countries, let alone the expropriation (which the Germans had in mind) of Briey and Calais on the coast of France itself, as well as Alsace-Lorraine.[56] Moreover, and a key point for Hitler, closer relations with France would certainly cause Italian hackles to rise—something he wanted at all costs to avoid. In any case, it seems doubtful that Hitler really wanted the French as fully fledged allies anyway. So the talks with Pétain amounted to no more than shadow-dancing.

In short, Hitler could not satisfy Spain without antagonizing France, and could not accommodate the French without upsetting his 'friend' Mussolini. Meanwhile, by the time the two dictators met again, in Florence on 28 October, his 'friend' had, to Hitler's fury, begun his ill-fated invasion of Greece—putting a further sizeable spanner in the works of any strategy revolving around German-Italian military co-operation in the Mediterranean.

Already on his way back from his meetings with Franco and Pétain, Hitler had indicated to his pliant head of *Wehrmacht* High Command, Field-Marshal Wilhelm Keitel, and to Jodl, that the war against Russia had to take place in the coming year.[57] Soon afterwards, on 4 November, while offering his military leaders a *tour d'horizon* of all current strategic possibilities which concentrated on the Mediterranean and Middle East, Hitler nevertheless remarked that Russia remained the 'great problem of Europe' and that 'everything must be done to be ready for the great showdown.'[58] Evidently, his failure to accomplish any breakthrough in engineering even a limited west European 'continental bloc' ranged against Great Britain had confirmed his own prior instinct that the only way to achieve final victory was through attacking and rapidly defeating the Soviet Union. The taking of Gibraltar (together with the Canaries and Cape Verde Islands) was still high on the agenda, and Hitler continued to cherish hopes of Franco joining in the war. He was prepared if need be, he said, to send troops into Portugal. But Mussolini's Greek adventure meant that the Italian offensive in Libya had to be deferred, and in consequence also the deployment of German troops in north Africa and the drive to Suez. It was the first clear sign of Hitler's lack of trust in the military capability of his Italian partner.[59]

As Molotov, the Soviet Commissar for Foreign Affairs, made his way to Berlin for talks with Hitler on 12–13 November, German war strategy was still unclear and undetermined. On the very day that discussions with Molotov began,[60] Hitler put out a military directive which ranged widely over potential fields of combat. The taking of Gibraltar to drive the British from the western Mediterranean and prevent them gaining a foothold on the Iberian peninsula or the Atlantic islands was the dominant item. Political efforts to bring Spain into the war were in train. France would for the time being provide co-operation short of full military engagement in the war against Britain. Deployment of German troops to support the planned Italian offensive against Egypt was put on hold. 'Operation Sealion', the invasion of Britain, was not formally abandoned, but no longer figured as anything remotely resembling a military priority. Thanks to Mussolini, preparations had to be undertaken for the occupation of Greece, north of the Aegean. But perhaps the most crucial consideration came towards the end of the directive: 'Political discussions with the aim of clarifying Russia's position in the near future are in progress. Whatever the results of these discussion, all preparations already verbally ordered for the east are to be continued.'[61] Though no military option had been closed off by this point, there is every indication that Hitler had become so sceptical about progress in the Mediterranean that he was returning, his ideas confirmed, to the strategy he had already favoured in the summer: the attack on the USSR. The unease prompted in his mind by the Molotov visit was the final determinant.[62] Raeder's renewed plea, on 14 November, for priority to be given to the Mediterranean, and to a push on Suez, could only fall, therefore, on deaf ears. Hitler made it plain that he was still inclined to press forward with the showdown with Russia. Raeder's recommendation to postpone this until victory over Britain had been attained was by now whistling in the wind. And when Raeder advised caution to obviate a possible occupation of the Portuguese Atlantic islands by the British or Americans, Hitler's reply was characteristic. He was not thinking of the Azores primarily in a defensive, but in an *offensive*, capacity, to allow the stationing of bombers capable of reaching America and therefore compelling the United States to build up air defences rather than providing aid to Britain.[63] It was an indication that the Iberian peninsula and the Spanish and Portuguese Atlantic islands now figured in his thinking as a deterrent to Anglo-American intervention while he was engaged in the east, rather than—as earlier in the summer—as part of a strategy aimed primarily at getting Britain to the conference table.[64]

Only a brief time later, Hitler dispatched his adjutants to find a field headquarters in East Prussia.[65] On 5 December he told Brauchitsch and Halder to prepare the army for an attack on Russia at the end of the coming May.[66] Three days later he heard that renewed attempts to win over Spain had failed. Franco had decided categorically to keep Spain out of the war. Hitler promptly called off preparations to take Gibraltar 'since the political conditions are no longer available'.[67] The operation was abandoned on 9 January, even if Hitler dreamt for some while longer of its possible resurrection.[68] Long before this, the eastward direction of German strategy had been fixed by Hitler's formal directive on 18 December for 'Operation Barbarossa', with the expressed aim, even before the war against Britain was won, 'to crush Soviet Russia in a rapid campaign'.[69] The decision reached in principle on 31 July was now enshrined in a military directive. There would be no turning back. The possibility of an alternative strategy which had briefly presented itself in the late summer and autumn could now be definitively ruled out.[70]

IV

So did Hitler miss his chance in 1940? In the light of what we have seen, the question has perhaps to be approached in different ways. The first and most important consideration relates to Hitler's own thinking. *He*, after all, determined policy. Others might seek to influence him. But, ultimately, he decided.

Hitler certainly did not think he had missed a chance. In his eyes, despite testing a number of possibilities in the late summer and autumn of 1940, none proved a practicable alternative to the course which he had already regarded by July as the most promising strategy—an attack on the Soviet Union to attain rapid victory before the winter, laying the ground for the wider struggle against Britain and America. This of course fitted his long-established and unchanging ideological convictions. But strategic considerations were paramount in determining the timing. The United States, he thought, would be ready to enter the war on Britain's side by 1942. He was convinced, therefore, that time was not on Germany's side. Continental dominance, the end of the European war and the impregnability that this would bring had to be attained during 1941 before any conflict with the USA. There is no indication that he considered postponing, let alone cancelling, the invasion of Russia that he had envisaged for spring 1941. The preparations set in train at the end of July 1940 were never halted. By containing Great Britain and deterring the USA, the 'peripheral strategy' offered for him a device for laying the ground for the attack on the Soviet Union, not a replacement for it. There is little doubt that he was serious in his support for both the military and diplomatic moves centring on the Mediterranean and the Iberian peninsula. But from his perspective there was nothing to be done during the war to reconcile or overcome the serious differences of interest which separated the main powers in the region—Italy, France and Spain. And since the necessary political framework could not be established, a military strategy for the Mediterranean was unlikely to pay a high dividend. Without Spain's entry into the war, an assault on Gibraltar, the key to the western Mediterranean, became a different proposition. It could be achieved. But the cost, militarily and politically, would be high. It was no wonder, therefore, that it was called off, once Franco made it clear that Spain would remain neutral. The other main prong of the Mediterranean military strategy, the push to Suez, depended upon the Italians, who soon proved themselves to be the weakest link in the military chain. Once Mussolini had invaded Greece—immediately and unsurprisingly branded by Hitler as an act of stupidity[71]—the prospects of Italian success in north Africa vanished. But with the weakened and stretched Italians up against it in Libya, the push for Suez obviously could not take place. Finally, there was little to be done with France. Until the end of 1940, when Italy's Greek venture had created such difficulties that Mussolini would have welcomed a German-French agreement, the Italians had been reluctant to see any rebuilding of French strength in the Mediterranean and north Africa.[72] For Hitler, therefore, an alternative to his chosen strategy never posed itself. And what he was aiming for—a prop for his chosen strategy—could not be accomplished. From Hitler's point of view, there was, therefore, no chance that was missed.

Did others, close to the heart of strategic planning, think a chance had been missed? The clearest alternative, as we have seen, was thought out by the navy. And it was put before Hitler by Grand Admiral Raeder on more than one occasion. We noted that Raeder did attempt, if not forcefully, to dissuade Hitler from pressing ahead with the attack on Russia. Hitler even agreed, before his tune changed later in the autumn, particularly following Molotov's visit, that the Soviet Union posed no imminent threat to Germany. But Raeder, for the reasons already adduced, never had any serious prospect of persuading Hitler to change his plans. Hitler never deviated from his conviction that destruction of the Soviet Union in a lightning campaign was the only route to overall victory. Moreover, Raeder, though he favoured another route, never actually *opposed* the invasion of Russia, even if he was lukewarm about it. And by the time the navy's preferred Mediterranean strategy had taken shape—leaving aside the grandiose utopian dreams of a vast colonial empire that had temporarily seemed so attractive in the wake of the defeat of France—both the political and military framework for its accomplishment were crumbling, leaving the force of Hitler's argument for the Russian option difficult to counter. The navy's alternative—the conclusion seems hard to resist—was a genuine policy option only in retrospect, not at the time.

In the High Command of the *Wehrmacht*, the most outspoken advocate of a Mediterranean strategy was Jodl's deputy in the *Wehrmacht* Operations Staff, and head of its strategic planning section, General Warlimont. But his advancement of proposals to focus Germany's military effort on the drive through north Africa became increasingly futile as the autumn progressed. Warlimont had little support from Jodl, his immediate superior and Hitler's closest adviser on strategic matters. Despite the fact that he himself had put forward the 'peripheral strategy' at the end of June, Jodl, as we have noted, viewed this as the basis for facilitating the strategic goal which Hitler had established: the attack on Russia.[73] Though Jodl was little involved before December 1940 in the detailed preparations for the war in the east, which were the province of the army's high command, not of the *Wehrmacht* Operations Staff, he did not question Hitler's fundamental decision to attack the Soviet Union. Uncritical belief in Hitler as a military genius, greatly magnified since the triumph over France, ruled out any conceivable opposition from this quarter,[74] and even more so if anything from the toadying Keitel. And whatever the initial doubts of Brauchitsch and Halder, the leaders of the army (which was evidently the key branch of the *Wehrmacht* in the forthcoming assault on Russia), they were quickly quelled. Both rapidly saw preparation for the war in the east as the outright priority. No serious consideration was given to any alternative. And, certainly, no alternative could be expected from the Luftwaffe, whose Commander-in-Chief was Göring.

The divided organizational structure of the German armed forces in itself hindered the promotion of any serious alternative to Hitler's own plans. The Chiefs of Staff of the Army, Navy, and Air Force, and the Chief of the Operations Staff of the *Wehrmacht* High Command (responsible for overall strategic planning) did not meet in a body to devise strategy. Nor did the commanders-in-chief come together, except in Hitler's domineering presence when genuine discussion was as good as impossible.[75] So the axis of common interest briefly forged between Warlimont's office and naval command both lacked support elsewhere within the armed forces and had no outlet to argue the case for an alternative which could have been put as a reasoned strategy in opposition to Hitler's. Structurally, therefore, it was impossible to construct a coherent alternative strategy. None was ever available to be put forward for consideration. But without that coherent alternative, it is difficult to argue that a chance was missed.

Finally, there was Ribbentrop. His own conception had certainly differed from that of Hitler. But Ribbentrop was Hitler's man through and through. The last thing he was going to do was to threaten his own position by opposing the man on whom it depended. Once it was plain both that the 'continental strategy' was doomed and that Hitler was set upon his war in the east, Ribbentrop's 'alternative' simply faded like the morning mist.

But even if Hitler did not see any other chance, and the armed forces were not capable of presenting a compelling alternative, is it possible, finally, to posit a *theoretical* chance—an option which could have won Germany the war, or at least have prevented such a disastrous outcome, if only the leadership had not been blind to it? Here, of course, we leave historical terrain—that which happened and the actual strategic considerations at the time—and move to the realm of counter-factual speculation. Given the number of possible variables to take into consideration, this rapidly degenerates into little more than an academic guessing game. But, staying with the thought-experiment for a moment, it is possible to imagine that a full German commitment to war in the Mediterranean and north Africa—demanding also a tougher policy towards the Italians, as well as the Spaniards, and full acceptance of the French as fighting allies—at the expense of preparation for a war in the east could have paid dividends in at least the short to medium term, would have given the overall war a different complexion and another possible outcome, and might have avoided the total calamity that came to befall Germany. The Mediterranean was, it must be admitted, not as vital to Britain's global empire as Raeder had claimed. Nevertheless, loss of control of the Mediterranean, followed by deprivation of possessions and oil in the Middle East, would unquestionably have been a grave blow. Britain and her empire would certainly have been seriously weakened, especially if national independence movements in the Middle East and India had, as most probably would have been the case, gained in strength and confidence as a result of British military set-backs. And it is far from certain that the United States, where even as it was Roosevelt had to struggle for months against strong isolationist tendencies, would have rushed to support a weakened Britain. The Japanese would doubtless have shown little hesitation in exploiting British discomfiture in the Far East, so that the Americans, instead of seeing the Atlantic as the main concern, might have found their attention diverted at an earlier stage than was historically the case towards the Pacific. Whether, given such a bleak scenario, Britain would have continued to hold out, or would have discarded the Churchill government and looked for peace terms with Germany is a moot point. With Britain subordinated, the European continent and north Africa under German control, and the Americans preoccupied with Japan, the 'Russian question' would have been seen in a different light. There would have been less urgency, less immediate strategic necessity, to crush the Soviet Union in 1941. The detestation for Bolshevism would have remained. But Stalin's regime would have appeared less of a threat, more capable of containment, and, therefore, perhaps not worth a dangerous military gamble in a lightning war of aggression, thus weakening Hitler's own case for the eastern war in the eyes of his military leaders.

But a Mediterranean strategy, even if followed through, would probably have led at some point to the war of the continents which Hitler envisaged. Most likely, it would have come sooner rather than later, with Germany, holding down massive imperial conquests by little more than brute force and tyranny, still unable to contend in the long run with the immensity of American resources. Conceivably, if circumstances had become favourable, the Soviet Union would have taken the opportunity to join in on the Allied side. Germany would have then faced the feared war on two fronts after all. A race to build nuclear weapons would have taken place and, as indeed happened, have most probably been won by American scientists (some of German descent). An imaginable outcome of such a contest would have been the dropping of American atom-bombs on Berlin and Munich, rather than Hiroshima and Nagasaki.

In the real world of Hitler, rather than the counter-factual world of fantasy and imagination, it seems clear that no chance was missed in 1940. No clear alternative strategy was available. Standing still, doing nothing, and awaiting the inevitable shift in the balance of power was obviously not an option. Given the leadership which Germany had, and the very reason she was facing a strategic dilemma in the summer and autumn of 1940 in the first place, the attack on the Soviet Union was indeed the only practicable way left open. It was Hitler's decision, though the blame for it does not stop at his door, as some post-war apologetics would have had it. It goes beyond him and ranges widely. The regime's military elite, though with extensive backing both among other power-groupings and within the German population, had supported the policies of a leader who had taken Germany into a gamble for world power with the odds in the long run stacked heavily against her and, crucially, without a 'get-out clause'. By 1940, unable to end the war, the only option for Hitler, and for the regime which had helped to put him in that position, was to gamble further, to take, as always, the bold, forward move, one that would sweep over the Russians 'like a hailstorm' and make the world 'hold its breath'.[76] It was madness, but there was method in it.

I wish to express my gratitude to the Leverhulme Trust, whose generous support allowed me the time to prepare this paper.

8

Shoot First and Ask Questions Afterwards?

Wannsee and the Unfolding of the Final Solution[1]

Mark Roseman

I

At the end of November 1941, Reinhard Heydrich, the head of the German Security Police, chief of the Security Service (SD) and protector of Bohemia and Moravia, sent out invitations to a meeting.[2] The invitees were civil servants, Nazi Party officials and senior SS men with responsibility for Jewish matters; the meeting, to be followed by a buffet, was to take place in a grand SD villa in the Berlin suburb of Wannsee.[3] Originally scheduled for 9 December, it was deferred indefinitely by a phone call on the day before.[4] After a new round of invitations early in the new year, the fifteen senior officials finally came together on 20 January 1942. After the discovery of the minutes in 1947, the ninety minutes they spent in each other's company came to be known as the 'Wannsee conference'—and as the most infamous meeting of modern times.[5]

The actual conference organization had been entrusted to Adolf Eichmann, one of Heydrich's underlings. At his trial in Jerusalem in 1961, Eichmann said that on the morning of 20 January the assembled officials had stood around in groups and chatted for a while before they got down to business. The formal proceedings were relatively short—perhaps an hour to an hour and a half in length.[6] With no agenda, much of the time was taken up by an extensive lecture from Heydrich. It seems there were some interjections from the other participants and a little more discussion afterwards. But these are conjectures. There is much in Eichmann's testimony that is open to question. We also have no direct transcript of what was said. A stenotypist took the minutes in shorthand but the notes have not been preserved. In any case they were not verbatim notes, according to Eichmann, and recorded only the salient points. What we have is

Eichmann's glossary of the notes, which Eichmann claimed was in turn heavily edited by Heydrich. These minutes, or 'protocol' as they have come to be known, in deference to the German term, are thus very far from a verbatim account. For a number of questions that discrepancy is not so important, since the written protocol represents what Heydrich wanted on record of the meeting; for others it raises real challenges of interpretation.[7]

According to the minutes, Heydrich began by reminding his guests that Göring had entrusted him with preparing the final solution of the European Jewish question. The purpose of the present meeting was to establish clarity on fundamental questions. The Reich Marshal's desire to be provided with an outline of the organizational, policy and technical prerequisites for the final solution of the European Jewish question made it necessary to ensure in advance that the central organizations involved be brought together and their policies properly co-ordinated. From Heydrich's point of view, probably the most important sentence of the minutes came right at the beginning: overall control of the final solution lay, irrespective of geographical boundaries, with the Reichsführer SS and chief of the German police (i.e. Himmler) and specifically with Heydrich as his representative. Heydrich then reminded his listeners of the recent history of Nazi action against the Jews. The principal goals had been to remove Jews from different sectors of German society and then from German soil. The only solution available at the time had been to accelerate Jewish emigration, a policy that had led in 1939 to the creation of the Reich Central Office for Jewish Emigration. But the Reichsführer SS had now stopped emigration in view of the dangers it raised during wartime and the new possibilities in the east. Instead of emigration, Heydrich continued, the Führer had given his approval for a new kind of solution—the evacuation of Jews to the east. The next, ambiguous, sentence reads, 'These actions are nevertheless to be seen only as temporary relief (*Ausweichmöglichkeiten*) but they are providing the practical experience which is of great significance for the coming final solution of the Jewish question.'[8]

With breathtaking calmness, the minutes continue with the observation that around eleven million Jews would be affected by the final solution. A table was provided listing European countries and their Jewish populations. The list included not only those countries under German occupation or control (Part A), but also Germany's European allies, neutral countries, and those with whom it was still at war (Part B). Some rather motley remarks followed about the difficulty of tackling the Jewish question in Romania and Hungary and the occupational composition of Jews in Russia. Whether Eichmann's protocol was just picking up fragments here, or Heydrich had been responding to questions, or his presentation really did offer these little snippets, we do not know. Then came one of the most significant section of the protocol:

> In the course of the final solution and under appropriate leader-
> ship, the Jews should be put to work in the east. In large, single-sex
> labour columns, Jews fit to work will work their way eastwards
> constructing roads. Doubtless the large majority will be eliminated
> by natural causes. And doubtless any final remnant that survives
> will consist of the most resistant elements. They will have to be
> dealt with appropriately, because otherwise, by natural selection,
> they would form the germ cell of a new Jewish revival. (See the
> experience of history).

Germany and the Czech Protectorate would have to be cleared first and then Europe would be combed from west to east. Bit by bit the Jews would be brought to transit ghettos and then sent further east.

Heydrich then identified some key prerequisites for the deportations (or 'evacuations' in the language of the protocol). There had to be clarity about who was going to be deported. Jews over 65, and those with serious war injuries or the Iron Cross First Class, would be sent to Theresienstadt. At a stroke, this would obviate the many interventions on their behalf. The larger evacuation actions would commence when the military situation allowed. There followed discussion involving Martin Luther from the Foreign Office about the situation in countries allied to Germany or under its influence—Slovakia, Croatia, Italy, France and so on.

A lengthy discussion of the issue of half-Jews and mixed marriages follows, taking up almost a third of the minutes. At this stage let us note his proposal that half- and quarter Jews, so-called first-degree *Mischlinge*, be evacuated to the east with the rest of the Jews. There would be a few exceptions, and in these cases the person concerned should be sterilized. As far as Jews in mixed marriages were concerned, Heydrich said that a decision should be made on the merits of each individual case as to whether the Jewish partner should be evacuated or, in view of the impact of such a measure on the German relatives, should be sent to an old-age ghetto.

The latter part of the minutes records a number of interventions from individual participants. Possibly the protocol gathered up individual inter-jections that had been made at various points in the meeting and inserted them here. However, in cross-examination in Jerusalem Eichmann indi-cated that towards the end of the Wannsee meeting, and somewhat fortified by brandy, the participants turned what had been a monologue from Heydrich into a bit more of a free for all. Dr Bühler from the *Generalgouvernement* asked for the final solution to be begun in Poland, since transport was no major problem and there were no serious manpower issues to be born in mind. Bühler 'had only one request—that the Jewish question be solved as quickly as possible'.

An ominous section at the end of the protocol noted that 'in conclusion the various possible kinds of solution were discussed.' A rather obscure sentence added that both Dr Meyer and Dr Bühler took the view that in the course of the final solution certain preparatory work should be carried out directly in the territories concerned, though without alarming the populace. With a final request for co-operation and assistance in carrying out his tasks Heydrich closed the meeting. Afterwards, says Eichmann, the guests stood around in small groups for a little while, and then left.

II

In March 1947, Robert Kempner and his US war crimes team were in search of material for the forthcoming indictment of German civil servants. In a German Foreign Office folder labelled 'Final solution of the Jewish question', they found the only surviving copy of the Wannsee protocol, no. 16 out of the original 30. Kempner, by background a German Jew and until 1933 a high-flying civil servant in the Prussian civil service, was staggered to discover what his former colleagues had been up to. Was such a thing possible?[9] More than that, he thought he had found the key deciding meeting that unleashed Nazi genocide.[10] The terminology of invitation and protocol suggested that it was here that the fundamental questions were clarified, prior to the formulation and execution of a 'total solution' to the Jewish question. The systematic listing of all the Jews of Europe added credence to the idea that here for the first time a comprehensive European solution was being proposed. But most important of all was the fact that the Allied investigators already knew from the official diary of Bühler's boss, Hans Frank, the Governor of occupied Poland, that in mid-December 1941 Frank and other Nazi officials were eagerly awaiting some fundamental meeting in Berlin that would find a solution to the intractable Jewish question.[11] Small wonder, then, that after the war 'Wannsee' rapidly became synonymous with the formulation of genocide, and to this day, it lives on in popular imagination as the meeting where the final solution was decreed.[12]

Over the following decades, however, historians grew less and less certain whether Wannsee could have the significance originally attributed to it. A few reputable historians, most notably Dieter Rebentisch (as well as the usual range of cranks and deniers), have wondered if the meeting ever really discussed genocide at all.[13] Based on civil servants' post-war denials of ever having seen the minutes or of having talked about murder, Rebentisch questions whether the text of the protocol bore any relation to the actual meeting and indeed whether the protocol reached the bulk of the delegates who had been present. The protocol is certainly a fairly amateurish typewritten summary rather than a formal document. Only the one copy has ever been found. The covering note that accompanied it, sent to the Foreign Office's Martin Luther, was written on an individual basis, rather than being a clear duplicate of multiple letters with the title of circular letter (or at least it is dated individually, suggesting it *may* not have been a circular letter).

It is just possible therefore that Luther received a document which other participants did not receive, and that those civil servants who denied having seen it at Nuremberg were justified. But the balance of probability is that the protocol was indeed dispatched to all who attended, and that it does convey a plausible summary of what took place. At the main Nuremberg Trials, before the Wannsee protocol had been discovered but after it was known that a key meeting had taken place in Berlin, the head of the Reich Chancellery, Heinrich Lammers, admitted to receiving the minutes (which he claimed contained nothing new). His subsequent denial followed discovery of the actual protocol and the revelation as to its contents.[14] We also have evidence that the protocol reached others in the Nazi hierarchy at the time.[15] The above-mentioned covering note to Luther, as well as accompanying the protocol, also contained an invitation to a follow-up meeting. Since we know the other ministries represented at Wannsee definitely received that invitation (because they sent representatives to the follow-up meeting), it seems most likely that they too received the protocol.[16] In Jerusalem, Eichmann claimed that not only did the meeting cover the ground claimed in the protocol, but that discussion of murder had been even more explicit than the written record allowed.[17] Some civil servants too, most notably Bernhard Lösener, a junior official for Jewish matters in the Interior Ministry, whose boss Wilhelm Stuckart had been one of those sitting round the table at Wannsee, also claimed after the war that the meeting really had discussed the issues outlined in the protocol.[18] This does not mean that we can take the protocol completely at face value; on some matters it uses euphemisms where the meeting probably did not, on others it suggests a consensus was reached where dissension probably remained. But overall, we can assume that it was the official and widely circulated record.

The more serious doubts about the conference's significance arise because it took place so late in the day, and because the people round the table were too junior. After all, by the time the *Staatssekretäre* (Permanent Secretaries) were sipping their cognacs at Wannsee, mass murder had been underway for six months or more. Since the invasion of the Soviet

Union in June 1941, the *Einsatzgruppen* had butchered more than half a million Jews. The Germany army had all but eliminated the Jewish population in Serbia. A special security police task force had conducted mass shootings in Polish Galicia. Gassing had started too. The Chelmno camp began operations in early December 1941, preparations at Bełżec were well underway, and 'test-gassings' had been undertaken at Auschwitz. If Wannsee was the time of 'asking questions', truly the Nazis had begun the shooting long before. What still needed to be decided when so many murderous facts had already been created? Even if major decisions were still required, was the group Heydrich gathered together empowered to make them? Neither Hitler nor Himmler attended; we do not know if Hitler was even informed about the meeting.[19] Indeed, there were no actual ministers present—not surprising since Heydrich, though enjoying a great deal of influence and power, held SS office equivalent to the post of *Staatssekretär*, a position that enabled him to give invitations to high civil servant rankings, but not to ministers.

As a result, many historians have questioned whether the Wannsee gathering could have had any programmatic significance. A lot of ingenuity has been applied to teasing out some special purpose or other to explain its existence. Wolfgang Scheffler, for example, claims the meeting was called because of Heydrich's concerns about his personal authority.[20] In the weeks and months before the conference Himmler had rapidly expanded the concentration camp empire—an empire over which Heydrich's security police had little control. Heydrich thus wanted to reassert his position, and counterbalance this potential loss of authority. The historian Eberhard Jäckel, on the other hand, while sharing the view that the meeting was about power, believes that far from feeling vulnerable, Heydrich—recently installed as protector of Bohemia and Moravia—wanted to demonstrate he was no longer simply Himmler's man.[21] Wannsee was an almost empty event in a classy venue stage-managed to show off Heydrich's newly acquired independence. Henry Huttenbach offers another variant of the power struggle story—the meeting was simply to ensure that the SS supremacy was accepted by other officials, a conclusion that is probably close to the mark.[22] Indeed, many of these interpretations have something to recommend them, as does Dieter Rebentisch's assumption that if the meeting had a point it was to achieve a common line on the 'borderline' cases—the half-Jews and mixed marriages.[23] But all proceed from the assumption that the meeting was largely irrelevant for explaining the final solution. They all thus dismiss the protocol's claim to be laying the foundations for a programme yet to be implemented. But why should the meeting be making that claim, if the general programme of murder was already decided? 'The most remarkable thing about Wannsee', concluded Eberhard Jäckel, pondering this question in a seminal article originally published on the conference's fiftieth anniversary, 'is that we do not know why it took place.'[24]

III

Over the last few years, German documents recovered from the archives of the former Soviet Union have begun to shed light on developments in the preceding months that help to give Wannsee greater coherence and 'logic'—if such a term can be used in this context. Above all, they show that we need to rethink the way in which the Soviet killings were extended in a European-wide programme of murder.

It used to be assumed that Göring's notorious instruction to Heydrich of 31 July 1941, to 'prepare the groundwork for a total solution of the European Jewish question' (the mandate Heydrich later used as the justification for the Wannsee conference) was a clear order to provide a blueprint for genocide. But recent discoveries suggest that Heydrich himself had drafted the document in March, and resubmitted it now after discussions with Rosenberg, in order to prepare for a huge deportation programme. In the summer of 1941, the terms 'final solution' and 'total solution' were not yet synonymous with murder. Other evidence, too (for example, testimony from Eichmann and Höß), once cited to demonstrate that the key decisions had been taken in the summer of 1941, no longer looks so compelling. What we find in spring and summer 1941, in fact, is growing clamour from different Nazi groups hoping to use the Soviet territory as a dumping ground for German and other European Jews. No one thought that the deportees were going to thrive there—and there was something implicitly genocidal about this. But it was not yet an overall plan for murder.[25]

If the summer was not the moment at which European Jewry's fate was sealed, other historians have seen the turning point as coming in mid-September 1941, when Hitler said that German Jews and those from the Czech Protectorate could be deported immediately. Not only was the green light being given in relation to Germany's Jews—other European Jews were also being readied for deportation. In the same month, the deportation of French Jews, initially limited to those in detention, was also announced. Since Hitler had given the green light for deportations under conditions no better than when he previously blocked them, some historians see in this crucial evidence that Hitler had now, in fact, either already decided on genocide, or was on the brink of doing so. Yet Hitler's command for deportation did not tie in with murder plans very neatly. Logically, if mass murder was already on the agenda, it would have made more sense to hold the Jews in Germany until the camps were ready.

Moreover, Hitler showed himself very uncertain over the following weeks as to whether the timing for deportations was opportune. Thus when, as a temporary step, Hitler and Himmler agreed in September that 60,000 Jews should be deported not to the *Generalgouvernement* but to the Łódź ghetto in the Wartheland, it seems that deportation rather than murder was what they had in mind. In early October, Hitler suggested that the Jews should not be sent to Poland but should immediately be directed further east, i.e. to the Soviet Union. It is obvious at the very least that the eventual extermination plan on Polish territory had not yet been arrived at, though unclear whether Hitler expected the deportees to be murdered on Soviet soil.[26]

Indeed, when we look at developments in the following months, we find ample evidence the key protagonists were not responding to a central plan of killing. Instead, from the summer of 1941 the notion spread that shooting Jews was an appropriate thing to do. In Serbia, for example the newly arrived commander, General Böhme, introduced a radical new reprisals policy against partisan attacks: all Jewish men of arms-bearing age were placed in a 'reservoir' of potential hostages and 100 shot for every German soldier killed. Though responding to central signals, Böhme had had no central instructions to make Jews his principal target. Instead, the historian Walter Manoschek has concluded that by the autumn of 1941 no special orders were necessary for such genocidal policy decisions to be taken. All the German authorities co-operated smoothly despite their disagreements in other questions. What is more, the willingness to kill was not the result of the special indoctrination given to SS men. It was ordinary soldiers who carried out most of the murders. By the end of the year, there was virtually no adult male Jewish population left in Serbia. Following the murder of the women and children in early 1942, Serbia became one of the first countries to be 'Jew free'.[27] In Eastern Galicia the activities of the local SS and police leader Katzmann may well also offer a similar picture of regional initiative in response to the shooting lessons from the Soviet Union.[28]

In the late summer and early autumn two new factors influenced policy in the annexed Polish provinces and in the *Generalgouvernement*. The first was Hitler's September decision to unleash the deportation trains. Whatever Hitler's immediate intentions, the planned eastward deportation of German Jews created new pressures and challenges for the receiving territories. Within two weeks of Himmler's edict that the first deportations should be sent to Łódź—an already overcrowded ghetto within the jurisdiction of the Wartheland authorities—construction began of the Chelmno gas camp. A letter sent by the Wartheland's Gauleiter Greiser to Himmler on 1 May 1942, looking back on events in 1941, indicates that the killing of 100,000 Polish Jews from the region was specifically authorized by Himmler, through Heydrich, as a quid pro quo for the willingness of the Wartheland authorities to receive deportees from Germany. While *authorization* for the killings came from the centre, the initiative had come from the locality, and the goal was the solution of a regional 'problem' rather than the implementation of a comprehensive programme.[29]

Unlike the annexed former Polish territory in the Wartheland, the *Generalgouvernement* proper was not directly affected by Hitler's deportations decision. Here, the biggest impact of the Soviet campaign in the autumn was to disappoint earlier expectations of offloading the region's Jews. In the course of 1941, the whole of the administration, from Hans Frank downwards, had been anticipating the Jews' rapid removal into former Soviet territory. But in mid-October Frank learned for sure that the slow progress of the war meant there was little prospect of such removals. The dragging Soviet campaign also had economic implications for his region. A fatal two-pronged development ensued. The hard-line radicals in Himmler's almost autonomous police-empire in Poland undertook violent initiatives, while the civilian administration imposed ordinances of exclusion and persecution on the Jewish population that made killing seem the only option. The Lublin district SS and police leader, Odilo Globocnik, had shown ruthless energy in developing murderous labour projects for Jews in the Bug region. The outcome of Globocnik's consultations was the decision to begin building an extermination camp at Bełżec.[30]

The implications of these recent findings, then, is to suggest that the slippage from murderously neglectful and brutal occupation policies to genocidal measures took place initially without a comprehensive set of commands from the centre. The centre, above all Himmler, was consulted in almost all cases we have looked at. But neither Hitler nor Himmler was providing a clear-cut plan or even a fundamental command for the lower echelons to carry out. What then happened was that in interaction with these developments, Hitler, Himmler and Heydrich began to treat the idea of a territorial solution more and more as a metaphor. In other words, even though there was not yet a precise concept of killing the deportees by gas, the dividing line between the territorial solution and that of outright murder was becoming very thin indeed. On 23 October, all Jewish emigration from the Reich was prohibited. On 25 October, Erhard Wetzel, the official in charge of race questions in Rosenberg's ministry of the east wrote to the Reich commissioner for the Ostland, Hinrich Lohse, recommending the deployment of the former euthanasia personnel to construct gas installations in order to eliminate deported Jews who were unfit to work.[31] The 'territorial' element of sending the Jews east was becoming simply a euphemism. Selection and attrition was becoming the central element of the process, rather than a desirable by-product.

In mid-November, Himmler and Rosenberg had a lengthy meeting after which Rosenberg provided a detailed press briefing. Here the distance between deportation and destruction had narrowed to nothing. Though the issue of killing—as against allowing to die—was not yet spelled out, and Rosenberg still used the metaphor of deportation, his reference to the 'biological eradication of the entire Jewry of Europe' made it absolutely explicit that extinction and not just removal of Jewish presence was the aim.[32] At almost exactly the same time, on 16 November, in the journal *Das Reich*, Goebbels published a leading article that was excerpted in many of the German regional papers.[33] Entitled 'The Jews are guilty', the piece provided one of the most explicit communications to the German people as a whole that Jews were going to be exterminated. World Jewry, Goebbels wrote, was suffering a gradual annihilation process. Jews were falling according to their own law—an eye for eye, a tooth for a tooth. In December Goebbels acknowledged in his diary that the deportation of Jews to the east was 'in many cases synonymous with the death penalty'.[34]

On 28 November, Hitler met the Grand Mufti of Jerusalem. Hitler was seeking to court the Grand Mufti—aware, no doubt, that just a few years earlier the Nazis had been working together with Jewish agencies to 'facilitate' Jewish emigration to Palestine. Some of what he said will have been for effect. But still, Hitler's declaration, which he requested the Mufti to 'lock deep into his heart', was striking. For the sake of pleasing the Grand Mufti, Hitler needed to have specified only that the Germans would deport the Jews to Siberia, along the lines of his statement to Kvaternik in the summer. But he went much further. After a successful war, Hitler said, Germany would have only one remaining objective in the Middle East: the annihilation of the Jews living under British protection in Arab lands. There was not a shadow of a territorial solution left.[35]

The argument here is thus that the dissemination and modification of the Soviet experiment took place piecemeal, by improvisation and example, over the period from September to November 1941. Himmler and Heydrich were closely involved; Hitler's involvement is less well documented, though he will at the very least have known what was happening, and at the very least will have decided not to prevent it. To stay his course Himmler will have needed Hitler's approving nod, though how emphatic that was, we do not know. In the course of October and November, Hitler, Himmler and those around them made statements showing how rapidly the idea of a territorial solution was dissolving into a mere metaphor. The territories were becoming holding bays before death. Whatever Hitler's green light for deportations had meant in September, by the end of November the idea of a reservation had effectively disappeared. In late

November, as we shall see, Himmler held a concerted series of consultations on the Jewish issue. It seems that as the overall concept of genocide crystallized in the heads of Nazi leaders, so other agencies had to be brought on board.[36]

IV

When we turn to the conference protocol, how far does it support this view of the evolution of policy? Part of the problem is that the protocol itself is a very ambiguous document. There are potentially at least three different narratives of genocide that can be read into it. In outlining the early history of Nazi measures towards the Jews, for example, Heydrich says that 'in pursuit of these ends [i.e. cleansing the Fatherland], the only provisional solution available had been a planned acceleration of Jewish emigration out of Reich territory' and that 'the drawbacks of such enforced accelerated emigration were clear to all involved'. This relegation of emigration to a mere provisional measure could be taken to imply that mass murder had *always* been the preferred strategy—but that in the past it had simply not been opportune. However, I think, this is a retrospective attempt by Heydrich to claim a continuity that was not there. It is true that emigration had always raised difficulties for the Nazis, but there is no evidence that Heydrich had been thinking of genocide in 1939 or that at the time Jewish emigration was seen merely as a temporary fall-back.

A second chronology—that of the early autumn decision—is suggested by a passage that follows a survey of the statistics of emigration up to October 1941. Heydrich says that, 'in the meantime the Reichsführer-SS and Chief of the German Police had prohibited emigration of Jews due to the dangers of an emigration in wartime and due to the possibilities of the east. . . Instead of emigration the new solution has emerged, after prior approval by the Führer, of evacuating Jews to the east.' At the time of Himmler's ban on emigration in October 1941, Hitler had just authorized the deportation of German Jews. Was Heydrich here talking about the beginning of the deportations—or was he implying in fact that this decision was the beginning of genocide? After all, elsewhere in the conference, there is no doubt that 'evacuation' was used as a euphemism for murder. Is that what the Führer had authorized in September? To make matters even more obscure, however, Heydrich goes on: 'These actions are nevertheless to be seen only as temporary relief but they are providing the practical experience which is of great significance for the coming final solution of the Jewish question.' That suggests, rather, a third chronology—that the programme he is talking about until now is in fact still something piecemeal—a mixture of deportations and regional killings, but that the practical experience thus gained is creating the basis for a future comprehensive programme of genocide.[37]

I think we can say the following. First, and most emphatically, there is no territorial solution left. Heydrich's comments about what will happen to Jewish labour show that all, even the fittest, are to be killed. Most will die through labour; those who do not must be eliminated. So Nazi policy towards European Jewry has crossed the Rubicon; death is the only outcome.[38] Secondly, however, the comprehensive programme is only now coming together; the gestation period is not yet over. Something that reinforces this point is not only Heydrich's description about collecting practical experience, but also his initial invitation list. When he initially drew up the guest list for the conference in November, his first draft did not include any representatives from Poland, suggesting that what was to be the eventual form of the final solution—the concentration of killings on Polish soil—had not yet reached the planning stage.[39] Heydrich's comments about forced labour are in line with other proposals being mooted by various Nazi figures at this time, and show that he was still toying with the idea of eliminating the Jews by deploying them to build roads under murderous conditions in the east.[40] At a confidential meeting with his senior advisers in Prague a week later, Heydrich reiterated this idea, talking about gigantic labour camps in the Soviet Union.[41] In other words, the final shape of the killing programme was not yet fully established. It may be there was some talk at Wannsee about gassings —Eichmann certainly asserted this in Jerusalem just as strenuously as the others denied it.[42] However, overall our sense from the protocol is indeed that the crucial shift of mood from territorial solution to genocide has been effected, but that the final form of that genocide is only now being established.

V

Wannsee, then, really does provide a window on an ongoing process, a process in which the essential points have been set, but the full timetable and exact course of the journey has not yet been finalized. This does not, in itself, explain Wannsee's function, but the meeting no longer appears so detached from the overall process. What, though, was the exact point of the conference? Why had it been called? Looking at the guest list, we can rule out from the beginning the idea sometimes still voiced that Heydrich was planning to talk about the technical details of transports.[43] Quite apart from the fact that the *Staatssekretäre* were too senior to be called together for such matters, Heydrich had not invited any transport specialist, or a military representative or indeed anyone from the finance ministry. Deportation arrangements were not to be on the agenda.

Amongst his many achievements, Jeremy Noakes has provided some of the most insightful work published to date on the development of Nazi policy towards the so-called *Mischlinge*.[44] At Wannsee the choice of guests and the length of time devoted to the matter in the meeting both indicate that the *Mischlinge* and other protected categories were an important item on the agenda.[45] This had been in the sights of party radicals for a long time and particular in the course of 1941. The radicals rejected the protection given to mixed marriages and particularly to first-degree *Mischlinge*. They were ranged up against the Ministry of the Interior and the Reich Chancellery, both of whom had committed themselves to protecting half-Jews, and they were in RSHA's sights.[46] A meeting convened by Eichmann in September 1941 had articulated almost word for word the same proposals that Heydrich now voiced.[47] So it is clear that the meeting was supposed to push forward the agenda on half-Jews.

Even so, that clearly was not the whole of the agenda. Instructive in this context is Heydrich's decision to include German representatives from Poland (for whom the half-Jewish question was not a major issue) only a day or two after drawing up his first draft guest list. What happened was that the Higher SS and Police Leader (HSSPF) for the *General-gouvernement* visited Himmler at the end of November, complaining about the conflicts he was having with Frank's civilian administration. A day later, Heydrich added SS and civilian representatives from Poland to the guest list.[48] It was clear, in other words, that this was a meeting designed to assemble those with whom the security police and SS had run into demarcation disputes. Indeed, the *Mischling* question was of such interest to Heydrich precisely because it was one of the few significant areas where other ministries retained a leverage on Jewish policy. The original invitation, which stressed the importance of 'achieving a common view among the central agencies involved in the relevant tasks' made clear from the start how important it was for Heydrich to bring the other bodies into line. The protocol itself, which re-emphasized the importance of the common line, is unwittingly revealing in this respect. Instead of saying (as was probably intended) that it was necessary that the bodies involved agree on a common treatment of the pertinent questions, the protocol offers a convoluted sentence that in fact says that the relevant bodies themselves should be given a prior common treatment (*'vorherige gemeinsame Behandlung'*) in order to achieve 'parallelization' of policy-making. Heydrich's desire to bring the others into line could hardly have been more explicit.

It is important to recognize that, in contrast to the view of Scheffler and Jäckel, this was not a solo effort by Heydrich. Instead, it was a concerted effort by Himmler and his deputy to ensure they were in control, at a time when the final solution was taking shape. Two weeks before the Wannsee invitations went out, both Himmler and Heydrich had arranged a series of meetings. In mid-November, Himmler and Rosenberg had a lengthy discussion. [49] A day later, Himmler and Heydrich spoke to co-ordinate their policy, among other things, on 'Eliminating the Jews'.[50] On 24 November it was Wilhelm Stuckart's turn to confer with Himmler. Number three of the four points in Himmler's appointments calendar was 'Jewish question—belongs to me.'[51] If the post-war testimony of Bernhard Lösener is to be believed, Stuckart complained in the following weeks that Jewish matters were being taken away from the Ministry. On 28 November Himmler had yet another meeting on the issue—this time conferring with the HSSPF of the *Generalgouvernement*, Friedrich-Wilhelm Krüger.[52] Between the invitation and the eventual Wannsee conference there were more such encounters, most notably between Himmler and Bühler on 13 January.

Himmler and Heydrich were thus making strenuous efforts to co-ordinate and centralize all initiatives on the Jewish question. 'This was the reason why Heydrich convened this Wannsee Conference', Eichmann said in Jerusalem, 'in order, as it were, to press through, on the highest level, his will and the will of the Reichsführer-SS and Chief of the German Police.'[53] Heydrich's real target was the civilian ministries—the other participants were brought along to strengthen his hand. In the weeks and months before the conference, Himmler and Heydrich had repeatedly clashed with civilian agencies over issues of competence. Both within Germany and in the occupied territories the demarcation lines were ill defined. In autumn 1941, Heydrich's security police experienced regular run-ins with the Ministry of the Eastern Territories and particular with the Ministry's Commissioners in the Baltic and White Russia.[54] In Poland the conflicts between Himmler's staff and the civilian administration were, as noted, if anything even more intense.[55] Other ministries too, particularly the Interior Ministry, had a contested relationship with the RSHA. Nominally, Himmler was the subordinate of the Minister of the Interior. In practice, Minister Frick had abandoned any pretence at controlling Himmler, indeed was giving up hope even of being informed what the RSHA was up to.[56] Yet some jealously guarded questions of prerogative remained, particularly the borderline of mixed-race Jews. Alone among the civilian representatives at Wannsee, probably only Martin Luther from the Foreign Ministry had already resigned himself to subordination and had adapted by trying to be as helpful to the RSHA as possible.[57]

It is perfectly possible that Himmler and Heydrich could have resolved demarcation issues on an individual basis with each agency. The series of November meetings suggests they were in the process of doing so. Yet, in the complicated power structure of the Third Reich, a collective acknowledgement among all the interested parties was of much greater worth in establishing power and precedents. Moreover, in the climate of a high-level meeting with a strong Party-SS presence, the other representatives would be much more susceptible to group pressure.

There was another aspect to the meeting too: Heydrich wanted to establish shared complicity. The shooting of a transport of Berlin Jews to Riga on 29/30 November, news of which rapidly spread through government circles, had brought to a head the growing disquiet among some Berlin officials over the treatment of the German-Jewish deportees.[58] Stuckart's deputy, Bernhard Lösener, later claimed that they represented a personal turning point.[59] Both Heydrich and Himmler were undoubtedly concerned to bind in all agencies to their enterprise and prevent further murmurings. The last thing they wanted was for Hitler to worry about morale and once again rein in their activities. Moreover, with the first premonitions in December that Germany might not win the war, Heydrich will have recognized that making other agencies complicit was a powerful means to bring them into line. It would encourage them to hand over responsibility to the SS to avoid taking on further responsibility. We know, for example, that Otto Bräutigam, who represented the Ministry for the Eastern Territories at one of the follow-up conferences after Wannsee, concluded in January that Germany could not win the war and showed ostentatious willingness to make concessions to Heydrich's men. 'As far as the Jewish question', he confided to one of his own colleagues, 'he was quite happy to emphasize the responsibility of the SS and the police.'[60]

Heydrich's aim of establishing shared knowledge of murder explains one of the real oddities of the Wannsee protocol, namely its peculiar juxtaposition of euphemism and undisguised murderousness. On the one hand, it is coy about killing and talks of 'evacuation to the east'. On the other hand, the language used about eliminating Jewish workers is so open, and the implications for the rest so clear, as to render the euphemisms useless as a disguise. The natural tendency of the security police was to be extremely guarded. The euphemisms were its normal mode of communicating about murder, and will have served here to remind recipients of the language codes they should use. At the same time it was so vital to establish the participants' shared knowledge in the killing programme that this overrode the need for caution. This was why Lammers, Stuckart and others were at such pains after the war to deny having seen the protocol, to escape from the trap that Heydrich had set them.

VI

1942 was the most astounding year of murder in the Holocaust, one of the most astounding years of murder in the whole history of mankind. The period from the beginning of killings at Bełżec in mid-March 1942 through to mid-February 1943 saw the extermination of over half of all the Jews who would die at the Nazis' hands. How significant was the Wannsee conference itself in unleashing this unbelievable tide?

Both Heydrich and Eichmann certainly talked up the meeting's significance at the time. Five days after Wannsee, Heydrich sent out a circular to all the regional security police chiefs, attaching Göring's mandate and assuring them the preparatory measures were now being implemented.[61] Towards the end of February, Heydrich sent out copies of the protocol, accompanying it with a note to the participants affirming that 'happily the basic line' had now been 'established as regards the practical execution of the final solution of the Jewish question'.[62] In the aftermath of the conference, Eichmann spread word among his subordinates about the plan to murder Europe's Jews.[63] In Jerusalem, too, Eichmann continued to underline Wannsee's significance. At the very least, Wannsee opened the way to a massive new wave of deportations, as soon as the transport situation permitted.[64]

There are signs too that the protocol spread waves through German officials in Europe. Thirty copies were produced; at a cautious estimate each one reached five to ten officials. We know that the officials in Minsk soon heard about it, whilst on 23 March, the Jewish expert in the German embassy in Paris, Carltheo Zeitschel, wrote to his superiors in the Foreign Office, saying he had heard that a *Staatssekretär* meeting had taken place and asking for a copy of the minutes.[65]

As has already been indicated, Wannsee itself was not *the* moment of decision. Nobody at Wannsee, not even Heydrich, was senior enough to settle the fate of European Jewry. Moreover, some of the breakthroughs on *Mischlinge* that Heydrich thought he had achieved there, in fact proved subsequently illusory.[66] The Wannsee protocol was rather a signpost indicating that genocide had become official policy. Yet Heydrich undoubtedly took the assent he had engineered at Wannsee very seriously. The signals he and Eichmann gave out after the event showed it had immeasurably strengthened their confidence. Even in May, visiting security officials in France for the last time before his assassination, Heydrich's account of the planning for the final solution emphasized the agreements reached on 20 January.[67] Wannsee really had helped to clear the way for genocide.

9

Auschwitz and the Germans

History, Knowledge, and Memory

Norbert Frei

(translated from the German by Alan Bance)

arianne B. was still living at home with her parents in Berlin when, in the summer of 1943, she was posted to a teaching appointment in the grammar school in Auschwitz, to begin with the new school year. Increasing numbers of air raids meant that her former school, in the south of the capital, could not resume classes at the end of the summer holidays; the children were being evacuated to the country-side. So the young woman had volunteered for 'service in the east'. From her memoirs, written half a century later,[1] it is apparent that her decision was based not solely on a sense of duty, but also on conviction. Like her two brothers, the elder of whom had been killed in action right at the beginning of the war, she wanted to do her bit in the struggle against Germany's enemies. She was just over 30 at the time of her move.

Among her family and her neighbours, 'nobody had ever heard the name of the place' where she would be working; Marianne had to look it up in the encyclopaedia. This paucity of information was more than made up for when, immediately upon the arrival of the new teacher and after a tour of the rectangular market-place ('typical of all the towns colonized by the Germans in the east'), the mayor of Auschwitz pointed out to her the significance of IG Farben's Buna Works.

> 'And now for the most important thing', said the mayor with a meaningful pause. 'Over there beyond the fields is a concentration camp. It occupies the territory of what used to be twelve Polish villages. At the centre of it is a former Austrian barracks. The guards consist of 500 men from the SS and the Waffen-SS. The

inmates are mostly Poles, and Jews from all over Europe. The proportions vary. *New prisoners arrive every week, but the total number never changes.*' As he said this, he fixed me with a piercing look, so that I dropped my gaze. Surely I could not have heard him correctly. He repeated his words. I would have to give them some thought in private. And that was the end of the guided tour'.[2]

It was not long before the teacher infiltrated the heart of Auschwitz camp; on the very evening of the day of her arrival, in fact. Her predecessor, who was pregnant, was married to an SS officer, and lived in the vicinity. She remembered that in school next day she was greeted by a 'crowd of distressed little second-year pupils' who had been watching the arrival of a goods train at the station. 'I was deeply saddened. Couldn't they have kept this cruel process they called selection (separating out those intended to die) out of the public eye, so that it could not be seen by small schoolchildren only two platforms away?!!'[3]

With the same twisted logic, Marianne B. soon found herself full of pity for the 'horrible situation' of Rudolf Höß.[4] The children of the Camp Commandant were among her pupils. And on one occasion, meeting at close quarters 'six most elegant ladies, undoubtedly very lovely, wealthy, and spoilt pure-bred Jewesses', guarded by SS men with German shepherd dogs, what she noticed was not only the 'degrading and cruel situation', but above all the women's 'hate-filled look'. 'They must have thought "SS tart", since I was coming from the direction of the camp.' Once more, with the account of this episode ending in a conclusion that reverses the blame, the morality of the Nazi 'People's Community' shows through as though still intact. 'With all their wealth, why didn't they manage to get out in time? After all, the anti-Jewish laws had been in place since 1934.'[5]

Anyone capable of writing with this kind of logic a whole lifetime later (the text dates from 1999) has to be credited with an unfeigned honesty that demonstrates rare resistance to the learning process. Even in old age, the former high-school teacher could still recall what it was like 'having to live as a "victor" in close proximity to "the defeated", without being able to avoid each other'.[6] Thus her self-pity and style of reasoning about the facts of Auschwitz, facts of which she very soon became fully aware, seem as fresh as they were in the last year of the war:

> The urge to write and tell my parents and friends about the crimes of Auschwitz, to relieve my guilty conscience of this burden, was overwhelming. But at the same time, it seemed to me unquestionably self-evident that I must control the urge to communicate, and remain silent about something I could do nothing about, absolutely

nothing. The truth would have to come out sooner or later; these crimes would have to be atoned for. But right then, during the war, when everything was in the balance, when everything depended on the front line and the home front holding out, was not the moment to besmirch the image of the leadership and weaken our fighting spirit. Germany itself was at risk! Just say nothing for the time being. I would not write about it to my brother or my friends, who were facing the toughest battles. It was not until many years after the war that I talked about it, by which time it was all an open secret. Passing it on at that time would only have made more people unhappy, put them in terrible danger. And sadly, nobody could do anything about it. It was embarrassing that foreign countries seemed to have found out about it.[7]

These comments, through which Marianne B. attempted to explain her insights into and knowledge of Auschwitz, and to rationalize how she dealt with that knowledge, represent more than merely a reflection of the way one individual 'eyewitness' perceived and came to terms with her experiences. Basically, her explanations serve as a key to the question of what Auschwitz represented to the Germans, during the Second World War and in the succeeding decades.

I

Auschwitz was one of the places in south-west Poland attacked by Göring's Luftwaffe as early as 1 September 1939.[8] What attracted the *Wehrmacht*'s attention were the strategically important rail station and the barracks of the 6th Polish Cavalry Squadron. Forced by the aerial attacks to pull out that same day, the squadron moved its base to Crakow, about 60 kilometres to the east. After a number of civilians had died in the bombardment, including a thirteen-year-old boy and an elderly woman, many inhabitants also hurriedly decided to flee. In the attack, one young man died of his wounds, and another, as recorded in the Catholic parish register of deaths, committed suicide 'out of agitation' because war had broken out.

In September 1939, the population of Auschwitz was about 14,000. Rather more than half were Jews, the rest Catholics. The Jews had been in the majority since the late nineteenth century, and were self-confident enough to refer to the town as their 'Oświęcim Jerusalem'. In the first few days after the beginning of the Second World War, they left in droves.

Meanwhile, the *Wehrmacht* began its advance on Oświęcim, and behind the army there followed an *Einsatzgruppe* 'for special purposes', which

Himmler had ordered to be hastily assembled to put down Polish resistance in the industrial area of Upper Silesia. The invaders took the town on 4 September, after overcoming a fierce defence. Just one week later, the market square bore the name of Adolf Hitler, and the town was now known as Auschwitz—as it had been at the end of the nineteenth century, when it belonged to Austria-Hungary.

Despite this rapid German relabelling, it was not all clear as yet whether Auschwitz was intended to be a part of eastern Silesia (known as East Upper Silesia), which was due for accelerated annexation and 'Germanization', or included in the planned 'Reichsgau Beskidenland', or the *Generalgouvernement*, an entity with no constitutional definition whatsoever. It was only after the establishment of new Reich frontiers by a boundary commission from the Reich Ministry of the Interior that a decision was made at the end of October 1939 in favour of incorporating the town into East Upper Silesia. Hitler's aim in carrying out the division of the conquered territories at this point was not primarily to cement German claims for all time. What he wanted was, first, to put in train as quickly as possible the 'Germanization' of western Poland, which, in addition to East Upper Silesia, included West Prussia-Danzig, the Wartheland, and East Prussia; and secondly, to lose no time in economically exploiting the *Generalgouvernement*.

From then on, Auschwitz belonged to the *Landkreis* (district) of Bielitz, in the newly formed *Regierungsbezirk* (region) of Katowice, in the Province of Silesia. At this time there were only a few *Volksdeutsche*, or ethnic Germans, living in the town, and—by National Socialist racial criteria— almost nobody who could claim to be German. This situation throws into sharp relief the size of the self-imposed task the conquerors thought they were facing in terms of 'population policy'.

With overstated historical reference to the medieval colonization of the east, an ideological programme of 'Germanization' was forcibly instituted throughout the annexed western Polish territories. Within the framework of the 'New European Order', 'germanizing' meant an unscrupulous 'reconfiguration of peoples'. The systematic displacement of the indigenous population was meant to turn the newly acquired territories as quickly as possible into an ethnically homogeneous and (when combined with fundamental economic and social reorganization measures) economically productive part of the German Reich. Correspondingly, besides installing German local government, the plans envisaged resettlement by 'racially valuable' Germans. In western Poland, this meant deporting all Jews and the majority of Poles, and 'inserting' Germans and those of German descent, who were to be strictly segregated from the remaining Poles.

In his new capacity as Reich Commissar for the Strengthening of

Germandom, the SS Reichsführer had devised a special role for Auschwitz, within the framework of his very first relocation project. Himmler proposed to develop the town as a political, economic and cultural centre for the South Tyroleans to be 'brought home' from fascist Italy. Of course, a precondition for this was that the Jews and Poles would first have to be removed. This requirement was wholeheartedly endorsed by the regional planners, architects, historians and anthropologists of the South-East German Research Association (*Südostdeutsche Forschungs-gemeinschaft*) in Vienna as they set about their cultural and area studies in support of the project. These plans never left the drawing-board, however, because the fall of France led Himmler to favour Burgundy instead as a new settlement area for the South Tyroleans. Lower Styria and the Crimea were other, later suggestions.

However, in the Auschwitz area the problems of the programme of ethnic reordering were beginning to emerge. It proved difficult to 'Germanize' the eastern part of the Katowice region, as the population consisted almost entirely of Poles and Jews. The resettlement strategists of the civilian authority and the SS were soon in agreement that the so-called 'eastern strip' was unsuitable as a 'placement area' for Germans and ethnic Germans. Separated from the western districts of the region by a border guarded by police, and classified as second-rate in terms of territorial status, the area was (at least temporarily) exempt from 'Germanization'. This was a significant move for Auschwitz, meaning that—for the time being—the native population was safe from deportation.

So it was that the start of Nazi relocation operations in western Poland saw an increase in the number of Jews in Auschwitz, rather than a decrease. The town now became a collecting point for Jews who were to be deported to the 'eastern strip' from the western parts of the Katowice region marked out for accelerated 'Germanizing'. The Jewish Council of Elders in Auschwitz, charged with accommodating and providing for all these additional arrivals, faced an impossible task. In the spring of 1940 the town harboured one of the biggest Jewish communities of the 'eastern strip'. The Jews were crammed into the alleys of the Old Town, isolated from the other inhabitants, and subject to the strict supervision of German guards.

Aside from administrators, among other Germans who settled in Auschwitz at this time were a number of businessmen, including trustees of the firms previously owned by Jews and Poles. Moving to the annexed territories opened up numerous opportunities for social advancement and self-enrichment. Particularly in the interim period between the withdrawal of the military government in autumn 1939 and the consolidation of the civil administration in spring 1940, anarchic conditions prevailed in occupied Poland. With the proliferation of countless offices and bureaucrats, there was increasing uncertainty about legality. Corruption was rife, and a mixture of the euphoria of war, the conqueror-mentality and the pioneer spirit frequently led to the suspending of all moral constraints. Lack of scruples became the hallmark of Germans 'in the east'. Freed from the traditional norms of bourgeois conduct, lacking any effective curb on their power, the German officials indulged every arbitrary impulse. This was the case in Auschwitz, too, as Sybille Steinbacher has shown.[9]

II

The first concentration camp to be built on former Polish territory took shape less than 3 kilometres from Auschwitz Old Town in spring 1940, in a disused military base that had housed Polish seasonal workers (*Sachsengänger*, or 'Saxony casuals') during the First World War. The spot was chosen in connection with the grand-scale plans of the SS, combing through all the border areas of the Reich for suitable sites for 'precautionary' facilities where political opponents could be interned, in the name of protecting German power. Although it took several visits to confirm their choice—the huts were dilapidated, and the site was on a flood-plain— the SS men were eventually swayed by a couple of advantages: the former seasonal workers' camp already had the necessary infrastructure, and it was easy to seal off from the outside world.

As is well known, more people were killed in Auschwitz than anywhere else in Hitler's sphere of influence. But Auschwitz was by no means the centre of the Holocaust from the beginning. When it was opened in June 1940, what was called the *Stammlager* (main camp), also known as Auschwitz I, was in fact a detention centre for Polish political prisoners. In addition, Auschwitz concentration camp was originally one of many enforcement facilities in the National Socialist camp network designed to isolate and 'discipline' those held to be 'community aliens'. The only unusual feature of Auschwitz was its capacity to hold up to 10,000 inmates, a figure that had been arrived at on the basis of the large numbers of political opponents the occupiers expected to intern in defeated Poland. In the early days it was not Jews who made up the bulk of the prison population, but members of the Polish intelligentsia and political groups identified as belonging to the Polish nationalist resistance.

Nonetheless, the first to suffer from the construction of the camp were Jews from the town. With enforced assistance from the Jewish Council, the SS recruited about 300 men to do the building work. The labourers were not told anything about the purpose of the construction, and were kept strictly isolated from the incoming prisoners. Others affected by the building of the camp were the roughly 1,200 unemployed and penniless Polish refugees who had moved into huts directly adjacent to the building site. Kommandant Höß was bothered by the presence of these 'asocial elements', and proposed to incorporate the site occupied by the huts into his building terrain. He wanted them moved out immediately, but they pre-empted his 'cleansing operation' by doing a moonlight flit—taking care not to leave any useful bits of the huts behind.

Only German firms profited from the building work in Auschwitz. Höß brought in workmen and materials from firms in the *Altreich* (Old Reich) part of Silesia. The first to be contracted, in June 1941, were the water-supply specialists Wodak from Beuthen, followed by the construction and civil engineering firm of Kluge, from Gleiwitz. Up until summer 1944, more than 500 large and small companies from all over the Reich contributed to the permanent enlargement of the camp, whether through planning and construction, through installation contracts, or as suppliers.[10] The leading role in financing the project was taken by the Deutsche Bank, which extended credit to at least ten construction companies. Considering the sums involved, it is safe to assume that the bank's directors were fully informed of these commitments.[11]

Whereas its ethnic composition and situation in the downgraded territory of the 'eastern strip' meant that the town of Auschwitz originally played only a marginal role in National Socialist 'Germanization policy', by the spring of 1941 its standing had altered radically. The reason was the construction of a new production plant for IG Farben. This state-of-the-art factory for the large-scale production of 'Buna' (synthetic rubber) and synthetic petroleum became one of the most expensive, largest and most ambitious investment projects of the Second World War. It quickly led to new town-planning and building policies that raised Auschwitz to the status of a leading project for the 'Germanization' of newly acquired *Lebensraum* (living-space): a 'model town' for settlement in the east.

With the construction of its Buna Works on the eastern edge of the Reich, IG Farben not only met the needs of military strategy and fulfilled one of the most urgent economic priorities of the Reich government; the company thereby also supported the resettlement policies of the National Socialist leadership. Its willingness to help construct a new 'Germanic bulwark' in the east would allow the firm profitably to combine pursuing its own commercial interests with demonstrating its ideological trustworthiness.

The business plan for this gigantic industrial project not only took into account the availability of Upper Silesian coal reserves: another commercial advantage of the site was perceived to be the presence of the prison workforce in Auschwitz. The latter was a miscalculation, however. Contrary to what was long asserted by later scholarly research, the use of rapidly burnt-out prisoners was not good business for IG Farben. Even the daily march by the prisoners from the mother-camp to the building site at Monowitz, some kilometres away, soon turned out to be so exhausting that the IG Farben managers, against the wishes of the SS, insisted on constructing their own camp near the works site. The first prisoners were moved into this new camp by October 1942. Auschwitz III was thus a novelty within the German system of terror in that it was a privately financed and privately maintained concentration camp, but with SS guards. After the war the IG Farben management claimed that 'Buna Camp' had its own sickbay for prisoners. However, if a worker could not regain his strength quickly enough, he was sent to the gas chambers of Auschwitz-Birkenau. Bernd Wagner, who has investigated in detail the use of prisoners at the IG Farben site, has concluded that this went on with the knowledge and approval of the management there, although those charged in the Nuremberg IG Farben trial refused to accept any blame for the deaths of more than 25,000 forced labourers.[12]

Not only did the management of IG Farben unhesitatingly enter into co-operation with the SS, they also took an active part in the enforced 'Germanization' of the town. The deportation of the Jewish population was a direct consequence of the decision to develop Auschwitz as an industrial complex. At the very moment, at the beginning of April 1941, when dignitaries from politics and industry were gathering in Katowice to celebrate the founding of the Buna Works, the Jews of Auschwitz were being forced out of their homes. When they were taken to the transit camps, and later ghettos, of Sosnowitz and Bendzin (Bendsburg), the more than 700-year-old history of the Jews in Auschwitz came to an end. Most of them were later murdered in the extermination camp outside the gates of their home town. The Polish inhabitants of the town, by contrast, stayed behind to work on the construction of the IG Farben factory. They disappeared only after its completion.

III

Whole villages were swallowed up by the expansion of the Auschwitz camp constellation. In March 1941 Himmler ordered a huge expanse of land to be cleared; it was henceforth designated an area of 'SS interest'. In September 1942 he gave orders for the construction of a second camp segment (Auschwitz II). Within the area of the main camp, meanwhile, about 11,000 inmates were registered. The new complex, to be built upon land previously covered by the village of Birkenau (whose population had consisted of about 3,800 Jews and Poles) was intended to hold a far greater number of prisoners. Probably early in the summer of 1942 Birkenau, initially planned as a POW camp for tens of thousands of Soviet soldiers, became—by a process we are now unlikely ever to be able to retrace in detail—the appointed place for the mass murder of European Jews to be carried out.[13]

At this time, the annihilation of the Jews in occupied Soviet territory was proceeding apace. Ever since the surprise invasion of the Soviet Union in June 1941, the Security Police and Security Service task forces had been systematically shooting men of military age; they also soon began gunning down women, children and old people in the conquered territories. At the same time, hundreds of Jews were dying of hunger and disease every day in the chronically overcrowded ghettos of the *Generalgouvernement* and the Warthegau. Despite the horrific conditions, when Hitler issued his order, in September 1941, that the pre-1938 'Old Reich' was to be made 'free of Jews', the German bureaucrats sent more and more transports to the ghettos, particularly to Łódź, where an SS commander had already broached the question of whether the 'most humane solution' might not be 'to dispatch those Jews unfit for work by some fast-acting method'.[14]

It was a feature of 'Jewish policy' in the conquered territories that SS and police functionaries, as well as the heads of the civilian authorities, seized the initiative and pressed for the disposal of the Jews. A large number of bureaucrats were involved in the preparation, logistical support and implementation of the Jewish extermination policy. Their demands for the 'disappearance' of the Jewish population were as a rule based on supposedly practical, 'factual' arguments: the Jews were spreading epidemics, occupying scarce accommodation, working inefficiently, involved in the black market, active as partisans. In short, they represented a danger or menace in every respect. Furthermore, to German minds, in Upper Silesia their very presence was an obstacle to 'Germanization'.

Supposedly in the cause of modernization, functionaries up to the level of mayor demanded that their area of responsibility should be made 'Jew-free'. As recent research has shown, it was often precisely middle- and lower-ranking officials who gave significant stimulus to the policy of murder.[15] Moreover, the scientific approach to planning the reshaping and remodelling of the towns selected for 'Germanizing' helped greatly to legitimize mass murder. But all of this does not constitute the root cause of the Holocaust: rather, it was the situation-specific expression of a racist ideology which was both widely accepted and raised to the level of a normative basis for action, and whose logic led ultimately to the 'Final Solution'.

Auschwitz-Birkenau was the last extermination camp to be 'set in motion' in occupied Poland. The first, at the beginning of December 1941, was installed in the village of Chelmno (Kulmhof) in the Warthegau. SS specialists under the command of Herbert Lange, some of whom had already taken part in the so-called 'euthanasia' operation, carried out killings using the exhaust gases of specially modified trucks.[16]

There followed the death centres of 'Operation Reinhard': Bełżec, Sobibor and Treblinka, where, under the direction of the SS leader and police chief of the Lublin district, Odilo Globocnik, the bulk of Polish Jews were killed. The three camps were established between November 1941 and June 1942, and from the middle of March 1942 onwards the rail transports trundled in their direction from the *Generalgouvernement*.

The first experiments in killing with the poison-gas Zyklon B, until then employed only to fumigate dwellings and clothes, had taken place in Auschwitz as early as September 1941. The victims of these trials were Russian POWs and other prisoners declared unfit for work. The first mass killings then took place in connection with the extension of the so-called euthanasia operation to the concentration camps.

Among Nazi extermination sites, Auschwitz-Birkenau (along with Majdanek, near Lublin, established at the same time) was exceptional in serving both as an extermination camp and a concentration camp at the same time. Given this double function from July 1942 onwards, the selection or separation of new arrivals there into 'fit to work' or 'unfit to work' represented a life-and-death decision.

After Himmler's second visit to Auschwitz in July 1942 (his first was in March 1941), transports of Jews from all over Western Europe began to arrive, especially from France, and, after the fall of Mussolini in autumn 1943, from Italy as well. By 1943 the construction of gigantic new crematoria had been completed; according to the experts, they were technically the most up-to-date to be found anywhere. The factory-style extermination of human beings reached a first peak at this time; a second one followed in early summer 1944, when some 400,000 Hungarian Jews were murdered within a few weeks.

Heinrich Himmler clearly intended to attend extermination proceedings regularly, for in summer 1943 he had quarters fitted out for him in the 'House of the Waffen-SS' opposite the railway station in Auschwitz—this at a time when the camps involved in 'Operation Reinhard' were being gradually wound down, and Auschwitz was being upgraded to the position of sole killing centre. Admittedly, Himmler never made use of his accommodation, probably because events crowded in upon him after the uprising in the Warsaw ghetto in May 1943, and the outbreaks of prisoners from Sobibor and Treblinka in August and October 1943.

As the development of the 'model town' of Auschwitz forged ahead, attracting hordes of planners and experts from the 'Old Reich', the 'Final Solution' was running at full speed. No one could ignore it. Until the new crematoria came into operation in spring 1943, the bodies of poison-gas victims in Auschwitz-Birkenau were burnt in the open air. Witnesses reported that the glow of the fires could sometimes be seen from Katowice, 30 kilometres away.

According to our current information, some 1.1 million people met their deaths in Auschwitz, just under a million of them Jews.[17] Trains bearing those deported rolled in literally from the whole of Europe. To facilitate the murder of the Hungarian Jews in the spring of 1944, a special rail spur was even put in, taking trains right into Birkenau camp. Nonetheless, it was impossible for anyone who lived around Auschwitz, and who wanted to know, to remain ignorant of the fact that terrible things were happening there. Even if one could not know all the details, it is apparent from the wealth of indicators evaluated in the course of recent research[18] that the SS did *not* succeed in keeping the murder operations secret. Even the existence of gas chambers was known about outside the strictly guarded camp area.

IV

But what could 'strictly guarded' mean anyway? The camp complex (only later, in post-war German consciousness, vaguely relegated to 'somewhere in the east') stood in the immediate vicinity of a developing middle-sized town, and had hundreds of work-sites. Contrary to what the Germans tried to convince themselves in the context of the Cold War and their collective denial of guilt, the Auschwitz of the 'Final Solution' lay not in the geographically nebulous east, but—like the killing centre of Chelmno in the Warthegau—stood until 1945 on territory that had been annexed: that is to say, on territory belonging to the Third Reich.

In the war years, Auschwitz was not only an important transport node, but also a new home for many thousands of Germans from the Reich; for the foremen and leading workers of IG Farben in Monowitz, as much as for the new proprietor of the previously Jewish-owned liqueur factory, or the pub landlord from Wuppertal, now running the best premises in town, and still enthusing about the glittering New Year's ball he had laid on for his 'Aryan' guests. Auschwitz was a German city, with its theatre performances and hunting parties for Nazi dignitaries, and its botanical guided tours and social evenings for the SS men from the camp.

Hundreds of SS guards—if their families were not already living on the edge of the camp area—received regular week-long and month-long visits from their wives and children. And so overjoyed were most participants in these thousand-fold visits to Auschwitz that Rudolf Höß eventually had to issue a special warning concerning the situation just at the end of the working day, when the SS men were bringing their work-groups back into the camp, reminding mothers to restrain their children from running out to meet their fathers while on guard duty, because the latter were obliged to shoot to kill if there were any escape bids.[19]

The so-called SS housing estate, which eventually expanded to become a separate district of Auschwitz, developed into a macabre idyll. While at first the guards were accommodated in a former barrack block outside the 'precautionary custody' camp or in the grammar school by the Soła Bridge, later on houses were requisitioned from town families. Furthermore, over a hundred buildings were blown up, in order to create a clear field of fire in case of escape attempts. In August 1944, 3,342 SS men were serving in Auschwitz, the high point being reached over about two weeks in January 1945 with 4,481 SS personnel in post. Altogether, by the end of the war about 7,000 people had served with the SS in the camp, including about 200 women. The number of people with whom these SS members shared at least some portion of the knowledge they had acquired in the course of their duties must have run to tens of thousands.

In the early days relatives were forbidden to stay in the camp. Soon, however, the authorities were permitting, and even positively encouraging, fiancées, wives and children to follow their men to Auschwitz, to allow them to live a normal family life. Consequently, the camp administration repeatedly approved a whole series of applications from family members to be allowed to stay.[20] Living on the SS estate brought many advantages. Among them was medical attention from the so-called garrison doctors of the SS, who held 'family surgeries' there.

Amazingly, the numbers of SS family members living in Auschwitz rose markedly precisely when the mass murders were at their height. The numbers of additional arrivals from the 'Old Reich' eventually reached such proportions that the camp command was reluctant to allocate any more accommodation to newly arrived families. In June 1944, at the height of the 'Hungarian operation', the camp authorities felt obliged to remind the SS guards that it was strictly forbidden for 'strangers to enter the camp area'.[21]

In the town, meanwhile, the specially commissioned architect Hans Stosberg was busy planning gigantic building projects on behalf of future German inhabitants, and in the name of 'raising the standard of civilization' there: wide streets, magnificent Party buildings, living quarters for the employees of IG Farben, stadiums, swimming pools, and parks. Whole districts of the town were redesigned, and the plan on the drawing-board envisaged that Auschwitz should sooner or later be able to accommodate 70,000 to 80,000 German inhabitants.

The town did, indeed, become a new home for several thousands of Germans from the Reich. While the mass extermination programme was running at full capacity, workers of IG Farben were moving to Auschwitz from other towns where the firm had branches. Among them were many younger people who were clearly intended to gain a part of their training in the new works. Settlers later came from all parts of the Reich, drawn by the generous tax concessions in the annexed eastern provinces. And in the end the region around Auschwitz—like the whole of Silesia—became attractive because for a long time it was free of air raids.

In comparison with the first year of the war, by 1943 the population of Auschwitz had doubled, to about 28,000. However, Jews no longer numbered among the residents. In their place, about 7,000 newly arrived Reich Germans had settled in. The amount of corruption, rapacity and individual and collective megalomania that was involved in this 'Germanization' cannot be described in detail here. Like the conquered east in general, Auschwitz was an El Dorado of amorality, and the exact reverse of the principles of 'honour and loyalty' upheld by SS propaganda.

As the memoirs of Marianne B. show, all sorts of partial information, rumours, suspicions and suppositions about the camp were in circulation among the civilian German population of Auschwitz. It was impossible not to be aware of the sweetish and penetrating smell of burnt flesh that hung so often over the town. If you were so inclined, of course you could always find 'harmless' explanations; for example, by telling yourself that in a large concentration camp there must 'obviously' be a high mortality rate, making it necessary to cremate corpses. This kind of comforting auto-suggestion enabled people to deal with clashing perceptions; latent fear must surely also have contributed to the suppression of curiosity. Added to this, there was the widespread indifference to the fate of the Jews, well attested in other contexts. It is hard to estimate the degree of approval of what was going on in the camp. Open protests were hardly to be expected, and were unknown, in contrast to complaints about 'the unpleasant smell'.

Despite the continuing lack of clarity around how much was generally known about these crimes, it has nonetheless now been established that certain circles in Auschwitz were very precisely informed; not only the SS people stationed there, but also the railway personnel who regularly brought the death-trains from the station into Birkenau camp. And it was an open secret among the IG Farben management that inmates who were no longer 'fit to work' were killed by poison-gas.[22]

In a constellation such as Auschwitz, where the exploitation and murder of the 'racially inferior' were seen as a guarantee of the permanent future of one's own race, and concepts of racial superiority ideologically justified the deed, it seems possible that the 'normal' population too were able to suspend their notions of right and wrong. The fact that the German population of Auschwitz largely remained so unaffected by what was going on in the camp—and moreover, that they obviously thought it inevitable, if not even necessary—indicates the effectiveness of antisemitism and other elements of the ideology ('people's community', 'racial purity', 'living space', 'Germanization') that the National Socialists had been propagating since well before 1933.

Where town and camp are in such close proximity, as in Auschwitz, there is a clear demonstration that mass extermination and 'the strengthening of Germandom' were not in opposition to each other, but could form a single conceptual, spatial, and temporal entity. The message could quite evidently be conveyed here 'in the east'—much more visibly than in the 'Old Reich'—that the removal of the 'racially worthless' served 'racial renewal', the latter being inconceivable without a parallel extermination programme.

While it was almost impossible for the average German 'national comrade' living for any length of time in Auschwitz to ignore the crimes taking place there, those simply travelling through could also learn of them. A vivid example is the surviving letter sent from the field by a young soldier to his relatives in December 1942, telling them with obvious satisfaction that it was 'good to see something of the world', and then continuing: 'every week 7–8,000 Jews arrive here, i.e. in Auschwitz, to die a "hero's death" shortly afterwards.'[23] There is a report on record from a group of grammar school pupils from Zittau, who were posted as anti-aircraft auxiliaries to defend the Buna Works and consequently spent two nights in the Auschwitz mother-camp, that they noticed a smell 'as though near a crematorium'.[24]

Although many Germans may never have heard the name of Auschwitz until after the end of the Third Reich, it already bore associations of death and extermination during the war, not only in the immediate vicinity, but without doubt also in the 'Old Reich'. In the hard-pressed situation of a Jew in a 'privileged mixed marriage', Victor Klemperer was among those who picked up horror reports. On 16 March 1942 he noted in his diary: 'I'm hearing the name of Auschwitz (or something like that), near Königshütte in Upper Silesia, mentioned these days as the most terrible KZ of all. Work in the mines, death after a few days.'[25] Seven months later, when he learned of the death of two women in Auschwitz, the former Dresden Professor of Romance Studies ('relieved' of his post in 1935) no longer had any doubts about the spelling of the place-name. 'Both women were taken from the women's camp in Mecklenburg to Auschwitz, which appears to be a fast-working slaughterhouse. Cause of death: "age and weak heart". Both were around sixty, one of them in particularly robust health.'[26]

Klemperer's diary entries prove that the question of what was known about Auschwitz and the murder of the Jews was already then what it has never ceased to be since 1945, despite all attempts at enlightenment: it was, among other things, a question of what one *wanted* to know.

V

The post-war history of the experience of Auschwitz from 1939 to 1945 has been scarcely less significant as part of the formation of European memory than the wartime history of the place itself. This is particularly the case for Jews, Poles, and Germans.

Before the Poles took charge of it, the site of Auschwitz or Oświęcim (which was situated within what were later to be their national borders, now shifted towards the west) was in the hands of the Red Army, which captured it on 27 January 1945. At first, field hospitals were set up for the remaining inmates, but there was also a Soviet camp for German POWs.[27] Just eight weeks later the Polish government drew up a plan for creating a memorial in the former mother-camp. Auschwitz II and Auschwitz III (Birkenau and Monowitz) were handed over for civilian use. While the Soviets dismantled the fully operational synthetic coal works and removed it to Kemerovo in Siberia, Poland developed the IG Farben installations they had inherited into one of the largest synthetic materials plants in the country.

Beginning in March 1947, the former commandant of the camp was tried by the People's High Court in Warsaw, especially created to deal with Nazi war crimes. The trial of Rudolf Höß, whose death sentence was carried out on the camp terrain, was followed, in Crakow, by that of his successor Arthur Liebehenschel and thirty-nine members of the camp SS. In addition, there were many hundreds of individual enquiries and court proceedings, but the Crakow trial was to remain the largest conducted in connection with Auschwitz.

Both the reckoning with the main perpetrators, and the establishment of a state museum on the site of the mother-camp, begun in summer 1947, reinforced the Polish national interpretation of Auschwitz which had evolved: it was first and foremost a symbol of Polish resistance to the German occupation. As befitted this version, whenever the topic of the four million people (according to Soviet estimates) killed in Auschwitz was raised, for decades there was no mention of the Jews, either in Poland or the USSR. As the SS had destroyed the deportation schedules, the International Military Tribunal likewise accepted this estimate, and it found its way into text-books and encyclopaedias. It took longer to rectify in Auschwitz than anywhere else in Eastern Europe. It was not until after the demise of the Soviet Union that the curators of the Auschwitz memorial dared to issue a correction.[28]

Even in the murky depths of this imposed official memorializing it was apparent that Poland was and is more powerfully involved in the post-war history of Auschwitz—as with the Holocaust as a whole, since it mainly took place in Poland—than any other country invaded by Germany. But it is also true that the wartime and post-war histories of Auschwitz take very different forms in the collective memories of Europe.

Perhaps we will eventually identify the European reception of Auschwitz as one of the few thin connecting threads that continued to stretch across a politically divided continent in the Cold War era: remnants of common experience and transnational memory preserved by the victims' associations that sprang up everywhere after 1945. At the moment, we know far too little about these networks of memory strung across Europe (even transcending the Iron Curtain, wherever and whenever possible) by groups of survivors, initially tending to be small, though very active. But there is much to suggest that these transnational recollections in European post-war societies have acted as a kind of catalyst of collective memory: not only the memory of the victims in each country respectively, but in a longer-term perspective also the memory of collaborating with the Germans—much harder to accept, and in many places often still highly controversial.

In connection with these networks of memory, one could think of the International Federation of the Resistance and of the Deportees (*Féderation Internationale de la Résistance et de la Déportation*), founded in 1951 with the aim of speaking up for 'freedom and peace in the world' and the prosecution of 'all crimes against humanity'. Such an objective makes it clear that, even at that time, more was involved than merely representing the interests of former inmates within the context of reparations. The moral-political impetus was as evident in the *Fédération* as it was in 1954 when the International Auschwitz Committee (*Comité Internationale d'Auschwitz*) was founded, although the latter organization had only a limited reach because of its recognized affiliation to the communist parties of East and West Europe.

There is a good deal left to do for future research. It is important, for example, to look into the extent to which the later formation of narrative memory has been influenced by the dominance of survivors who were deported to Auschwitz for being communists, and assumed important roles in organizing camp society. To put it another way: there is work to be done in clarifying how the camp memoirs that appeared in the 1950s and 1960s of the last century are to be understood. What Auschwitz reality do they stand for? To what extent are they shaped by the political and social contexts in which they were produced? And how do these accounts, written close in time to the events by survivors who were then still young, relate to autobiographical texts only produced decades later? One might think, for instance, of the books by the literary scholar Ruth Klüger, or by Anita Lasker-Wallfisch, who survived as a cellist in the Auschwitz girls' orchestra, and only began to talk about it in recent years.[29]

To mention, by contrast, just a few of the early writings: Primo Levi's profoundly thoughtful book *If This is a Man*, reflecting his experiences as a Jewish chemist in Monowitz, certainly also conveyed his experience of Italian fascism.[30] For Elie Wiesel, deported as a youth with his family from Romania to Auschwitz, the central theme of his first book, *Night*, published in 1960, was the justification of God, which was to be at the heart of his lifelong quest for ways of telling a tale that to him seemed impossible to tell.[31] A sharp contrast is Ella Lingens, who wrote from the perspective of a non-Jewish Viennese doctor sent to Auschwitz for aiding Jews, and whose social status enabled her to gather a good deal of information there, for example about the so-called 'gypsy camp'.[32]

The questions that arise, in view of these contrasts, concerning autobiography, eyewitness accounts and the formation of memory remain to be discovered by intellectually and methodologically open-minded historians who are seriously interested in the post-1945 history of National Socialism. This is especially applicable to survivors who, like Hermann Langbein, combine authorship with commitment to the politics of history. General Secretary of the International Auschwitz Committee until he broke with the Austrian Communist Party, author of numerous books and what is still the most important documentation of 'people in Auschwitz', he combines in his person the European history of Auschwitz since the war with the history of the successor states that replaced the Third Reich.[33]

VI

In the German-speaking area, the achievements and omissions of contemporary historians working on Auschwitz were for decades closely connected with degrees of willingness, or unwillingness, to engage with those events at the level of politics, society and, above all, criminal law.

If we compare developments in the GDR, Austria and the Federal Republic, it is in West Germany where—after a decade of juridical inactivity and historiographical sloth—things first began to move. Worthy of special mention is the determination shown by Fritz Bauer, the Prosecutor General of the state of Hesse. Decisively influenced by Hermann Langbein, from 1962 he began preparations for what has come to be known in National Socialism studies as 'the Frankfurt Auschwitz Trial'.[34] Empirical contemporary history, still in its infancy, provided at Bauer's request a series of expert reports on the historical background, which were introduced into the trial. Published in book form under the title *Anatomy of the SS State*, they were to become nothing short of famous over the course of the subsequent decades.[35] But one monograph on Auschwitz did as little to bring a West German historiography into being as it did an East German one.

In a certain sense, the opening of the Auschwitz trial in December 1963 marked the symbolic end of that phase of a policy for dealing with the past in which (in a way that one now finds hard to imagine) the political agenda was determined by the preservation of the interests of the perpetrators.[36] A social critique of 'the past that had not been overcome' had emerged in the meantime, which was able to latch on to the Frankfurt proceedings 'versus Mulka and others' and which made them its most important focus so far. In this sense it really is possible to say—adopting Fritz Bauer's formulation about 'holding a Day of Judgement upon ourselves'[37]—that the Auschwitz trial represented the first stage of West Germany's self-enlightenment as a society, a process which, from then on, despite all setbacks, developed its own momentum.

It was quite different in the GDR. In terms of the doctrine of anti-fascism, postulated even before the East German state was founded, 'Auschwitz' automatically stood for the genocidal outcome of a capitalist system that inevitably led to fascism. If proof were needed, then it seemed to be very clearly provided by the presence of IG Farben in Auschwitz-Monowitz. For a long time, this was the level at which East German historiography operated. Basically, the murder of European Jews never developed into a topic of itself there.

If we wanted to identify a moment when the Auschwitz debate became a matter for the whole of Germany, it would be the time after the end of the Frankfurt proceedings, in autumn 1965, when Peter Weiss's *Die Ermittlung* (The Investigation), a dramatized reading of evidence given in the trial, was simultaneously premiered in fourteen West and East German theatres.[38] Admittedly, the bias of the playwright—living in exile in Sweden—in favour of the GDR deprived the play of some of its impact in the Federal Republic; what is more, it made it easier for those looking for excuses yet again to denounce the debate about the Nazi past as an affront coming 'from the East'.

In retrospect, almost more irritating than the hesitance shown by German society at large to take up the topic of Auschwitz was the histo-riographical standstill in the 1970s in the Federal Republic. In those years concentration camp research made little if any progress.[39] Perhaps a personal recollection will serve to illustrate the situation at the end of the decade. The 'Auschwitz myth' had just put in its first appearance, a terrible farrago assembled by right-wing apologists, which I had been commissioned to refute in the public forum of an extended radio programme.[40] In the course of preparing for the broadcast, it became clear that there were no contemporary German historians currently working specifically on Auschwitz. My most important interviewees, therefore, were two survivors who had dedicated themselves for many years to investigating and publicizing this topic: Hermann Langbein and Simon Wiesenthal.

Both were based in Vienna, but with the best will in the world this could not to be regarded as a particular inclination on the part of Austrian society to confront the subject of Auschwitz. On the contrary: in the 1980s the prevailing interpretation in the third successor state of the 'Greater German Reich' was that the Republic of Austria was Hitler's 'first victim', thus exempting Austrians from guilt for his crimes. Studies like that of Hans Safrian about 'Eichmann's men' have contributed to the development of more nuanced views than this, but as yet the old interpretation does not seem to have been completely displaced. [41]

If Vienna was nonetheless for decades the place where the memory of Auschwitz was kept alive, then surely a contributory factor, apart from the size of the Jewish community deported from there, was the role of the city—at the height of the Cold War and amidst the resulting communication difficulties between East and West—as a kind of turntable for the exchange of information and documents. But this again remains to be researched.

What seems clear, however, is that neither the history nor the subsequent story of Auschwitz has been entirely absorbed into the metaphorical significance attached, in present-day European or even global memory, to the largest Nazi concentration and extermination camp. This significance is currently, at the beginning of a new century, acquiring renewed topicality. Auschwitz is more than the sum of partial memories; Auschwitz is more than the memory associated with it by Jews from the whole of Europe, by the Poles and by the Germans. We must at least mention also the Sinti and Roma murdered in Auschwitz, as well as the Soviet prisoners of war who were the first, experimental victims of gas there.

All of these partial memories will continue, so that the task of historical study must be continually to make clear the plurality of perspectives and the complexity of events. It does not necessarily follow from this that ambitions to create a unified European approach to historical memory— currently being widely discussed, and advocated by many in the name of increasing European integration—should be discouraged. But it does mean a warning against being over-ambitious, and thereby asking too much of those whose connection with Auschwitz is more than just an ethical postulate directed towards the future—above all of the last survivors, and the descendants of the victims.

Notes

All references to Noakes and Pridham *Nazism 1919–1945* vols 1, 2 and 3 are to the revised second editions with indexes; published, respectively, in 1998, 2000 and 2001.

1: Nazism—A Political Religion? Rethinking the Voluntarist Turn

1   Of the countless examples of such local and regional studies see W.S. Allen, *The Nazi Seizure of Power. The Experience of a Single German Town 1930–1935* (London, 1965); Rudy Koshar, *Social Life, Local Politics and Nazism. Marburg 1880–1935* (Chapel Hill, 1986); Walter Struve, *Aufstieg und Herrschaft des Nationalsozialismus in einer industriellen Kleinstadt: Osterode am Harz, 1918–1945* (Essen, 1992); Wolfram Pyta, *Dorfgemeinschaft und Parteipolitik 1918–1933. Die Verschränkung von Milieu und Parteien in den protestantischen Landgebieten Deutschlands in der Weimarer Republik* (Düsseldorf, 1996); Stefan Klemp, *'Richtige Nazis hat es hier nicht gegeben.' Nationalsozialismus in einer Kleinstadt am Rande des Ruhrgebiets* (Münster, 1997). Jeremy Noakes's *The Nazi Party in Lower Saxony 1921–1933* (Oxford, 1971) remains an iconic study.

2   See, for example, Hans Mommsen with Manfred Grieger, *Das Volkswagenwerk und seine Arbeiter im Dritten Reich* (Düsseldorf, 1996); Neil Gregor, *Daimler-Benz in the Third Reich* (New Haven, 1998); Gerald Feldman, *Allianz and the German Insurance Business, 1933–1945* (Cambridge, 2001); Jonathan Steinberg, *Die Deutsche Bank und ihre Goldtransaktionen während des Zweiten Weltkrieges* (Munich, 1999); Peter Hayes, *Industry and Ideology. IG Farben in the Nazi Era* (2nd edn, Cambridge, 2001); Harold James, *The Deutsche Bank and the Nazi Economic War against the Jews* (Cambridge, 2001); Peter Hayes, *From Cooperation to Complicity. Degussa in the Third Reich* (Cambridge, 2005).

3   Gerhard Paul, *Staatlicher Terror und Gesellschaftliche Verrohung: Die Gestapo in Schleswig-Holstein* (Hamburg, 1996); Hans-Dieter Schmid, *Gestapo Leipzig: Politische Abteilung des Polizeipräsidiums und Staatspolizeistelle Leipzig 1933–1945* (Beucha, 1997); Gerhard Wysocki, *Die Geheime Staatspolizei im Land Braunschweig: Polizeirecht und Polizeipraxis im Nationalsozialismus* (Frankfurt/M., 1997); see also the numerous case studies in Gerhard Paul and Klaus-Michael Mallmann (eds), *Die Gestapo im Zweiten Weltkrieg. 'Heimatfront' und besetztes Europa* (Darmstadt, 2000).

4   Ursula Büttner, *'Gomorrha'—Hamburg im Bombenkrieg* (Hamburg, 1993); Volker Zimmermann, *In Schutt und Asche: Das Ende des Zweiten Weltkrieges in Düsseldorf* (Düsseldorf, 1995); Gerhard Sollbach (ed.), *Dortmund.*

Bombenkrieg und Nachkriegszeit 1939–1948 (Hagen, 1996); more generally Stephan Burgdorff and Christian Habbe (eds), *Als Feuer vom Himmel fiel. Der Bombenkrieg in Deutschland* (Munich, 2003).

5   For judicious reflections on the current 'memory boom' see Omer Bartov, Atina Grossmann and Mary Nolan, 'Introduction', to Omer Bartov, Atina Grossmann and Mary Nolan, *Crimes of War. Guilt and Denial in the Twentieth Century* (New York, 2002), pp. ix–xxxiv.

6   David Blackbourn, 'A Sense of Place. New Directions in German History', 1998 Annual Lecture, German Historical Institute, London, p. 8.

7   Sybille Steinbacher, *'Musterstadt' Auschwitz. Germanisierungspolitik und Judenmord in Ostoberschlesien* (Munich, 2000); Bernd C. Wagner, *IG Auschwitz. Zwangsarbeit und Vernichtung von Häftlingen des Lagers Monowitz, 1941–1945* (Munich, 2000); see also the associated collection of documents *Standort- und Kommandaturbefehle des Konzentrationslagers Auschwitz 1940–1945*, ed. by Norbert Frei, Thomas Grotum, Jan Parcer, Sybille Steinbacher and Bernd C. Wagner (Munich, 2000); Sybille Steinbacher, *Auschwitz. Geschichte und Nachgeschichte* (Munich, 2004); in English, see Yisrael Gutman and Michael Berenbaum (eds), *Anatomy of the Auschwitz Death Camp* (Bloomington, IN, 1994).

8   Yitzhak Arad, *Belzec, Sobibor, Treblinka. The Operation Reinhard Death Camps* (Bloomington, IN, 1987).

9   Miroslav Kárný, Margita Kárná, Vojtech Blodig (eds), *Theresienstadt in der 'Endlösung' der Judenfrage* (Prague, 1992); see also Ruth Bondys, 'Women in Theresienstadt and the Family Camp in Birkenau', in Dalia Ofer and Lenore J. Weitzman (eds), *Women in the Holocaust* (New Haven, 1998), pp. 310–326. Since 1994 the *Theresienstädter Studien und Dokumente* yearbook, produced by the Theresienstadt Initiative Institute, has published a considerable volume of material related to the ghetto and the Holocaust in Bohemia and Moravia.

10 Sybille Steinbacher, *Dachau—Die Stadt und das Konzentrationslager in der NS-Zeit: Die Untersuchung einer Nachbarschaft* (Frankfurt/M., 1993); Harald Marcuse, *Legacies of Dachau. The Uses and Abuses of a Concentration Camp, 1933–2001* (Cambridge, 2001); of older literature, see Günther Kimmel, 'Das Konzentrationslager Dachau. Eine Studie zu den nationalsozialistischen Gewaltverbrechen', in Martin Broszat and Elke Fröhlich (eds), *Bayern in der NS-Zeit*, vol. 2, *Herrschaft und Gesellschaft in Konflikt* (Munich, 1979), pp. 349–413; Hans-Günther Richardi, *Schule der Gewalt. Das Konzentrationslager Dachau* (Munich, 1983).

11 Ulrich Bauche et al (eds), *Arbeit und Vernichtung: Das Konzentrationslager Neuengamme 1938–1945* (2nd edn, Hamburg, 1991); Hermann Kaienburg, *'Vernichtung durch Arbeit': Der Fall Neuengamme* (Bonn, 1990).

12 Günter Morsch (ed.), *Konzentrationslager Oranienburg* (Berlin, 1994).

13 See, for example, Claus Füllberg-Stolberg et al. (eds), *Frauen in Konzentrationslagern: Bergen-Belsen Ravensbrück* (Bremen, 1994); Hermann Kuhn (ed.), *Stutthof: Ein Konzentrationslager vor den Toren Danzigs* (Bremen, 1995); of the many recent overviews, the following are among the most important: Klaus Drobisch and Günther Wieland, *System der NS-Konzentrationslager 1933–1939* (Berlin, 1993); Johannes Tuchel, *Die*

Inspektion der Konzentrationslager 1938–1945 (Berlin, 1994); Hermann Kaienburg (ed.), *Konzentrationslager und Deutsche Wirtschaft 1939–1945* (Opladen, 1996); Ulrich Herbert, Karin Orth, Christoph Dieckmann (eds), *Die Nationalsozialistischen Konzentrationslager: Entwicklung und Struktur* (Göttingen, 1998); Karin Orth, *Das System der Nationalsozialistischen Konzentrationslager* (Hamburg, 1999); Norbert Frei, Sybille Steinbacher, Bernd C. Wagner (eds), *Ausbeutung, Vernichtung, Öffentlichkeit. Neue Studien zur nationalsozialistischen Lagerpolitik* (Munich, 2000).

14 Toni Siegert, *30,000 Tote mahnen! Die Geschichte des Konzentrationslagers Flossenbürg und seiner 100 Aussenlager von 1938 bis 1945* (Weiden, 1984); Edith Raim, *Die Dachauer KZ-Aussenkommandos Kauerfering und Mühldorf. Rüstungsbauten und Zwangsarbeit im letzten Kriegjahr 1944/45* (Munich, 1991); Hans Müller, *'Wir haben verzeihen aber nicht vergessen. . .' Das KZ-Aussenlager Buchenwald in Dortmund* (Dortmund, 1994); Bärbel Maul und Axel Ulrich, *Das KZ-Aussenkommando 'Unter den Eichen'* (Wiesbaden, 1995); Karola Fings, *Messelager Köln: Ein KZ-Aussenlager im Zentrum der Stadt* (Cologne, 1996).

15 For example Isabell Sprenger, *Groß-Rosen: Ein Konzentrationslager in Schlesien* (Cologne, 1996); Dietfried Krause-Vilmar, *Das Konzentrationslager Breitenau. Ein staatliches Schutzhaftlager* (Marburg, 1997); Markus Kienle, *Das Konzentrationslager Heuberg bei Stettin am Kalten Markt* (Ulm, 1998); more generally Wolfgang Benz and Barbara Distel (eds), *Geschichte der Nationalsozialistischen Konzentrationslager* (2 vols, Berlin, 2001–).

16 On ghettos see most recently Gustavo Corni, *Hitler's Ghettos. Voices from a Beleaguered Society* (London, 2002); on labour education camps see Gabriele Lotfi, *KZ der Gestapo. Arbeitserziehungslager im Dritten Reich* (Stuttgart, 2000); more specifically Detlef Korte, *'Erziehung' ins Massengrab: Die Geschichte des 'Arbeitserziehungslagers Nordmark' Kiel Russee 1944–1945* (Kiel, 1991); on prisons Nikolaus Wachsmann, *Hitler's Prisons. Legal Terror in Nazi Germany* (New Haven, 2004).

17 Of key older studies see Helmuth Krausnick and Hans-Heinrich Wilhelm, *Die Truppe des Weltanschauungskrieges: Die Einsatzgruppen der Sicherheitspolizei und des SD 1938–1942* (Stuttgart, 1981); Eberhard Jäckel and Jürgen Rohwer (eds), *Der Mord an den Juden im zweiten Weltkrieg* (Stuttgart, 1985); Gerhard Hirschfeld (ed.), *The Policies of Genocide. Jews and Soviet Prisoners of War in Nazi Germany* (London, 1986); more recently David Cesarani (ed.), *The Final Solution. Origins and Implementation* (London, 1994); Ralf Ogorreck, *Die Einsatzgruppen und die Genesis der Endlösung* (Berlin, 1996); Peter Klein (ed.), *Die Einsatzgruppen in der besetzten Sowjetunion 1941/42. Die Tätigkeits- und Lageberichte des Chefs der Sicherheitspolizei und des SD* (Berlin, 1997).

18 See above all the work of Christopher Browning: Christopher R. Browning, *Ordinary Men. Reserve Police Battalion 101 and the Final Solution in Poland* (New York, 1992); Christopher R. Browning, 'German Killers: Orders from Above, Initiative from Below, and the Scope of Local Autonomy—the Case of Brest-Litovsk', in id., *Nazi Policy, Jewish Workers, German Killers* (Cambridge, 2000), pp. 116–142.

19 This historiographical turn is exemplified by two important studies of the

Holocaust in Galicia: Dieter Pohl, *Nationalsozialistische Judenverfolgung in Ostgalizien 1941–1944. Organisation und Durchführung eines staatlichen Massenverbrechens* (Munich, 1996); Thomas Sandkühler, *'Endlösung' in Galizien. Der Judenmord in Ostpolen und die Rettungsinitiativen von Berthold Beitz 1941–1944* (Bonn, 1996); for a good introduction to the wave of recent studies of the implementation of the Holocaust 'on the ground' see Ulrich Herbert, *National Socialist Extermination Policies: Contemporary German Perspectives and Controversies* (Oxford, 2000).

20 The best English-language account of the 'racial state' is Michael Burleigh and Wolfgang Wippermann, *The Racial State: Germany, 1933–1945* (Cambridge, 1991). For detailed accounts of various aspects see Gisela Bock, *Zwangssterilisation im Nationalsozialismus: Studien zur Rassenpolitik und Frauenpolitik* (Opladen, 1986); Burkhard Jellonneck, *Homosexuelle unter dem Hakenkreuz. Die Verfolgung von Homosexuellen im Dritten Reich* (Paderborn, 1990); Wolfgang Ayaß, *'Asoziale' im Nationalsozialismus* (Stuttgart, 1995); Michael Zimmermann, *Die Nationalsozialistische Lösung der Zigeunerfrage* (Hamburg, 1996); Robert Gellately and Nathan Stoltzfus (eds), *Social Outsiders in Nazi Germany* (Princeton, 2001).

21 Hans-Walter Schmuhl, *Rassenhygiene, Nationalsozialismus, Euthanasie: von der Verhütung zur Vernichtung 'lebensunwerten Lebens' 1890–1945* (Göttingen, 1987); Norbert Frei (ed.), *Medizin und Gesundheitspolitik in der NS-Zeit* (Munich, 1991); Götz Aly, Peter Chroust and Christian Pross, *Cleansing the Fatherland: Nazi Medicine and Racial Hygiene* (Baltimore, 1994); Michael Burleigh, *Death and Deliverance: 'Euthanasia' in Germany 1900–1945* (Cambridge, 1994); Henry Friedlander, *The Origins of Nazi Genocide: From Euthanasia to the Final Solution* (Chapel Hill, 1995); Michael Burleigh, *Ethics and Extermination: Reflections on Nazi Genocide* (Cambridge, 1997); Francis Nicosia and Jonathan Huener (eds), *Medicine and Medical Ethics in Nazi Germany. Origins, Practices, Legacies* (Oxford, 2000).

22 Bernhard Richarz, *Heilen, Pflegen, Töten. Zur Alltagsgeschichte einer Heil- und Pflegeanstalt bis zum Ende des Nationalsozialismus* (Göttingen, 1987); Gerhard Baader et al., *'Verlegt nach Hadamar': Die Geschichte einer NS 'Euthanasie'- Anstalt* (Kassel, 1991); Thomas Schilter, *Unmenschliches Ermessen. Die Nationalsozialistische 'Euthanasie'-Tötungsanstalt Pirna-Sonnenstein 1940–41* (Leipzig, 1999); Frank Hirschinger, *'Zur Ausmerzung freigegeben': Halle und die Landesheilsanstalt Altscherbitz 1933–1945* (Cologne, 2001).

23 The classic study remains Christian Streit, *Keine Kameraden: Die Wehrmacht und die sowjetischen Kriegsgefangenen 1941–1945* (Stuttgart, 1978); more recently Reinhard Otto, *Wehrmacht, Gestapo und sowjetische Kriegsgefangene im deutschen Reichsgebiet 1941/42* (Munich, 1998); Hannes Heer and Klaus Naumann (eds), *War of Extermination. The German Military in World War II 1941–1944* (Oxford, 2000). For forced labour, see the pioneering study by Ulrich Herbert, *Hitler's Foreign Workers. Enforced Foreign Labour in Germany in the Third Reich* (Cambridge, 1997); for individual case studies Christa Tholander, *Fremdarbeiter 1939–1945. Ausländische Arbeitskräfte in der Zeppelin-Stadt Friedrichshafen* (Essen, 2001); Clemens von Looz-Corswarem (ed.), *Zwangsarbeit in Düsseldorf. 'Ausländer-Einsatz' während des Zweiten*

Weltkrieges in einer rheinischen Großstadt (Essen, 2002).

24 An excellent overview of recent work is offered by Gerhard Paul (ed.), *Die Täter der Shoah. Fanatische Nationalsozialisten oder ganz normale Deutsche?* (Göttingen, 2002); see also Wolf Kaiser (ed.), *Täter im Vernichtungskrieg. Der Überfall auf die Sowjetunion und der Völkermord an den Juden* (Berlin, 2002).

25 Karin Orth, 'Experten des Terrors. Die Konzentrationslager-SS und die Shoah', in Paul (ed.), *Täter der Shoah*, pp. 93–108; more generally Karin Orth, *Die Konzentrationslager—SS. Sozialstrukturelle Analysen und biographische Studien* (Göttingen, 2000).

26 Ulrich Herbert, *Best. Biographische Studien über Radikalismus, Weltanschauung und Vernunft, 1903–1989* (Bonn, 1996); Michael Wildt, *Generation des Unbedingten. Das Führungskorps des Reichssicherheitshauptamptes* (Hamburg, 2003); see also Claudia Steur, *Theodor Dannecker. Ein Funktionär der Endlösung* (Essen, 1997); Lutz Hachtmeister, *Der Gegnerforscher. Die Karriere des SS-Führers Franz Alfred Six* (Munich, 1998); Jens Banach, *Heydrichs Elite. Das Führerkorps der Sicherheitspolizei und des SD 1936–1945* (Paderborn, 1998).

27 Michael Thad Allen, *The Business of Genocide. The SS, Slave Labor and the Concentration Camps* (Chapel Hill, 2002); Hermann Kaienburg, *Die Wirtschaft der SS* (Berlin, 2003).

28 Christopher Browning, *Ordinary Men*; see especially also the work of Edward B. Westermann: '"Friend and Helper": German Uniformed Police Operations in Poland and the General Government, 1939–1941', *Journal of Military History* 58 (1994), pp. 643–661; 'Himmler's Uniformed Police on the Eastern Front: The Reich's Secret Soldiers 1941–1942', *War in History* 3 (1996), 309–330; '"Ordinary Men" or "Ideological Soldiers"? Police Battalion 310 in Russia, 1942', *German Studies Review* 21 (1998), pp. 41–48; 'Shaping the Police Soldier as an Instrument of Annihilation', in Alan E. Steinweis and Daniel E. Rogers (eds), *The Impact of Nazism. New Perspectives on the Third Reich and its Legacy* (Lincoln, NE, 2003), pp. 129–150.

29 Andrew Ezergailis, *The Holocaust in Latvia, 1941–1944* (Riga, 1996); Martin Dean, *Collaboration in the Holocaust: Crimes of the Local Police in Belorussia and Ukraine 1941–1944* (London, 1999); Radu Ioanid, *The Holocaust in Romania* (Chicago, 2000); also the relevant essays in Vincas Bartusevičius, Joachim Tauber and Wolfram Wette (eds), *Holocaust in Litauen. Krieg, Judenmorde und Kollaboration im Jahre 1941* (Cologne, 2003).

30 See, for example, Omer Bartov, *Hitler's Army. Soldiers, Nazis and War in the Third Reich* (Oxford, 1991); Walter Manoschek (ed.), *Die Wehrmacht im Rassenkrieg* (Vienna, 1996); Karl-Heinz Pohl (ed.), *Wehrmacht und Vernichtungspolitik. Militär im nationalsozialistischen System* (Göttingen, 1999); Hannes Heer and Klaus Naumann (eds), *War of Extermination*.

31 Walter Manoschek, *'Serbien ist Judenfrei'. Militärische Besatzungspolitik und Judenvernichtung in Serbien, 1941/42* (Munich, 1993).

32 Christian Gerlach, *Kalkulierte Morde. Die deutsche Wirtschafts- und Vernichtungspolitik in Weissrussland 1941 bis 1944* (Hamburg, 1999).

33 Alexander B. Rossino, *Hitler Strikes Poland. Blitzkrieg, Ideology, and Atrocity* (Kansas, 2003).

34 Manoschek, *Serbien ist Judenfrei*, pp. 86–91, 98.

35 Gerlach, *Kalkulierte Morde*, pp. 13–80.

36 For introductions to the recent development of the debate concerning women's involvement in Nazism see Adelheid von Saldern, 'Victims or Perpetrators? Controversies about the Role of Women in the Nazi State', in David Crew (ed.), *Nazism and German Society* (London, 1994), pp. 141–165; A. Ebbinghaus (ed.), *Opfer und Täterinnen. Frauenbiographien des Nationalsozialismus* (Frankfurt/M., 1996); Gisela Bock, 'Ordinary Women in Nazi Germany: Perpetrators, Victims, Followers and Bystanders', in Dalia Ofer and Lenora J. Weitzman (eds), *Women in the Holocaust* , pp. 85–100.

37 Claudia Koonz, *Mothers in the Fatherland: Women, the Family and Nazi Politics* (New York, 1987).

38 Gudrun Schwarz, 'During War, We Girls want to be somewhere where we can really accomplish Something', in Bartov, Grossmann, Nolan (eds), *Crimes of War*, pp. 121–137, here 131–132.

39 Elizabeth Harvey, *Women and the Nazi East. Agents and Witnesses of Germanization* (New Haven, 2003).

40 The document is reprinted in J. Noakes and G. Pridham (eds), *Nazism 1919–1945* vol. 3: *Foreign Policy, War and Racial Extermination: A Documentary Reader* (Exeter, 2nd edn, 2001), pp. 499–501.

41 Steinbacher, *Dachau*; Jens Schley, *Nachbar Buchenwald. Die Stadt Weimar und ihr Konzentrationslager* (Cologne, 1999).

42 Gerlach, *Kalkulierte Morde*, p. 657.

43 Ibid., p. 721.

44 Harvey, *Women and the Nazi East*, pp.133–134.

45 Steinbacher, *Musterstadt Auschwitz* , pp. 178–194.

46 Noakes and Pridham, *Nazism*, vol. 3, p. 400; for soldiers' letters Walter Manoschek (ed.), *'Es gibt nur eines für das Judentum: Vernichtung'. Das Judenbild in deutsche Soldatenbriefen 1939–1944* (Hamburg, 1995); slightly more cautious, but highly valuable, conclusions are to be found in Klaus Latzel, *Deutsche Soldaten—nationalsozialistischer Krieg? Kriegserlebnis— Kriegserfahrung 1939–1945* (Paderborn, 1998).

47 Saul Friedländer, 'The Wehrmacht, German Society, and the Knowledge of the Mass Extermination of the Jews', in Bartov, Grossmann, Nolan (eds), *Crimes of War*, pp. 17–30, here 28.

48 Bernd Ogan and Wolfgang Weiss (eds), *Faszination und Gewalt. Zur politischen Ästhetik des Nationalsozialismus* (Nuremberg, 1992); Peter Reichel, *Der Schöne Schein des Dritten Reiches. Faszination und Gewalt des Faschismus* (Frankfurt/M., 1993); Sabine Behrenbeck, *Der Kult um die Toten Helden. Nationalsozialistische Mythen, Riten und Symbole* (Vierow, 1996).

49 The classic exploration of these issues remains Ian Kershaw, *The Hitler Myth: Image and Reality in the Third Reich* (Oxford, 1987).

50 See the pioneering work of Robert Gellately, *The Gestapo and German Society. Enforcing Racial Policy 1933–1945* (Oxford, 1990); also Gisela Diewald-Kerkmann, *Politische Denunciation im NS-Regime, oder die kleine Macht des Volksgenossen* (Bonn, 1995); Katrin Dördelmann, *Die Macht der Worte: Denunziationen im Nationalsozialistischen Köln* (Cologne, 1997); a useful

overview of recent work on denunciations is provided in Gerhard Paul, 'Private Konfliktregulierung, gesellschaftliche Selbstüberwachung, politische Teilhabe? Neuere Forschungen zur Denunziation im Dritten Reich', *Archiv für Sozialgeschichte* 42 (2002), pp. 380–402.

51 Frank Bajohr, *'Aryanisation' in Hamburg. The Economic Exclusion of Jews and the Confiscation of their Property in Nazi Germany* (Oxford, 2001).

52 Omer Bartov, *Germany's War and the Holocaust. Disputed Histories,* (Ithaca, 2003) pp. 96–97. Perhaps the best recent example of these historiographical shifts is Robert Gellately, *Backing Hitler: Consent and Coercion in Nazi Germany* (Oxford, 2001).

53 Michael Burleigh, *The Third Reich. A New History* (Basingstoke, 2000).

54 See for example Klaus Vondung, *Magie und Manipulation: Ideologischer Kult und politische Religion des Nationalsozialismus* (Göttingen, 1971).

55 Omer Bartov, *Germany's War and the Holocaust* , p. 191.

56 Burleigh, *The Third Reich*, p. 91.

57 Ibid., p. 210.

58 Ibid., p. 194.

59 For a powerful critique of the book which explores the significance of such comments at length see Geoff Eley, 'Hitler's Silent Majority? Conformity and Resistance under the Third Reich (Part One)' *Michigan Quarterly Review* 42 (2003), pp. 389–425.

60 Burleigh, *The Third Reich*, p. 42.

61 Ibid., p. 91.

62 Ibid., p. 187.

63 Ibid., pp. 372–373.

64 Timothy W. Mason, 'Intention and Explanation: A Current Controversy about the Interpretation of National Socialism', reprinted in id., *Nazism, Fascism and the Working Class*, (ed.) Jane Caplan (Cambridge, 1995), pp. 212–230, here 230.

65 Eric Voegelin, *Die Politischen Religionen* (Vienna, 1938); the quote is from the 1993 reprint (ed.) by Peter J. Opitz (Munich, 1993), pp. 6–7.

66 Clemens Vollnhals, *Evangelische Kirche und Entnazifizierung 1945–1949. Die Last der nationalsozialistischen Vergangenheit* (Munich, 1989).

67 Wolfram Pyta, 'Ländlich-evangelisches Milieu und Nationalsozialismus bis 1933', in Horst Möller, Andreas Wirsching and Walter Ziegler (eds), *Nationalsozialismus in der Region* (Munich, 1996), pp. 199–212, here 204.

68 See the examples and discussion in Dennis Showalter, *Little Man, What Now? Der Stürmer in the Weimar Republic* (Hamden, CT, 1982).

69 For a reading of *Mein Kampf* which emphasizes this see Neil Gregor, *How to Read Hitler* (London, 2005).

70 Paul Gilroy, *Between Camps. Nations, Cultures and the Allure of Race* (London, 2000), p. 94

71 Richard Steigmann-Gall, *The Holy Reich. Nazi Conceptions of Christianity, 1919–1945* (Cambridge, 2003).

72 See, for example, Beth A. Griech-Polelle, *Bishop von Galen. German Catholicism and National Socialism* (New Haven, 2002).

73 Ian Kershaw, 'Hitler and the Uniqueness of Nazism', *Journal of Contemporary History* 39 (2004), pp. 239–254.

74 For stimulating treatments see the classic Detlev Peukert, *The Weimar Republic. The Crisis of Classical Modernity* (London, 1991); Hans Mommsen, *The Rise and Fall of Weimar Democracy* (North Carolina, 1996); most recently Richard J. Evans, *The Coming of the Third Reich* (2003); in German see the essays in H.A. Winkler (ed.), *Die Deutsche Staatskrise 1930–1933* (Munich, 1993).

75 This is the thrust of Hans Mommsen's powerful critique of the term: see Hans Mommsen, 'Der Nationalsozialismus als säkulare Religion', in Gerhard Besier (ed.), *Zwischen 'Nationaler Revolution' und militärischer Aggression. Transformationen in Kirche und Gesellschaft 1934–1939* (Munich, 2001), pp. 43–54.

76 Burleigh, *The Third Reich*, p. 615.

77 Ibid., p. 331; p. 8.

78 Banach, *Heydrichs Elite*, p. 325; pp. 330–332; Herbert, *Best* and Wildt, *Generation des Unbedingten* make a similar case.

79 Gerhard Paul, 'Die Täter der Shoah im Spiegel der Forschung', in Paul (ed.), *Die Täter der Shoah* , p. 62.

80 Elizabeth D. Heineman, 'Sexuality and Nazism: The Doubly Unspeakable?', *Journal of the History of Sexuality* 11 (2002), pp. 22–66, here 29.

81 For excellent overviews of the debate see Christopher R. Browning, 'German Killers. Behaviour and Motivation in the Light of New Evidence', in Browning, *Nazi Policy*, pp. 143–169; Gerhard Paul, 'Die Täter der Shoah im Spiegel der Forschung', in Paul (ed.), *Die Täter der Shoah*, pp. 13–90.

82 The best statement of this position is to be found in Ian Kershaw's two-volumed political biography *Hitler 1889–1936. Hubris* (London, 1998) and *Hitler 1936–1945. Nemesis* (London, 2000).

83 Kershaw, *Hitler 1889–1936. Hubris*, p. 244. For one interested in notions of political religion Burleigh is, in fact, surprisingly dismissive of the movement's founding texts.

84 Gerhard Weinberg (ed.), *Hitler's Second Book. The Unpublished Sequel to Mein Kampf by Adolf Hitler*. Tr. Krista Smith (New York, 2003).

85 David Cesarani, *Eichmann: His Life and Crimes* (London, 2004).

86 The most obvious recent example of this is Daniel J. Goldhagen, *Hitler's Willing Executioners: Ordinary Germans and the Holocaust* (New York, 1996).

87 Manoschek, *'Serbien ist judenfrei'*, p. 12.

88 Christopher R. Browning, 'The Wehrmacht in Serbia Revisited', in Bartov, Grossman, Nolan (eds), *Crimes of War*, pp. 31–40, here 32–33; for similar emphasis on the continued presence of older, colonial visions and their significance see Harvey, *Women and the Nazi East*.

89 On the SA see Richard Bessel, *Political Violence and the Rise of Nazism. The Storm Troopers in Eastern Germany 1925–1934* (New Haven, 1984); Eric Reiche, *The Development of the SA in Nuremberg 1922–1934* (Cambridge, 1986); P. Longerich, *Geschichte der SA* (Munich, 2003); of comparative studies see Hans Mommsen (ed.), *Der Erste Weltkrieg und die europäische Nachkriegsordnung. Sozialer Wandel und Formveränderung der Politik* (Cologne, 2000); most recently Sven Reichardt, *Faschistische Kampfbünde. Gewalt und Gemeinschaft im italienischen Squadrismus und in der deutschen SA* (Cologne, 2002).

90 Benjamin Ziemann, 'Germany after the First World War—A Violent Society? Results and Implications of Recent Research on Weimar Germany', *Journal of Modern European History* 1 (2003), 80–94.
91 Reichardt, *Faschistische Kampfbünde*, p. 370.
92 Burleigh, *The Third Reich*, p. 64.
93 Martin Döring, *'Parlamentarischer Arm der Bewegung'. Die Nationalsozialisten im Reichstag der Weimarer Republik* (Düsseldorf, 2001), pp. 309–311.
94 Ibid., pp. 413–418.
95 Dirk Walter, *Antisemitische Kriminalität und Gewalt. Judenfeindschaft in der Weimarer Republik* (Bonn, 1999).
96 Ibid., p. 42.
97 This is emphasized by Richard Evans' excellent recent study: Richard J. Evans, *The Coming of the Third Reich*, especially chapters 4 and 5.
98 *Deutschland-Berichte der Sozialdemokratischen Partei Deutschlands (SOPADE) 1934–1940* (7 vols, Salzhausen, 1980).
99 Evans, *The Coming of the Third Reich*, p. xviii.
100 Bartov, *Germany's War and the Holocaust*, pp. 12–14.
101 Timothy W. Mason, 'Intention and Explanation', p. 229.

2: Political Detention and the Origin of the Concentration Camps in Nazi Germany, 1933–1935/6

1 Direktor des Provinzial-Werkhauses [Hugo Krack] to Landesdirektorium in Hannover, 23 March 1933 (Niedersächsisches Hauptstaatsarchiv Hannover (NSHA), Hann. 158 Moringen, acc. 84/82, Nr. 1, p. 90).
2 Verordnung zum Schutze von Volk und Staat, 28 February 1933 (RGBl, I 1933, p. 83); this translation in J. Noakes and G. Pridham, (eds), *Nazism 1919–1945* vol. 1: *The Rise to Power 1919–1934: A Documentary Reader* (Exeter, 1998), p. 134.
3 Klaus Drobisch and Günther Wieland, *System der NS-Konzentrationslager 1933–1939* (Berlin,1993), p. 38.
4 Johannes Tuchel, *Konzentrationslager. Organisationsgeschichte und Funktion der 'Inspektion der Konzentrationslager' 1934–1938* (Boppard am Rhein, 1991), p. 107; the estimate of 100,000 is given by Johannes Tuchel and Reinold Schattenfroh, *Zentrale des Terrors. Prinz-Albrecht-Strasse 8: Das Hauptquartier der Gestapo* (Berlin, 1987), p. 114; the derivation of this figure is unclear, and it may just repeat the estimate (likewise unsourced) offered by Wolfgang Sauer in 'Die Mobilmachung der Gewalt', his contribution to the pioneering and still essential study of the Nazi seizure of power, in Karl Dietrich Bracher, Wolfgang Sauer and Gerhard Schulz, *Die nationalsozialistische Machtergreifung. Studien zur Errichtung des totalitären Herrschaftssystems in Deutschland 1933/34* (Cologne/Opladen,1962), p. 871. For a recent account of the repressive violence of the seizure of power, see Richard J. Evans, *The Coming of the Third Reich* (London, 2003), ch. 5.
5 Figures cited from interior ministry documentation in Drobisch and Wieland, *System der NS-Konzentrationslager*, p. 134.
6 Tuchel, *Konzentrationslager*, pp. 37, 51f.
7 Nikolaus Wachsmann, *Hitler's Prisons. Legal Terror in Nazi Germany* (New

Haven, 2004), p. 55.

8   Wolfgang Sofsky, *Die Ordnung des Terrors: Das Konzentrationslager* (Frankfurt, 1997), p. 41; English translation, *The Order of Terror. The Concentration Camp* (Princeton, 1997).

9   Drobisch and Wieland, *System der NS-Konzentrationslager*, p. 12.

10 Ulrich Herbert, Karin Orth and Christoph Dieckmann (eds), *Die national-sozialistischen Konzentrationslager. Entwicklung und Struktur* (Göttingen, 1998), vol. 1, pp. 19–20.

11 Eugen Kogon, *Der SS-Staat. Das System der deutschen Konzentrationslager* (Berlin, 1946); English translation, *The Theory and Practice of Hell. The German Concentration Camps and the System Behind Them* (London, 1950).

12 Hans Buchheim, Martin Broszat, Hans-Adolf Jacobsen and Helmut Krausnick, *Anatomie des SS-Staates* (Olten/Freiburg,1965). English translation, *Anatomy of the SS State* (New York, 1968).

13 Gudrun Schwarz, *Die nationalsozialistischen Lager* (Frankfurt /M., 1996; orig. edn 1990), p. 9, citing Andrzej Kamínski.

14 The death statistics are discussed in Karin Orth, *Das System der national-sozialistischen Konzentrationslager. Eine politische Organisationsgeschichte* (Zürich/Munich, 2002; orig. edn, 1999), pp. 343–50.

15 See e.g. Tuchel, *Konzentrationslager*, pp. 359–366.

16 In addition to works already cited, see especially the series of *Dachauer Hefte*, and Wolfgang Benz and Barbara Distel (eds), *Geschichte der Konzentrations-lager*, 3 vols (Berlin, 2001–); also Karl Giebeler, Thomas Lutz and Silvester Lechner (eds), *Die frühen Konzentrationslager in Deutschland. Austausch zum Forschungsstand und zur pädagogischen Praxis in Gedenkstätten* (Bad Boll: Evangelische Akademie, 1995). An authoritative summary is Johannes Tuchel, 'Organisationsgeschichte der "frühen" Konzentrationslager", in Benz and Distel (eds), *Geschichte der Konzentrationslager*, vol. 3, pp. 9–27. For extensive documentation of one institution in the early camp system, Erich Kosthorst and Bernd Walter, *Konzentrations- und Strafgefangenenlager im Dritten Reich. Beispiel Emsland*, 3 vols (Düsseldorf, 1983). For the legal system, Lothar Gruchmann, *Justiz im Dritten Reich 1933–1940. Anpassung und Unterwerfung in der Ära Gürtner* (Munich, 1988). For the Gestapo, Gerhard Paul and Klaus-Michael Mallmann, (eds), *Die Gestapo. Mythos und Realität* (Frankfurt, 2003; 1st edn, 1995). For the relationship between the concentration camp and prison systems, Wachsmann, *Hitler's Prisons*.

17 Robert Gellately, *The Gestapo and German Society. Enforcing Racial Policy 1933–1945* (Oxford, 1990); Eric A. Johnson, *Nazi Terror. The Gestapo, Jews, and Ordinary Germans* (New York, 2000); Wachsmann, *Hitler's Prisons*.

18 Michael Burleigh, *The Third Reich. A New History* (New York, 2000), pp. 198–205; Robert Gellately, *Backing Hitler. Consent and Coercion in Nazi Germany* (New York, 2001); literature reviews in Herbert et al. (eds), *Die nationalsozialistischen Konzentrationslager*, vol. 1, Introduction, and Orth, *Das System der nationalsozialistischen Konzentrationslager*, Introduction.

19 In English see e.g. Hans Buchheim, 'The SS—Instrument of Domination', in *Anatomy of the SS-Staat*, pp. 143–166 especially; Shlomo Aronson, *Beginnings of the Gestapo System. The Bavarian Model in 1933* (New

Brunswick NJ, 1969); George Browder, *Foundations of the Nazi Police State. The Formation of Sipo and SD* (Lexington, 1990) and *Hitler's Enforcers. The Gestapo and the SS Security System in the Nazi Revolution* (New York, 1996); Gellately, *The Gestapo and German Society*, pp. 21–43; J. Noakes and G. Pridham (eds), *Nazism 1919–1945* vol. 1: *The Rise to Power 1919–1934: A Documentary Reader* (Exeter, 1998), ch. 22. For the Weimar police, Hsi-Huey Liang, *The Berlin Police Force in the Weimar Republic* (Berkeley, 1970). In German, see Christoph Graf, *Politische Polizei zwischen Demokratie und Diktatur* (Berlin, 1983) and id., 'Kontinuitäten und Brüche. Von der Politischen Polizei der Weimarer Republik zur Geheimen Staatspolizei', in Paul and Mallmann (eds), *Die Gestapo*, pp. 73–83; Tuchel and Schattenfroh, *Zentrale des Terrors*; Ulrich Herbert, *Best. Biographische Studien über Radikalismus, Weltanschauung und Vernunft 1903–1989* (Bonn, 1996), pp. 133–163; further German sources on the Weimar police noted in Evans, *The Coming of the Third Reich*, p. 511, fn. 92.

20 This account is drawn from Günther Wieland, 'Die normativen Grundlagen der Schutzhaft in Hitlerdeutschland', *Jahrbuch für Geschichte* vol. 26 (1982), pp. 75–102, and Drobisch and Wieland, *System der NS-Konzentrationslager*, pp. 16–21.

21 Wieland, 'Die normative Grundlagen', p. 85.

22 Andrzej Kaminski has traced the term back to the colonial wars in Cuba in the 1890s; it referred to camps in which civilian non-combatants were ordered to assemble if they did not wish to be treated as rebels, i.e. ostensibly for their own protection; Andrzej Kaminski, *Konzentrationslager 1896 bis heute. Geschichte, Funktion, Typologie* (Munich/Zürich, 1990), pp. 34ff. ; a brief summary of German precedents in Evans, *The Coming of the Third Reich*, pp. 345f.

23 Tuchel and Schattenfroh, *Zentrale des Terrors*, p. 42.

24 Graf, *Politische Polizei*, p. 257.

25 Partial translation in Noakes and Pridham (eds), *Nazism*, vol. 1, p. 142; discussion in Bracher, Sauer and Schulz, *Die nationalsozialistische Machtergreifung*. Strictly speaking the first move by the new government to equip itself with wider powers of arrest was the presidential decree 'for the protection of the German people' issued on 3 February, which authorized 'special police detention' for up to three months on suspicion of treasonable or similar activities. This decree still set narrow limits for summary arrest and retained an element of judicial review.

26 Other terms drawn from the historic repertoire of police detention were employed in other *Länder*, e.g. *Polizeihaft, vorbeugender Polizeihaft, Sicherungshaft* and *Sicherungs-verwahrung*, i.e. 'police arrest', 'preventive police arrest', 'security arrest' and 'security detention'; see Drobisch and Wieland, *Die nationalsozialistischen Konzentrationslager*, p. 31. For the subsequent national regulations on protective custody issued on 12/26 April 1934 and 25 January/1 February 1938, see Gerhard Werle, *Justiz-Strafrecht und polizeiliche Verbrechensbekämpfung im Dritten Reich* (Berlin, 1989, pp. 537–600, and Ulrich Herbert, 'Von der Gegnerbekämpfung zur "rassischen Generalprävention". "Schutzhaft" und Konzentrationslager in der Konzeption der Gestapo-Führung 1933–1939', in Herbert et al. (eds), *Die*

nationalsozialistischen Konzentrationslager, vol. 1, pp. 61–66.

27 Graf, *Politische Polizei*, pp. 262–263.

28 Tuchel, *Konzentrationslager*, pp. 48–49.

29 Rudolf Diels, *Lucifer ante Portas. Zwischen Severing und Heydrich* (Zürich, 1949), p. 190.

30 Evidence for Prussia set out in Graf, *Politische Polizei*, pp. 273–284 and Tuchel, *Konzentrationslager*, pp. 38–120; for other *Länder*, see Drobisch and Wieland, *Die nationalsozialistischen Konzentrationslager*, pp. 45–53, 62.

31 See Klaus Mlynek, 'Der Aufbau der Geheimen Staatspolizei in Hannover und die Errichtung des Konzentrationslagers Moringen', in Anke Dietzler et al. (eds) *Hannover 1933. Eine Großstadt wird nationalsozialistisch* (Hannover, 1981); documentation for the following account in NSHA Hann. 180/Hannover, Nr. 752 (files of *Regierungspräsident* Hannover) and Hann. 158/Moringen, acc. 84/82.

32 The Reich interior ministry announced that it would offer financial subventions to *Länder* camps on 13 May 1933, and on 20 May the Prussian interior ministry undertook to cover the costs of its camps; Graf, *Politische Polizei*, p. 264. The problem of cost was referred to in a discussion between an official of the Hanover *Regierungspräsident* and a representative of the Prussian police authorities on 1 April 1933; see report in NSHA Hann. 180/Hannover, Nr. 752, pp. 54–5.

33 Quoted in Dietfried Krause-Vilmar, *Das Konzentrationslager Breitenau. Ein staatliches Schutzhaftlager* (Marburg, 1997), p. 41.

34 For Moringen, see Cornelia Meyer, 'Abschreckung, Besserung, Unschädlichmachung: Die Disziplinierung gesellschaftlicher Randgruppen im Werkhaus Moringen (1871–1944)', Magisterarbeit, University of Göttingen, 2000, pp. 129f.

35 Hans Hesse, *Das Frauen-KZ Moringen 1933–1938* (Moringen: Lagergemeinschaft und KZ-Gedenkstätte, 2000), p. 19. Prussia had as many workhouses as the other Länder together.

36 Examples of disused prisons/cellblocks: Lichtenburg, the Berlin Columbia-Haus, Sonnenburg (Prussia), Gotteszell (Württemberg), Fuhlsbüttel (Hamburg); workhouses: Moringen, Brauweiler, Breitenau (Prussia), Kislau (Baden), Glückstadt (Schleswig-Holstein); labour service and similar camps: Kuhlen (Schleswig-Holstein), Ankenbuck (Baden); disused military facilities: Heuburg (Baden), Kuhberg (Württemberg), Nohra (Thuringia); empty factories: Bremen-Missler, Holstendorf (Oldenburg), Oranienburg (Prussia), Dachau (Bavaria). Individual details on these and other camps in Benz and Distel (eds), *Geschichte der Konzentrationslager*, vols. 1 and 2; exhaustive listing of early camps in Drobisch and Wieland, *Die nationalsozialistischen Konzentrationslager*, Table 12, pp. 73–75.

37 Benz and Distel (eds), *Geschichte der Konzentrationslager*, vol. 1, p. 8.

38 For a conceptual and historical approach to this, see respectively David Garland, *Punishment and Welfare. A History of Penal Strategies* (London, 1985), and Norbert Finzsch and Robert Jütte (eds), *Institutions of Confinement. Hospitals, Asylums, and Prisons in Western Europe and North America* (Cambridge, 1996).

39 For the history of poor relief and workhouses see Christoph Sachsse and

Klaus Tennstedt, *Geschichte der Armenfürsorge in Deutschland*, 3 vols (Stuttgart, 1988–92); for late nineteenth-century workhouse types, Wolfgang Ayass, *Das Arbeitshaus Breitenau. Bettler, Landstreicher, Prostituierte, Zuhälter und Fürsorgeempfänger in der Korrektions- und Landarmenanstalt Breitenau (1874–1949)* (Kassel, 1992), pp. 25–68.

40 Warren Rosenblum, 'Vagabonds, Prostitutes, and the Concept of the Asocial, 1900–1929', paper read at German Studies Association annual conference, New Orleans, September 2003.

41 Wolfgang Ayass, *'Asoziale' im Nationalsozialismus* (Stuttgart, 1995), pp. 17, 57–61.

42 This is a riskily compressed summary of what is naturally a much more complex history, for which see Sachsse and Tennstedt, *Geschichte der Armenfürsorge in Deutschland*; David Crew, *Germans on Welfare. From Weimar to Hitler* (New York, 1998); Ayass, *'Asoziale' im Nationalsozialismus*; Uwe Lohalm, 'Die Wohlfahrtskrise 1930–1933. Vom ökonomischen Notprogramm zur rassenhygienischen Neubestimmung', in Frank Bajohr (ed.), *Zivilisation und Barbarei. Die widersprüchliche Potentiale der Moderne* (Hamburg: Hans Christians Verlag, 1991), pp. 193–225.

For a summary of long-term attitudes to social outsiders in Germany, see Richard Evans, 'Social Outsiders in German History: From the Sixteenth Century to 1933', in Robert Gellately and Nathan Stoltzfus (eds), *Social Outsiders in Nazi Germany* (Princeton, 2001), pp. 20–44.

43 This account is drawn largely from Henning Köhler, *Arbeitsdienst in Deutschland. Pläne und Verwirklichungsformen bis zur Einführung der Arbeitsdienstpflicht im Jahre 1935* (Berlin, 1967), and Wolfgang Benz, 'Vom freiwilligen Arbeitsdienst zur Arbeitsdienstpflicht', *Vierteljahrshefte für Zeitgeschichte*, vol. 16 (1968), pp. 317–346.

44 Köhler, *Arbeitsdienst in Deutschland*, p. 144.

45 For the origins of the Nazi concept of work, see Wolfgang Brückner, *"Arbeit macht frei". Herkunft und Hintergrund der KZ-Devise* (Opladen, 1998). For work in the concentration camps, see *Dachauer Hefte*, vol.16 (2000), 'Zwangsarbeit', and Michael Thad Allen, *The Business of Genocide. The SS, Slave Labor and the Concentration Camps* (Chapel Hill, 2002).

46 For labour in the early camps, see Johannes Tuchel, '"Arbeit" in den Konzentrationslagern im Deutschen Reich 1933–1939", in *Arbeiterschaft und Nationalsozialismus—in memoriam Karl Stadler* (Vienna/Zürich, 1990), pp. 455–467, and Klaus Drobisch, 'Hinter der Torschrift "Arbeit macht frei". Häftlingsarbeit, wirtschaftliche Nützung und Finanzierung der Konzentrationslager 1933 bis 1939', in Hermann Kaienburg (ed), *Konzentrationslager und deutsche Wirtschaft 1939–1945* (Opladen, 1996), pp. 17–27. For press publicity, see Gellately, *Backing Hitler*, ch. 3; Sybil Milton, 'Die Konzentrationslager der dreissiger Jahre im Bild der in- und ausländischen Presse', in Herbert et al. (eds), *Die nationalsozialistische Konzentrationslager*, vol. 1, pp. 135–147; Lee Kersten, '"The Times" und das KZ Dachau', *Dachauer Hefte*, vol. 12 (1996). For local knowledge, see *Dachauer Hefte*, vol. 17 (2001), 'Öffentlichkeit und KZ—Was wusste die Bevölkerung?'; Sybille Steinbacher, *Dachau—die Stadt und das Konzentrationslager in der NS-Zeit. Die Untersuchung einer Nachbarschaft*

(Frankfurt, 1993), pp. 81, 181–193.

47 Lawrence D. Stokes, 'Das Eutiner Schutzhaftlager 1933/34. Zur Geschichte eines 'wilden' Konzentrationslagers', *Vierteljahrshefte für Zeitgeschichte*, vol. 27 (1979), pp. 570–625; id., 'Das oldenburgische Konzentrationslager in Eutin, Neukirchen und Nüchel 1933', in Benz and Distel (eds), *Geschichte der Konzentrationslager*, vol. 1, pp. 189–210; see also Jörg Wollenberg, 'Das Konzentrationslager Ahrensbök-Holstendorf im oldenburgischen Landesteil Lübeck', in ibid., pp. 223–250. My account rests on these sources.

48 Wollenberg, 'Das Konzentrationslager Ahrensbök-Holstendorf', p. 228; Ayass, *'Asoziale' im Nationalsozialismus*, pp. 20–47.

49 Stokes, 'Das oldenburgische Konzentrationslager', p. 200.

50 Harald Jenner, *Konzentrationslager Kuhlen 1933* (Rickling, 1988), and id., 'In Trägerschaft der Inneren Mission: Das Konzentrationslager Kuhlen', in Benz and Distel (eds), *Geschichte der Konzentrationslager*, vol. 2, pp. 111–127.

51 Jenner, *Konzentrationslager Kuhlen*, p. 41.

52 Angela Borgstedt, 'Der südbadische Ankenbuck: Arbeiterkolonie und Konzentrationslager', in Benz and Distel (eds), *Geschichte der Konzentrationslager*, vol. 2, pp. 211–216.

53 For the example of Breitenau, which has been studied in most detail, see Gunnar Richter, 'Das frühe Konzentrationslager Breitenau (1933/34)' in Gunnar Richter (ed.), *Breitenau. Zur Geschichte eines nationalsozialistischen Konzentrations- und Arbeitserziehungslagers* (Kassel, 1993), pp. 80–84 especially, and Krause-Vilmar, *Das Konzentrationslager Breitenau*, pp. 122–124; for the others, see the following essays in Benz and Distel (eds), *Geschichte der Konzentrationslager*, vol. 2: Reimer Möller, 'Schutzhaft in der Landesarbeitsanstalt: Das Konzentrationslager Glückstadt', pp. 101–109; Josef Wisskirchen, 'Schutzhaft in der Rheinprovinz: Das Konzentrationslager Brauweiler 1933–1934', pp. 129–156; Hermann Daners, *'Ab nach Brauweiler!'. Nutzung der Abtei Brauweiler als Arbeitsanstalt, Gestapogefängnis, Landeskrankenhaus. . .*, (Pulheim: Verein für Geschichte und Heimatkunde, 1996); Angela Borgstedt, 'Das nordbadische Kislau: Konzentrationslager, Arbeitshaus und Durchgangslager für Fremdenlegionäre', pp. 217–229; for Moringen, Mlynek, 'Der Aufbau der Geheimen Staatspolizei in Hannover', and Hesse, *Das Frauen-KZ Moringen*.

54 Tuchel, *Konzentrationslager*, pp. 60–89.

55 Ibid., pp. 76f.

56 See Elke Suhr, *Die Emslandlager. Die politische und wirtschaftliche Bedeutung der Emsländischen Konzentrations- und Strafgefangenlager 1933–1945* (Bremen, 1985), p. 188; Wachsmann, *Hitler's Prisons*, passim; also Dirk Lüerssen, '"Moorsoldaten" in Esterwegen, Börgermoor, Neusustrum: Die frühen Konzentrationslager im Emsland 1933 bis 1936', in Benz and Distel (eds), *Geschichte der Konzentrationslager*, vol. 2, pp. 157–211, and Kosthorst and Walter, *Konzentrations- und Strafgefangenenlager im Dritten Reich*.

57 Tuchel, *Konzentrationslager*, pp. 117–120.

58 For a discussion of this Reich interior ministry decree (12/26 April 1934), see Drobisch and Wieland, *System der NS-Konzentrationslager*, p. 36.

59 See Tuchel, *Konzentrationslager*, pp. 160ff.

60 For Dachau, see Harold Marcuse, *Legacies of Dachau. The Uses and Abuses of*

a Concentration Camp 1933–2001 (Cambridge, 2001); Tuchel, Konzentrationslager, pp. 121–158; Stanislav Zámecnik, 'Das frühe Konzentrationslager Dachau', in Benz and Distel (eds), Geschichte der Konzentrationslager, vol. 1, pp. 13–39; Lothar Gruchmann, 'Die bayerische Justiz im politischen Machtkampf 1933/34. Ihr Scheitern bei der Strafverfolgung von Mordfällen in Dachau', in Martin Broszat and Elke Fröhlich (eds), Bayern in der NS-Zeit, vol. 2 (Munich/Vienna, 1979), pp. 415–428,

61   Marcuse, Legacies of Dachau, pp. 24–26, 28.

62   For this analysis, see Herbert, 'Von der Gegnerbekämpfung zur "rassischen Generalprävention"', and Tuchel, Konzentrationslager, pp. 297–306.

63   For this legislation see Wachsmann, Hitler's Prisons, pp. 114–117 and references therein; extracts from the legislation in Noakes and Pridham (eds), Nazism, vol. 2, pp. 284–287.

64   Tuchel, Konzentrationslager, pp. 308f; Herbert, 'Von der Gegnerbekämpfung zur "rassischen Generalprävention"', pp. 72f.

65   For this decision on 20 June and its consequences, see Tuchel, Konzentrationslager, pp. 307–317.

66   Drobisch and Wieland, System der NS-Konzentrationslager pp. 251–256. In February 1936 the Gestapo drew up a list that came to include 47,000 named people (the 'A-List') to be taken into protective custody in the event of war.

67   Karl-Leo Terhorst, Polizeiliche planmässige Überwachung und polizeiliche Vorbeugungshaft im Dritten Reich (Heidelberg, 1985), pp. 49–59; Herbert, 'Von der Gegnerbekämpfung zur "rassischen Generalprävention"', pp. 68–73.

68   The foundation and development of the IKL are discussed in detail in Tuchel, Konzentrationslager, pp. 159–296. For a summary account in English, see Broszat, 'The Concentration Camps', pp. 436–446.

69   i.e. by the 3rd Gestapo Law, 10 February 1936, and the nomination of Himmler on 17 June 1936 to the amalgamated post of 'Reichsführer-SS und Chef der Deutschen Polizei'; see Graf, Politische Polizei, pp. 128–153; summary in Buchheim, 'The SS', pp. 145–166.

70   Tuchel and Schattenfroh, Zentrale des Terrors, pp. 114–124.

71   For the construction and financing of these camps see Drobisch and Wieland, System der NS-Konzentrationslager, pp. 262–279; for the systematic SS exploitation of concentration camp labour after 1938, see Allen, The Business of Genocide.

72   Orth, Das System der nationalsozialistischen Konzentrationslager, pp. 35–39; Drobisch and Wieland, System der nationalsozialistischen Konzentrationslager, pp. 262–279. This 1939 total hides fluctuations in 1938: 24,000 in custody in November 1938, immediately before the mass but temporary incarceration of Jewish men following the pogrom of 'Kristallnacht'; the mid-1939 total of 21,000 also reflects releases by amnesty to mark Hitler's fiftieth birthday; see Tuchel, Konzentrationslager, pp. 203f.

73   For post-1933 policies in general, see Ayass, 'Asoziale' im Nationalsozialismus, and Gellately and Stoltzfus (eds), Social Outsiders in Nazi Germany; for a wealth of documentation Wolfgang Ayass (ed.), 'Gemeinschaftsfremde'. Quellen zur Verfolgung von 'Asozialen' 1933–1945

(Koblenz, 1998).

74 Zámecnik, 'Das frühe Konzentrationslager Dachau', p. 31. For other examples, see Ayass, *'Asoziale' im Nationalsozialismus*, pp. 138f.

75 Herbert Diercks, 'Fuhlsbüttel—das Konzentrationslager in der Verantwortung der Hamburger Justiz', in Benz and Distel (eds), *Geschichte der Konzentrationslager*, vol. 1, pp. 277–284.

76 'Gesetz gegen gefährliche Gewohnheitsverbrecher und über Massregeln der Sicherung und Besserung', 24 November 1933 (RGBl 1933 I, 996); for details of this and subsequent legislation and arrests, see Wachsmann, *Hitler's Prisons*, pp. 128–139; Patrick Wagner, '"Vernichtung der Berufsverbrecher". Die vorbeugenden Verbrechensbekämpfung der Kriminalpolizei bis 1937', in Herbert et al. (eds), *Die nationalsozialistischen Konzentrationslager*, pp. 86–110; and Terhorst, *Polizeiliche planmässige Überwachung*; also Herbert, 'Von der Gegnerbekämpfung zur "rassischen Generalprävention"'; some four thousand such security detainees were incarcerated in 1934. For attitudes towards criminals, see Richard Wetzell, *Inventing the Criminal. A History of German Criminology, 1880–1945* (Chapel Hill/London, 2000), ch. 6.

77 Terhorst, *Polizeiliche planmässige Überwachung*, p. 111.

78 'Grundlegende Erlass über die vorbeugende Verbrechensbekämpfung durch die Polizei', 14 December 1937; full details in *ibid.*, ch. 4.

79 For the arrest campaigns and this judgment, see Ayass, *'Asoziale' im Nationalsozialismus*, chs 6 and 10; also Sachsse and Tennstedt, *Geschichte der Armenfürsorge in Deutschland*, vol. 3, pp. 222ff., 261; figures discussed in Drobisch and Wieland, *System der NS-Konzentrationslager*, pp. 284–289, and summarized in Herbert, 'Von der Gegnerbekämpfung zur "rassischen Generalprävention"', p. 81. For the detention of women, see Christa Schikorra, *Kontinuitäten der Ausgrenzung. 'Asoziale' Häftlinge im Frauen-Konzentrationslager Ravensbrück* (Berlin, 2001), pp. 60–112. For the distribution of political prisoners between judicial prisons and concentration camps, see Wachsmann, *Hitler's Prisons*, pp. 113–128, also ch. 4 and Figure 2, pp. 394–395.

80 Bernward Dörner, 'Ein KZ in der Mitte der Stadt: Oranienburg', in Benz and Distel (eds), *Geschichte der Konzentrationslager*, vol. 1, pp. 123–138.

81 As described in detail by Wachsmann, *Hitler's Prisons*.

3: Working-Class Identities in the Third Reich

1 For a summary and critique of this literature see Dick Geary, 'Nazis and Workers before 1933', *Australian Journal of Politics and History* 48 (2002), 1, pp. 40–51.

2 Geoff Eley, 'Hitler's Silent Majority? Conformity and Resistance under the Third Reich (Part One)', *Michigan Quarterly Review* 42 (2003), 2, pp. 398–399.

3 Inge Marßoleck and René Ott, *Bremen im Dritten Reich. Anpassung, Widerstand, Verfolgung* (Bremen, 1986); Klaus-Michael Mallmann and Gerhard Paul, *Das zersplitterte Nein: Saarländer gegen Hitler. Herrschaft und Alltag: Ein Industrierevier im Dritten Reich*, unter Mitarbeit von Hans-Henning Krämer. *Milieus und Widerstand: Eine Verhaltensgeschichte der*

Gesellschaft im Nationalsozialismus, 3 vols (Bonn, 1989–1995).

4 Ulrich Herbert, *Hitler's Foreign Workers. Enforced Foreign Labor under the Third Reich* (Cambridge, 1997). Also Ulrich Herbert, 'The Real Mystery in Germany. The German Working Class during the Nazi Dictatorship', in Michael Burleigh (ed), *Confronting the Nazi Past. New Debates on Modern German History* (London, 1996) and Ulrich Herbert (ed.), *Europa und der 'Reichseinsatz'. Ausländische Zivilarbeiter, Kriegsgefangene und Zivilhäftlinge in Deutschland 1938–1945* (Essen, 1991). Alf Lüdtke, 'The Appeal of Exterminating "Others": German Workers and the Limits of Resistance', in Christian Leitz (ed.), *The Third Reich. The Essential Readings* (Oxford, 1999), pp. 156 and 169 for quotations and pp. 155–177 more generally. See also Alf Lüdtke, 'What happened to the "Fiery Red Glow"? Workers' Experience and German Fascism', in Alf Lüdtke (ed.), *The History of Everyday Life. Reconstructing Historical Experiences and Ways of Life* (Princeton, 1995), pp. 198–251; Alf Lüdtke, 'The "Honor of Labour": Industrial Workers and the Power of Symbols under National Socialism', in David Crew (ed.), *Nazism and German Society* (London, 1994), pp. 67–109.

5 Robert Gellately, *Backing Hitler. Consent and Coercion in Nazi Germany* (Oxford, 2001); Eric Johnson, *The Nazi Terror. Gestapo, Jews and Ordinary Germans* (London, 2000).

6 Lutz Niethammer (ed.), *'Die Jahre weiss man nicht, wo man die heute hinsetzen soll'. Faschismuserfahrungen im Ruhrgebiet: Lebensgeschichten und Sozialkultur im Ruhrgebiet 1930 bis 1960* (Berlin, 1983); Lutz Niethammer (ed.), *'Hinterher merkt man, dass es richtig war, dass es schiefgegangen ist'. Lebensgeschichten und Sozialkultur im Ruhrgebiet 1930–1960,* (Berlin, 1983); Lutz Niethammer and Alexander von Plato (eds), *'Wir kriegen jetzt andere Zeiten'. Auf der Suche nach der Erfahrung des Volkes in nachfaschistischen Ländern* (Berlin, 1985); Alexander von Plato, *'Der Verlierer geht nicht leer aus'. Betriebsräte geben zu Protokoll* (Berlin, 1984).

7 Mark Roseman, 'National Socialism and Modernisation', in Richard Bessel (ed.), *Fascist Italy and Nazi Germany. Comparisons and Contrasts* (Cambridge, 1996), pp. 196–229.

8 Mallmann and Paul, *Herrschaft,* p. 162.

9 David Schoenbaum, *Hitler's Social Revolution. Class and Status in Nazi Germany, 1933–1939* (London, 1967).

10 Michael Prinz and Rainer Zitelmann (eds), *Nationalsozialismus und Modernisierung* (Darmstadt, 1991); Rainer Zitelmann, *Hitler: Selbstverständnis eines Revolutionärs* (Hamburg, 1987); Michael Prinz, *Vom neuen Mittelstand zum Volksgenossen. Die Entwicklung des sozialen Status der Angestellten von der Weimarer Republik bis zum Ende der NS-Staat* (Munich, 1986); Jeremy Noakes and Geoffrey Pridham (eds), *Nazism 1919–1945* vol. 2: *State, Economy and Society 1933–1939: A Documentary Reader* (Exeter, 2000), pp. 152–159. The Ley proclamation is reproduced in ibid., pp. 331–332. See also Stephen Salter, 'Structures of Consensus and Coercion: Workers' Morale and the Maintenance of Work Discipline', in David Welch (ed.), *Nazi Propaganda. The Power and the Limitations* (Beckenham, 1983), pp. 86–116.

11 Lüdtke, 'The Appeal', p. 167.

12 Mary Nolan, 'Work, Gender and Everyday Life: Reflections on Continuity, Normality and Agency in 20th-Century Germany', in Ian Kershaw and Moshe Lewin (eds.) *Stalinism and Nazism. Dictatorships in Comparison* (Cambridge, 1998) pp. 311–342; Mary Nolan, 'Rationalization, Racism and *Resistenz*: Recent Studies of Work and the Working Class in Nazi Germany', in *International Labor and Working-Class History* 48 (1995), pp. 213–230; Tilla Siegel, *Leistung und Lohn in der Nationalsozialistischen 'Ordnung der Arbeit'* (Opladen, 1989); Rüdiger Hachtmann, *Industriearbeit im Dritten Reich. Untersuchungen zu den Lohn- und Arbeitsbedingungen im Dritten Reich 1933–1945* (Göttingen, 1989); Tilla Siegel and Thomas von Freyberg, *Industrielle Rationalisierung unter dem Nationalsozialismus* (Frankfurt/M., 1991); Dagmar Reese et al. (eds), *Rationale Beziehungen? Geschlechterverhältnisse im Rationalisierungsprozess* (Frankfurt/M., 1993); Tilla Siegel, 'Whatever was the Attitude of German Workers? Reflections on Recent Interpretations', in Bessel (ed.), *Fascist Italy and Nazi Germany*, pp. 67–74; Tilla Siegel, 'Rationalizing Industrial Relations', in Thomas Childers and Jane Caplan (eds), *Reevaluating the Third Reich* (New York, 1993), pp. 139–160; Carola Sachse, *Betriebliche Sozialpolitik als Familienpolitik in der Weimarer Republik und im Nationalsozialismus* (Hamburg, 1987); Carola Sachse, *Siemens, der Nationalsozialismus und die moderne Familie. Eine Untersuchung zur sozialen Rationalisierung in Deutschland im 20. Jahrhundert* (Hamburg, 1990).

13 *Deutschland-Berichte der Sozialdemokratischen Partei Deutschlands (SOPADE) 1934–1940*, 7 vols (Salzhausen, 1980). *Dritter Jahrgang: 1936*, pp. 482–483. The report is reproduced in Noakes and Pridham, *Nazism*, vol. 2, pp. 178–179.

14 The classic account of the racial restructuring of the working class is Herbert, *Foreign Workers*. Jeremy Noakes, *Nazism 1919–1945* vol. 4: *The German Home Front in World War II: A Documentary Reader* (Exeter, 1998), discusses evacuation (pp. 359–365) and the differential treatment of racial groups within the labour force (p. 247).

15 *Deutschland-Berichte der SOPADE, Fünfter Jahrgang: 1938*, p. 980. The report is repinted in Noakes and Pridham, *Nazism*, vol. 2, pp. 179–180.

16 Noakes and Pridham, *Nazism*, vol. 2, p. 177.

17 Tilla Siegal, 'Rationalizing', p. 155.

18 David Crew, *Germans on Welfare. From Weimar to Hitler* (Oxford, 1998).

19 On various kinds of control over labour see Carola Sachse et al., *Angst, Belohnung, Zucht und Ordnung. Herrschaftsmechanismen im Nationalsozialismus* (Opladen, 1982) and especially Tim Mason's essay therein: 'The Containment of the Working Class in Nazi Germany', reproduced in Timothy W. Mason, *Nazism, Fascism and the Working Class* (Cambridge, 1995), pp. 231–73. Also Noakes and Pridham, *Nazism*, vol. 2, pp. 175–179; Tilla Siegel, 'Attitudes', in Bessel (ed.), *Fascist Italy and Nazi Germany*, pp. 65–72; Matthias Frese, *Betriebspolitik im Dritten Reich. Deutsche Arbeitsfront, Unternehmer und Staatsbürokratie in der westdeutschen Großindustrie, 1933–1939* (Paderborn, 1991); Tim Mason, *Social Policy in the Third Reich. The Working Class and the National Community* (Oxford, 1993), p. 141.

20 A very differentiated picture of living standards is presented in Günther Morsch, *Arbeit und Brot. Studien zu Lage, Stimmung, Einstellung und Verhalten der Deutschen Arbeiterschaft 1933–1936/7* (Frankfurt/M., 1993). See also Noakes and Pridham, *Nazism*, vol. 2, pp. 155, 176–177. Gerhard Bry, *Wages in Germany 1871–1945* (Princeton, 1966) gives real wage indices over the whole period. See also the statistical appendix of Tim Mason, *Arbeiterklasse und Volksgemeinschaft. Dokumente und Materialien zur Deutschen Arbeiterpolitik 1933–1939* (Opladen, 1975); Tim Mason, *Social Policy*, p. 132. On the failure to pass on cheaper world food prices to the German consumer see Richard Overy, *The Nazi Economic Recovery 1932–1938* (Cambridge, 1996), pp. 26–31; and Siegel, 'Rationalizing', p. 147.

21 There is a large body of labour history which stresses the centrality of skill and resources for labour protest and solidarity. See Dick Geary, *European Labour Protest, 1848–1939* (London, 1981); Dick Geary (ed.), *Labour and Socialist Movements in Europe before 1914* (Oxford, 1989); Dick Geary, *European Labour Politics from 1900 to the Depression* (London, 1991); Dick Geary, 'Working-Class Identities in Europe, 1850s–1930s', *Australian Journal of Politics and History* 45 (1999), 1, pp. 20–34; and multiple references in these works.

22 Nolan, 'Work', p. 324

23 Tilla Siegel, *Leistung und Lohn*; Rüdiger Hachtmann, *Industriearbeit im Dritten Reich*; Tilla Siegel and Thomas von Freyberg, *Industrielle Rationalisierung*; Carola Sachse, *Betriebliche Sozialpolitik als Familienpolitik*; idem., *Siemens, der Nationalsozialismus und die moderne Familie*.

24 See note 12 above for the literature on rationalization. Also Richard Overy, *War and Economy in the Third Reich* (Oxford, 1994), pp. 343–375. For its limits see Lüdtke, 'Honour of Labour', pp. 90–91; and Morsch, *Arbeit und Brot*, which shows how differentiated was the situation of German labour. Richard Overy identifies high growth in certain new areas—motorcar and aircraft manufacture, electrical goods and chemicals—but points out that structural shifts in the German economy under the Nazis were not as great as those which took place before 1929 or after 1945: Overy, *Nazi Economic Recovery*, pp. 22–23, 28 and 53. He also shows that high investment did not lead to a corresponding increase in productivity (pp. 38–39 and 51–53). See also Harold James, *The German Slump. Politics and Economics 1924–1936* (Oxford, 1986), and Volker Berghahn, *The Americanisation of German Industry 1945–1973* (Leamington Spa, 1986).

25 Nolan, 'Work', pp. 324–325. On women in the Third Reich see Renate Bridenthal, Atina Grossmann and Marion Kaplan (eds), *When Biology Became Destiny: Women in Weimar and Nazi Germany* (New York, 1984); Claudia Koonz, *Mothers in the Fatherland: Women, the Family and Nazi Politics* (New York, 1987); Adelheid von Saldern, 'Victims or Perpetrators? Controversies about the Role of Women in the Nazi State', in David Crew (ed.), *Nazism and German Society* (London, 1994), pp. 141–165; Atina Grossmann, 'Feminist Debates about Women and National Socialism', *Gender and History* 3 (1991), pp. 350–358; Tim Mason, 'Women in Germany, 1925–1940. Family, Welfare, Work', in Mason, *Nazism, Fascism and the Working Class*, pp. 131–211; Gabriele Czarnowski, 'The Value of

Marriage for the *Volksgemeinschaft*', in Bessel (ed.), *Fascist Italy and Nazi Germany*, p. 94. See also (for female labour in the War) Noakes, *Nazism*, vol. 4, p. 247.

26 On class formation and the difficulties that surround it see Geary, *European Labour Protest*; Ira Katznelson and Aristide R. Zollberg (eds), *Working Class Formation. Nineteenth Century Patterns in Western Europe and the United States* (Princeton, 1986); Marcel van der Linden and Jürgen Rojahn (eds), *The Formation of Labour Movements 1870–1914. An International Perspective* (Leiden, 1990); Jürgen Kocka, *Lohnarbeit und Klassenbildung. Arbeiter und Arbeiterbewegung in Deutschland, 1800–1875* (Berlin, 1983); Gareth Rees et al. (eds), *Political Action and Social Identity. Class, Locality and Ideology* (London, 1985); S.G. McNall et al. (eds), *Bringing Class Back in Contemporary and Historical Perspectives* (Oxford, 1991); Michael Hanagan and Charles Stephenson (eds), *Proletarians and Protest. The Roots of Class Formation in an Industrialising World* (New York, 1986).

27 On the multiple identities of workers see Geary, 'Working-Class Identities' (see note 21) and Geary, 'The Prussian Labour Movement', in Philip Dwyer (ed.), *Modern Prussian History, 1830–1947* (Harlow, 2000), pp. 126–145. The same point is also made forcefully by Tim Mason, 'Containment', p. 245.

28 On the many ways in which mass unemployment between 1929 and 1933 fragmented and demobilized the German working class see Dick Geary, 'Unemployment and Working-Class Solidarity in Germany, 1929–1933', in Richard J. Evans and Dick Geary (eds), *The German Unemployed. Experiences and Consequences of Mass Unemployment from the Weimar Republic to the Third Reich* (London, 1987), pp. 261–280.

29 John J. Kulczycki, *The Foreign Worker and the German Labor Movement. Xenophobia and Solidarity in the Coal Fields of the Ruhr, 1871–1914* (Oxford, 1994); Ulrich Herbert, *A History of Foreign Labour in Germany 1860–1960. Seasonal Workers, Forced Laborers, Guest Workers* (Ann Arbor, 1990); Stefan Berger and Angel Smith (eds), *Nationalism, Labour and Ethnicity 1870–1939* (Manchester, 1999); E. Cahm and V. Fisera (eds), *Socialism and Nationalism*, 2 vols (Nottingham, 1979); Th. Van Thijn, 'Nationalism and the Socialist Workers' Movement', in Frits van Holthoon and Marcel van der Linden, *Internationalism in the Labour Movement 1830–1940* (Leiden, 1988), vol. 2, pp. 611–623. On Germans disliking their Italian co-workers see Herbert, *Hitler's Foreign Workers*, p. 134.

30 The significance of chronology and widely differing views is central to Ian Kershaw, *Popular Opinion and Public Dissent in the Third Reich. Bavaria 1933–1945* (Oxford, 1983), pp. 66–110.

31 The Lüdtke quotation is from 'The Appeal', p. 158. Tilla Siegel also stresses the very different attitudes present amongst the German working class: Siegel, 'Attitudes', in Bessel (ed.), *Fascist Italy and Nazi Germany*, pp. 62 and 67.

32 Realization that the Gestapo relied on denunciations from the general public in its quest for information is central to Reinhard Mann, *Protest und Kontrolle im Dritten Reich. Nationalsozialistische Herrschaft im Alltag einer rheinischen Grossstadt* (Frankfurt/M., 1987); Robert Gellately, *The Gestapo and German*

Society. Enforcing Racial Policy 1933–1945 (Oxford, 1990); Gerhard Paul and Klaus-Michael Mallmann (eds), *Die Gestapo. Mythos und Realität* (Darmstadt, 1995). See also Johnson, *Terror*, pp. 368–373; Klaus-Michael Mallman and Gerhard Paul, 'Omniscient, Omnipotent, Omnipresent?', in David Crew, *Nazism and German Society* (London, 1994), pp. 166–196.

33 Noakes and Pridham, *Nazism*, vol. 2, pp. 178–179. See also Hans-Josef Steinberg, 'Die Haltung der Arbeiterschaft zum NS-Regime', in J. Schmädecke and P. Steinbach (eds), *Der Widerstand gegen den National- sozialismus* (Munich, 1994), pp. 871–873. For other perceptions of a variety of attitudes see note 31.

34 W.S Allen, *The Nazi Seizure of Power. The Experience of a Single German Town, 1930–1935* (London, 1966)

35 Mallmann and Paul, 'Omniscient', p. 169; Eley, 'Hitler's Silent Majority (Part Two)' *Michigan Quarterly Review* 42 (2003), p. 555. That violence characterized the Nazi regime and its reorganization of German society is a central theme of Pierre Ayçoberry, *The Social History of the Third Reich* (New York, 1999) and is also stressed in Michael Burleigh's *The Third Reich. A New History* (London, 2000), pp. 157–182. See also Mason, 'Containment', pp. 238–243. On the repression of communists see Alan Merson, *Communist Resistance in Nazi Germany* (London, 1985), pp. 32–34 , 61.

36 Eley, 'Hitler's Silent Majority (Part Two), pp. 555–559; Francis L. Carsten, *The German Workers and the Nazis* (Aldershot, 1995), p. 157. On the spread of terror in the war see also Noakes, *Nazism*, vol. 4, pp. 121–184 and Ian Kershaw, *Hitler. 1936–45: Nemesis* (London, 2000), pp. 762–763.

37 For detailed references see Dick Geary, 'Social Protest in Germany after 1945', *Contemporary German Studies* 1 (1985), pp. 39–45. A revised and extended version will appear as Dick Geary, 'Social Protest in the Ruhr, 1945–49', in Eleonore Breuning, Jill Lewis and Gareth Pritchard (eds), *A Social History of Central European Politics, 1945–53* (Manchester, forth- coming).

38 Roseman, 'National Socialism and Modernisation', p. 224.

4: Social Outsiders and the Consolidation of Hitler's Dictatorship, 1933–1939

1 For an introduction see Robert Gellately and Nathan Stoltzfus (eds), *Social Outsiders in Nazi Germany* (Princeton, 2001) and Jeremy Noakes, 'Social Outcasts in the Third Reich', in Richard Bessel (ed.), *Life in the Third Reich* (Oxford, 1987), pp. 83–96.

2 For an insightful recent account, see Helmut Walser Smith, *The Butcher's Tale: Murder and Anti-Semitism in a German Town* (New York, 2002).

3 For an overview see Richard Bessel, 'Germany from War to Dictatorship', in Mary Fulbrook (ed.), *German History Since 1800* (London, 1997), pp. 235–257.

4 M. Rainer Lepsius, 'From Fragmented Party Democracy to Government by Emergency Decree and National Socialist Takeover: Germany', in Juan L. Linz and Alfred Stepan (eds), *The Breakdown of Democratic Regimes* (Baltimore, 1978), pp. 34–79, here 46–49.

5 For an overview, see Eberhard Jäckel, *Hitler's World View: A Blueprint for*

Power (Cambridge, MA, 1981), p. 79.

6   Robert Gellately, *Backing Hitler: Consent and Coercion in Nazi Germany* (Oxford, 2001).

7   Jürgen W. Falter, *Hitlers Wähler* (Munich,1991), p. 225.

8   Historians in the former German Democratic Republic stated that of 300,000 members in the KPD up to 1933, around half experienced some form of persecution. These figures are cited by Hartmut Mehringer, *Widerstand und Emigration: Das NS-Regime und seine Gegner* (Munich, 1997), here p. 84.

9   Hans-Ulrich Wehler, *Deutsche Gesellschaftsgeschichte: Vom Beginn des Ersten Weltkriegs bis zur Gründung der beiden deutschen Staaten 1914–1949* (Munich, 2003), p. 676.

10 Detlef Schmiechen-Ackermann, *Nationalsozialismus und Arbeitermilieus: Der nationalsozialistische Angriff auf die proletarischen Wohnquartiere und die Reaktion in den sozialistischen Vereinen* (Bonn, 1998), p. 712.

11 Mehringer, *Widerstand*, p. 84. See also Ulrich Herbert, 'Arbeiterschaft im "Dritten Reich"', in his *Arbeit, Volkstum, Weltanschauung: Über Fremde und Deutsche im 20. Jahrhundert* (Frankfurt/M., 1995), pp. 79–119.

12 See Alf Lüdtke, 'The Appeal of Exterminating "Others": German Workers and the Limits of Resistance', in Michael Geyer and John W. Boyer (eds) *Resistance against the Third Reich 1933–1990* (Chicago, 1994) pp. 53–74, here 66–67.

13 For the concept of 'legal revolution', see Karl Dietrich Bracher, *The German Dictatorship: The Origins, Structure, and Effects of National Socialism* (Harmondsworth, 1973), pp. 243–252.

14 See Wehler, *Gesellschaftsgeschichte*, pp. 679, 734.

15 Golo Mann, *Deutsche Geschichte des 19. und 20. Jahrhunderts* (Frankfurt/M., 1967), p. 811.

16 Martin Broszat, *The Hitler State* (New York, 1981), p. 349.

17 See Max Domarus (ed.), *Hitler Reden und Proklamationen 1932–1945*, 4 vols (Leonberg, 1973), vol. 1, pp. 229–37, here 232–233.

18 For the pre-1914 background, see Brigitte Hamann, *Hitler's Vienna: A Dictator's Apprenticeship* (Oxford, 1999), pp. 78–85.

19 For an account of the enormous publicity surrounding the camps, which went well beyond the odd story in the press, see Gellately, *Backing Hitler*, pp. 51–69.

20 'Konzentrationslager für Berufsverbrecher', *Völkischer Beobachter* (26/27 Nov. 1933), henceforth cited as VB, with appropriate dates.

21 Ian Kershaw, *The "Hitler Myth": Image and Reality in the Third Reich* (Oxford, 1987), pp. 232–234.

22 See Saul Friedländer, *Nazi Germany and the Jews*, vol. 1, *The Years of Persecution, 1933–1939* (New York, 1997), p. 15.

23 See Ian Kershaw, *Hitler 1889–1936: Hubris* (London, 1998), pp. 472–473.

24 'Der Reichskanzler rechtfertigt den Lügen-Abwehrkampf vor dem Kabinett', *VB* (30 Mar. 1933).

25 See Michael Burleigh and Wolfgang Wippermann, *The Racial State: Germany 1933–1945* (Cambridge, 1991), pp. 77–78; Ian Kershaw, *Popular Opinion and Political Dissent in the Third Reich: Bavaria 1933–1945* (Oxford, 1983), p. 232.

26 For a copy of the law and others applying to the civil service, see Ingo von Münch (ed.), *Gesetze des NS-Staates*, 3rd edn (Paderborn, 1994), pp. 26–28.

27 Jane Caplan, *Government without Administration: State and Civil Society in Weimar and Nazi Germany* (Oxford, 1988), pp.143–146.

28 For the decision-making process and Hitler's stance, see esp. Kershaw, *Hitler 1889–1936*, pp. 559–571.

29 See Saul Friedländer, *Nazi Germany and the Jews*, p. 148.

30 In 1935, the Ministry of the Interior overestimated the number of 'mixed race' people at 750,000. In the census of May 1939, the total of 'mixed race' of the 'first grade' and of the 'second grade' in Germany (not counting Austria) was 84,674. For this 'grading' and the complex issues, see the classic account of Jeremy Noakes, 'The Development of Nazi Policy towards the German-Jewish "Mischlinge" 1933–1945', *Leo Baeck Institute Year Book* (1989), pp. 291–354.

31 For a detailed local account, see Robert Gellately, *The Gestapo and German Society: Enforcing Racial Policy 1933–1945* (Oxford, 1990).

32 See David Bankier, *The Germans and the Final Solution: Public Opinion under Nazism* (Oxford, 1992), p. 80.

33 Otto Dov Kulka, 'Die Nürnberger Rassengesetze und die deutsche Bevölkerung im Lichte geheimer NS-Lage- und Stimmungsberichte', *Vierteljahrshefte für Zeitgeschichte* (1984), pp. 582–624. Henceforth cited as *VfZ*

34 V. Klemperer, *Ich will Zeugnis ablegen bis zum letzten: Tagebücher 1933–1941*, 2 vols (Berlin, 1995), p. 215.

35 Bankier, *Germans*, pp. 38–40. For a recent analysis, see Peter Longerich, *Politik der Vernichtung: Eine Gesamtdarstellung der nationalsozialistischen Judenverfolgung* (Munich, 1998), pp. 70–101.

36 See the detailed reports *Deutschland-Berichte der Sozialdemokratischen Partei Deutschlands 1934–1940* (Nördlingen, 1980), (July and Aug., 1935), pp. 800–814 and 920–937, for the remark, p. 922. Henceforth cited as *SOPADE* (with pages and dates).

37 See the November report *SOPADE* (1938), pp. 1177–1211, here 1177.

38 See Elke Fröhlich et al. (eds), *Die Tagebücher von Joseph Goebbels*, 24 vols (Munich, 1993 ff.), here part 1, vol. 6 (10 Nov. 1938), 180.

39 *Der Prozess gegen die Hauptkriegsverbrecher vor dem internationalen Militärgerichtshof*, 42 vols. (Nuremberg, 1949), vol. 32: pp. 1–2, Dokument 3058-PS, 'Schnellbrief an Göring'. Henceforth cited as *IMT*.

40 Konrad Kwiet and Helmut Eschwege, *Selbstbehauptung und Widerstand. Deutsche Juden im Kampf um Existenz und Menschenwürde 1933–1945* (Hamburg, 1984), pp.199, 202.

41 Figures cited in Heinz Lauber, *Judenpogrom 'Reichskristallnacht' November 1938 in Großdeutschland* (Gerlingen, 1981) p. 124, suggest that 10,911 were sent to Dachau, 9,815 to Buchenwald and 5,000 to 10,000 to Sachsenhausen. The larger figure for Buchenwald, based on a closer study, is given by Rudi Goguel, 'Vom großen Pogrom bis zur Entfesselung des Krieges (1938/39)', in Klaus Drobisch et al., *Juden unterm Hakenkreuz* (Frankfurt/M., 1973), p. 194.

42 See accounts from December reports *SOPADE* (1938), pp. 1332–1350.

43 Bankier, *Germans*, pp. 86–87.
44 See the February report *SOPADE*(1939), pp. 201–2; and for April *SOPADE* (1940), pp. 256–68.
45 Noakes, 'Nazi Policy towards the German-Jewish "Mischlinge"1933–1945,' p. 293.
46 See Henry Friedlander, *The Origins of Nazi Genocide: From Euthanasia to the Final Solution* (Chapel Hill, 1995), p. 23.
47 Friedlander, *Origins of Nazi Genocide*, p. 27.
48 See esp. Gisela Bock, *Zwangssterilisation im Nationalsozialismus: Studien zur Rassenpolitik und Frauenpolitik* (Opladen, 1986), pp. 230–238.
49 Christine Charlotte Makowski, *Eugenik, Sterilisationspolitik, 'Euthanasie' und Bevölkerungspolitik in der nationalsozialistischen Parteipresse* (Husum, 1996), pp.151–152.
50 See Richard F. Wetzell, *Inventing the Criminal: A History of German Criminology 1880–1945* (Chapel Hill, 2000), pp. 249–250.
51 Lothar Gruchmann, *Justiz im Dritten Reich 1933–1945: Anpassung und Unterwerfung in der Ära Gürtner* (Munich, 1988), pp. 719–721.
52 The concept is 'gefährliche Gewohnheitsverbrecher'. In the Prussian decree the concept is 'Berufsverbrecher'. For the background, see Karl-Leo Terhorst, *Polizeiliche planmäßige Überwachung und polizeiliche Vorbeugungshaft im Dritten Reich* (Heidelberg, 1985), pp. 75 ff. The extension (*Erweiterung*) of the Prussian decree was 10 February 1934.
53 See 'Neue Reichsgrundsätze für den Vollzug von Freiheitsstrafen und von sichernden Maßnahmen', *VB* (19 May 1934).
54 *IMT*, vol. 29, p. 220: Dokument 1992(A)-PS, 'Vortrag Himmlers über Wesen und Aufgabe der SS und der Polizei', from 'Nationalpolitischer Lehrgang der Wehrmacht vom Januar 1937'.
55 The passage, from Hitler's *Mein Kampf*, is cited by Oberregierungsrat Dr. Albrecht Böhme, 'Die Vorbeugungsaufgaben der Polizei', *Deutsches Recht*, (15 Apr. 1936), p. 142.
56 'Konzentrationslager für Berufsverbrecher', *VB* (26/27 Nov. 1933).
57 'Unsicherheit läßt nach. Heute kann man wieder ruhig in der Nacht nach Hause gehen', *VB* (29 Dec. 1933).
58 They fell to 1,464 (in 1935); 946 (in 1936); and 765 (in 1937); thereafter there was an increase, to 964 (in 1938); 1,827 (in 1939); 1,916 (in 1940) and 1,651 (in 1941), the last year for which we have complete statistics. For the statistics, see Christian Müller, *Das Gewohnheitsverbrechergesetz vom 24. November 1933: Kriminalpolitik als Rassenpolitik* (Baden-Baden, 1997), p. 54. For slightly different figures, see Gruchmann, *Justiz*, p. 727–728.
59 Between 1934 and 1939, the courts sent 5,142 people to state hospitals; 885 alcoholics to rehabilitation institutes; 7,503 individuals to workhouses; and 1,808 people to be sterilized. Müller, *Gewohnheitsverbrecher*, p. 53.
60 Gruchmann, *Justiz*, p. 729.
61 Martin Broszat, 'Zur Perversion der Strafjustiz im Dritten Reich', *VfZ* (1958), pp. 390–443, here 395–396.
62 See Michael Zimmermann, *Rassenutopie und Genozid: Die nationalsozialistische 'Lösung der Zigeunerfrage'* (Hamburg, 1996), pp. 93–934.
63 Sybil Milton, 'Vorstufe der Vernichtung: Die Zigeunerlager nach 1933', *VfZ*

(1995), pp. 115–130.

64 For isolated statistics see Zimmermann, *Rassenutopie,* pp. 115–116.
65 See Schriftenreihe des Reichskriminalpolizeiamtes, Nr. 45, *Vorbeugende Verbrechensbekämpfung, Erlaßsammlung,* Rund Erl. RFSS, 'Bekämpfung der Zigeunerplage' (8 Dec. 1938), henceforth cited as RKPA VE.
66 Zimmermann, *Rassenutopie,* p. 127.
67 RKPA VE: 'Ausführungsanweisung' (1 Mar. 1939); RKPA VE: RKPA to Kripo, 'Erfassung aller wehrunwürdigen Personen' (7 July 1939).
68 See Hans Peter Bleuel, *Sex and Society in Nazi Germany* (Philadelphia, 1973), p. 211.
69 The phrase is from a Bremen law (11 Aug. 1933), reprinted in Wolfgang Ayaß (ed.), *'Gemeinschaftsfremde': Quellen zur Verfolgung von 'Asozialen' 1933–1945* (Koblenz, 1998), p. 33.
70 See Ayaß (ed.), *Gemeinschaftsfremde,* pp. 42–43.
71 RKPA VE communications of 27 Jan. 1937; 23 and 27 Feb. 1937.
72 Terhorst, *Polizeiliche planmäßige Überwachung,* p. 109.
73 Ibid., p. 113.
74 RKPA VE: Rund Erl. RFSS (19 Nov. 1937).
75 Gruchmann, *Justiz,* p. 725.
76 The professional criminal (*Berufsverbrecher*) was defined as someone who made crime their business and who lived in part or whole from the gains of their crimes; they were sentenced at least three times for a minimum of three months. The repeat offender (*Gewohnheitsverbrecher*), was not a professional, but, driven by a criminal drive and predisposition (*Trieben* or *Neigungen*), had a similar record.
77 RKPA VE: Erlaß RMI, 'Grundlegender Erlaß über die vorbeugende Verbrechensbekämpfung durch die Polizei' (14 Dec. 1937); RKPA VE: Rund Erl. RKPA, 'Vorbeugende Verbrechensbekämpfung durch die Polizei' (8 Feb. 1938).
78 'Vorbeugende Verbrechensbekämpfung,' *VB* (16 Jan. 1938).
79 Kripo Gleiwitz to Oberstaatsanwalt in Neisse (15 June 1938), reprinted in Ayaß (ed.), *Gemeinschaftsfremde,* pp. 135–136.
80 Gerhard Werle, *Justiz-Strafrecht und polizeiliche Verbrechensbekämpfung im Dritten Reich* (Berlin, 1989), p. 507. See also Wolfgang Ayaß, *Das Arbeitshaus Breitenau* (Kassel, 1992), pp. 319–327.
81 RKPA VE: Rund Erl. Reichskriminalpolizeiamt: 'Richtlinien des Reichskriminalpolizeiamtes über die Durchführung der vorbeugenden Verbrechensbekämpfung', (4 Apr. 1938).
82 RKPA VE: Himmler to Gestapa and RKPA, 'Schutzhaft gegen Arbeitsscheue' (26 Jan. 1938).
83 Wolfgang Ayaß, *'Asoziale' im Nationalsozialismus* (Stuttgart, 1995), p. 143.
84 See e.g. the later communication on this point in RKPA VE: RKPA an Kripostellen, 'Vorbeugende Verbrechensbekämpfung' (1 Sept. 1938).
85 SS-Oberführer Ulrich Greifelt, Chef der Dienststelle Vierjahresplan im Persönlichen Stab des Reichsführers SS (Jan. 1939): Nürnberg Dokument NO-5591, reprinted in Hans Buchheim, 'Aktion "Arbeitsscheu Reich"', *Gutachten des Instituts für Zeitgeschichte,* vol. 2 (Stuttgart, 1966), pp. 189–195, here 192–193.

86 See the reminder in RKPA VE, RKPA to Kripostellen, 'Vorbeugende Verbrechensbekämpfung durch die Polizei' (23 June 1938).

87 RKPA VE (25 May 1939).

88 Johannes Tuchel, *Konzentrationslager. Organisationsgeschichte und Funktion der 'Inspektion der Konzentrationslager' 1934–1938* (Boppard, 1991), p. 361.

89 See RKPA VE, 'Erfassung arbeitsscheue Personen' (18 Oct. 1939).

90 Tuchel, *Konzentrationslager*, p. 361. These figures, from 28 October, were before the mass arrests of the Jews that followed in the wake of the 'Night of Broken Glass' in November 1938.

91 See the table in Zimmermann, *Rassenutopie*, p.120.

92 See Terhorst, *Polizeiliche planmäßige Überwachung*, p. 153.

93 For a useful collection of documents, see Ayaß (ed.), *Gemeinschaftsfremde*, here, 3–5: Erlaß Göring to Police (22 Feb. 1933); Gesetz zur Abänderung strafrechtlicher Vorschriften (26 May 1933).

94 Ayaß, *Asoziale*, p. 187.

95 Bock, *Zwangssterilisation*, pp. 417–418, suggests that "tens of thousands" were rounded up in 1933 and sent to concentration camps or workhouses.

96 See David F. Crew, *Germans on Welfare: From Weimar to Hitler* (New York, 1998), pp. 150–151.

97 See Claudia Schoppmann, 'National Socialist Policies towards Female Homosexuality', in Lynn Abrams and Elizabeth Harvey (eds), *Gender Relations in German History: Power, Agency and Experience from the sixteenth to the twentieth Century* (Durham, 1997), pp. 177–187.

98 For evidence of Hitler's early aversion to homosexuality, see Hamann, *Hitler's Vienna*, p. 362.

99 See '"Säuberungsaktion" gegen Homosexuelle in Hamburg', (28 Aug. 1936), in the documentary collection Günter Grau (ed.), *Homosexualität in der NS-Zeit: Dokumente einer Diskriminierung und Verfolgung* (Frankfurt/M., 1993), p. 173.

100 During the war, the numbers declined further, to 3,773 in 1940; 3,739 in 1941; 2,678 in 1942; 2,218 in 1943, which was the last year for which we have figures. Statistics are reprinted in Grau (ed.), *Homosexualität*, p. 197.

101 See Cornelia Limpricht, Jürgen Müller and Nina Oxenius (eds), *'Verführte' Männer: Das Leben der Kölner Homosexuellen im Dritten Reich* (Cologne, 1991), pp. 96–103 and 82–94.

102 See Elke Fröhlich, 'Die Herausforderung des Einzelnen', in Martin Broszat and Elke Fröhlich (eds), *Bayern in der NS-Zeit*, vol. 6 (Munich, 1983), pp. 76–114.

103 Burkhard Jellonnek, *Homosexuelle unter dem Hakenkreuz: Die Verfolgung von Homosexuellen im Dritten Reich* (Paderborn, 1990), p. 328.

104 Burleigh and Wippermann, *Racial State*, p. 196, say that the 'usual figure' is 10,000, but believe that as many as 15,000 homosexuals may have died in the camps. Jellonnek, *Homosexuelle*, p. 328, puts the limits at between 5,000 and 15,000.

105 Christopher R. Browning, *The Origins of the Final Solution: The Evolution of Nazi Jewish Policy, September 1939–March 1942* (Lincoln, 2004), p. 10.

106 Detlev Peukert, *Volksgenossen und Gemeinschaftsfremde: Anpassung, Ausmerze und Aufbegehren unter dem Nationalsozialismus* (Cologne, 1982), pp.

260–261.
107 See J. Noakes and G. Pridham (eds), *Nazism 1919–1945* vol. 2: *State, Economy and Society 1933–1939: A Documentary Reader* (Exeter, 2000), p. 380.
108 Ibid., p. 380.
109 Wehler, *Gesellschaftsgeschichte*, p. 681.
110 Alison Owings, *Frauen: German Women Recall the Third Reich* (New Brunswick, 1993).
111 See Gellately, *Backing Hitler*, p. 258.
112 See Robert Gellately, 'Surveillance and Disobedience: Comments on the Political Policing of Nazi Germany', in Christian Leitz (ed.), *The Third Reich: The Essential Readings* (Oxford: Blackwell, 1999), pp. 183–203.

5: 'Soldiers of the Home Front': Jurists and Legal Terror during the Second World War

1 This essay focuses on criminal law, examining courts and prisons linked to the Ministry of Justice. Other courts, such as military courts or judicial courts set up outside Germany, are generally excluded from consideration. The term prisons encompasses all penal institutions controlled by the legal authorities.

2 For the death penalty, see R.J. Evans, *Rituals of Retribution. Capital Punishment in Germany, 1600–1987* (London, 1996). For imprisonment, see N. Wachsmann, *Hitler's Prisons. Legal Terror in Nazi Germany* (New Haven, 2004). Statistical references to the death penalty and imprisonment in this chapter are taken from these two sources, unless otherwise stated.

3 For the use of this term see M. Burleigh and W. Wippermann, *The Racial State: Germany 1933–1945* (Cambridge, 1991).

4 For this research, see R. Gellately, *Backing Hitler. Consent and Coercion in Nazi Germany* (Oxford, 2001); E. Johnson, *The Nazi Terror. Gestapo, Jews and Ordinary Germans* (London, 2000).

5 For a succinct picture of the legal profession in the Third Reich, see R. Angermund, *Deutsche Richterschaft 1919–1945* (Frankfurt/M., 1990), quote on p. 201. For a detailed portrayal of Franz Gürtner, see L. Gruchmann, *Justiz im Dritten Reich 1933–1940. Anpassung und Unterwerfung in der Ära Gürtner*, 2nd edn (Munich, 1990), pp. 9–83.

6 Much of the legislation is translated and contextualized in J. Noakes (ed.), *Nazism 1919–1945* vol. 4: *The German Home Front in World War II: A Documentary Reader* (Exeter, 1998), pp. 124–135.

7 For the Hamburg special court, see K. Bästlein, 'Sondergerichte in Norddeutschland als Verfolgungsinstanz', in F. Bajohr (ed.), *Norddeutschland im Nationalsozialismus* (Hamburg, 1993), pp. 218–238, here 228. In recent years, German scholars have published a wide range of valuable studies on individual special courts. For an overview of some of this literature, see H. Hirsch's review article in *Ius Commune* 26 (1999), pp. 498–505.

8 The most comprehensive study of the People's Court is W. Wagner, *Der Volksgerichtshof im nationalsozialistischen Staat* (Stuttgart, 1974). Important recent studies include K. Marxen, *Das Volk und sein Gerichtshof*

(Frankfurt/M., 1994) and H. Schlüter, *Die Urteilspraxis des nationalsozialis-tischen Volksgerichtshofs* (Berlin, 1995).

9   For the punishment of 'dangerous habitual criminals', see C. Müller, *Das Gewohnheitsverbrechergesetz vom 24. November 1933* (Baden-Baden, 1997). For indefinite confinement, see N. Wachsmann, 'From Indefinite Confinement to Extermination. "Habitual Criminals" in the Third Reich', in R. Gellately, N. Stoltzfus (eds), *Social Outsiders in Nazi Germany* (Princeton, 2001), pp. 165–191.

10 Schlüter, *Urteilspraxis*, pp. 50, 189–202; Marxen, *Gerichtshof*, p. 36.

11 For a brief account of police terror in Poland, see P. Longerich, *Politik der Vernichtung. Eine Gesamtdarstellung der nationalsozialistischen Judenverfolgung* (Munich, 1998), pp. 243–248.

12 For the most comprehensive study of racism and the law in Nazi Germany, see D. Majer, *'Non-Germans' under the Third Reich. The Nazi Judicial and Administrative System in Germany and Occupied Eastern Europe, with Special Regard to Occupied Poland, 1939–1945* (Baltimore, 2003), first published in German in 1981. For Nazi legal terror in occupied Poland, see also E. Zarzycki, *Besatzungsjustiz in Polen. Sondergerichte im Dienste deutscher Unterwerfungsstrategie* (Berlin, 1990).

13 G. Weckbecker, *Zwischen Freispruch und Todesstrafe: Die Rechtsprechung der nationalsozialistischen Sondergerichte Frankfurt/Main und Bromberg* (Baden-Baden, 1998), pp. 441–445, 722–726, 782–784, Freisler quote on p. 445.

14 Quotes in H. Michelberger, *Berichte aus der Justiz des Dritten Reiches* (Pfaffenweiler, 1989), p. 227; K.H. Keldungs, *Das Duisburger Sondergericht 1942–1945* (Baden-Baden, 1998), p. 93.

15 For the special court figures, see Weckbecker, *Rechtsprechung*, p. 443. For the death penalty figure, see BA Berlin, R 3001/alt R 22/1160, Bl. 48.

16 For foreign workers, see U. Herbert, *Fremdarbeiter. Politik und Praxis des 'Ausländer-Einsatzes' in der Kriegswirtschaft des Dritten Reiches* (Berlin, 1985).

17 Majer, *'Non-Germans'*, pp. 339–340; H.-E. Niermann, *Die Durchsetzung politischer und politisierter Strafjustiz im Dritten Reich* (Düsseldorf, 1995), pp. 353–357.

18 For a detailed discussion of 'radio offences', see M.P. Hensle, '"Rundfunkverbrechen" vor NS-Sondergerichten', *Rundfunk und Geschichte* 26 (2000), pp. 111–26. A useful, brief account can be found in Johnson, *Nazi Terror*, pp. 322–333.

19 Schlüter, *Urteilspraxis*, p. 50.

20 For the quotes, see H. Boberach (ed.), *Meldungen aus dem Reich*, 17 vols (Herrsching, 1984), vol. 9, pp. 3496, 3520. For popular opinion in general, see I. Kershaw, *The 'Hitler Myth'. Image and Reality in the Third Reich* (Oxford, 1989), pp. 169–189.

21 H. Picker, *Hitlers Tischgespräche im Führerhauptquartier* (Berlin, 1997), pp. 218–226.

22 L. Gruchmann, '"Generalangriff gegen die Justiz"? Der Reichstagsbeschluß vom 26. April 1942 und seine Bedeutung für die Maßregelung der deutschen Richter durch Hitler', *Vierteljahrshefte für Zeitgeschichte 51* (2003), pp. 509–520.

23 For the Braunschweig general state prosecutor, see Michelberger, *Berichte*,

p. 321. The concept of 'working towards the Führer' is introduced in I. Kershaw, '"Working towards the Führer". Reflections on the Nature of the Hitler Dictatorship', *Contemporary European History* 2 (1993), pp. 103–118.

24 Schlüter, *Urteilspraxis*, pp. 200–202, quote on p. 202.

25 N. Wachsmann, '"Annihilation through Labor": The Killing of State Prisoners in the Third Reich', *The Journal of Modern History* 71 (1999), pp. 624–659.

26 L. Gruchmann, '"Nacht- und Nebel"-Justiz. Die Mitwirkung deutscher Strafgerichte an der Bekämpfung des Widerstandes in den besetzten westeuropäischen Ländern 1942–1944', *Vierteljahrshefte für Zeitgeschichte* 29 (1981), pp. 342–396.

27 Majer, *'Non-Germans'*, pp. 332–333, 343, 433–436, quote on p. 332.

28 For the assessment of the SS security service, see Boberach (ed.), *Meldungen*, vol. 9, pp. 3307–3308. For the number of death sentences, see Bundesminister der Justiz (ed.), *Im Namen des Deutschen Volkes. Justiz und Nationalsozialismus* (Cologne, 1989), p. 228.

29 For this case, see H. Wüllenweber, *Sondergerichte im Dritten Reich* (Frankfurt/M., 1990), pp. 168–171.

30 Wachsmann, *Hitler's Prisons*, pp. 279–282.

31 Richterbrief Nr. 1, 1 Oct. 1942, reprinted in H. Boberach (ed.), *Richterbriefe. Dokumente zur Beeinflussung der deutschen Rechtsprechung 1942–1944* (Boppard, 1975), pp. 5–20, here 18–19.

32 For the punishment of 'race defilement', see A. Przyrembel, *'Rassenschande'. Reinheitsmythos und Vernichtungslegitimation im Nationalsozialismus* (Göttingen, 2003). The two examples are taken from Wüllenweber, *Sondergerichte*, pp. 199–210.

33 B. Dörner, 'Justiz und Judenmord: Todesurteile gegen Judenhelfer in Polen und der Tschechoslowakei 1942–1944', in N. Frei, S. Steinbacher, B.C. Wagner (eds), *Ausbeutung, Vernichtung, Öffentlichkeit. Neue Studien zur nationalsozialistischen Lagerpolitik* (Munich, 2000), pp. 249–263, quote on p. 251.

34 Id., *'Heimtücke': das Gesetz als Waffe: Kontrolle, Abschreckung und Verfolgung in Deutschland 1933–1945* (Paderborn, 1998), here pp. 233–241, quote on p. 234.

35 Wachsmann, *Hitler's Prisons*, pp. 223–225, 285–292.

36 For the People's Court, see Marxen, *Gerichtshof*, pp. 36, 43. The figures referring to the People's Court count 'ethnic Germans' as Germans. For popular opinion, Kershaw, *'Hitler Myth'*, pp. 189–219.

37 For the rise of property crime, see P. Wagner, *Volksgemeinschaft ohne Verbrecher. Konzeptionen und Praxis der Kriminalpolizei in der Zeit der Weimarer Republik und des Nationalsozialismus* (Hamburg, 1996), pp. 319–329. The Hamburg reference is given in Boberach (ed.), *Meldungen*, vol. 16, p. 6261.

38 For the background, see Boberach (ed.), *Richterbriefe*, pp. 250–309. For the examples, see ibid., pp. 286, 302 and K. Fricke, *Die Justizvollzugsanstalt 'Roter Ochse' Halle/Saale 1933–1945* (Magdeburg, 1997), p. 41.

39 Public Record Office, WO 309/199, IMT, testimony R. Havemann, 10 Apr. 1947.

40   W.-D. Mechler, *Kriegsalltag an der 'Heimatfront'. Das Sondergericht Hannover im Einsatz gegen 'Rundfunkverbrecher', 'Schwarzschlachter', 'Volksschädlinge' und andere 'Straftäter' 1939 bis 1945* (Hanover, 1997), p. 45.

41   Noakes (ed.), *Nazism*, vol. 4, pp. 655–656. For a more detailed discussion, see K.-D. Henke, *Die amerikanische Besetzung Deutschlands* (Munich, 1995), pp. 845–853.

42   Wachsmann, *Hitler's Prisons*, pp. 323–338, quote on p. 325.

43   H. Wrobel, *Verurteilt zur Demokratie. Justiz und Justizpolitik in Deutschland 1945–1949* (Heidelberg, 1989), p. 95; Angermund, *Richterschaft*, p. 219.

44   For police terror, see G. Paul, '"Diese Erschießungen haben mich innerlich gar nicht mehr berührt". Die Kriegsendphasenverbrechen der Gestapo 1944/45', in id., and K.-M. Mallmann (eds), *Die Gestapo im Zweiten Weltkrieg* (Darmstadt, 2000), pp. 543–568. For the People's Court, see Marxen, *Gerichtshof*, p. 36.

45   C. Oehler, *Die Rechtsprechung des Sondergerichts Mannheim 1933–1945* (Berlin, 1997), p. 250; Mechler, *Kriegsalltag*, p. 45; Bästlein, 'Sonder-gerichte', p. 228.

46   For the last point, see also Kershaw, *'Hitler Myth'*, p. 258.

47   The judgement is available in electronic form on CD-Rom as *Nuremberg War Crimes Trials Online* (Seattle, 1995).

6: Germans, Slavs and the Burden of Work in Rural Southern Germany during the Second World War

1   On the complex Nazi categories of foreigners' 'value', see U. Herbert, *Fremdarbeiter. Politik und Praxis des 'Ausländer-Einsatzes' in der Kriegswirtschaft des Dritten Reichs* (Berlin/Bonn, 1985), pp. 98–100. (English translation *Hitler's Foreign Workers. Enforced Foreign Labor in Germany under the Third Reich* [Cambridge, 1997]).

2   'Aus Monatsbericht der Gendarmerie-Station Aufsess, 26.1.41' in M. Broszat, E. Fröhlich, F. Wiesemann (eds), *Bayern in der NS-Zeit*, vol. I: *Soziale Lage und politisches Verhalten der Bevölkerung im Spiegel vertraulicher Berichte* (Munich/Vienna, 1977), p. 145. See also I. Kershaw, *Popular Opinion and Political Dissent in the Third Reich. Bavaria 1933–1945* (Oxford, 1983), pp. 287–288; J. Stephenson, 'Triangle: Foreign Workers, German Civilians and the Nazi Regime. War and Society in Württemberg, 1939–1945', *German Studies Review*, vol. XV, no. 2 (1992), p. 342–345, 350–351.

3   M. Spoerer and J. Fleischhacker, 'Forced Laborers in Nazi Germany: Categories, Numbers, and Survivors', *Journal of Interdisciplinary History*, vol. 33, no. 2 (2002), p. 196, table 8.

4   B. Schönhagen, *Tübingen unterm Hakenkreuz. Eine Universitätsstadt in der Zeit des Nationalsozialismus* (Stuttgart, 1991), pp. 357–358.

5   Stephenson, 'Triangle: Foreign Workers, German Civilians and the Nazi Regime', p. 354.

6   Herbert, *Hitler's Foreign Workers*, pp. 296–298.

7   T. Weger, *Nationalsozialistischer 'Fremdarbeitereinsatz' in einer bayerischen Gemeinde 1939–1945. Das Beispiel Olching (Landkreis Fürstenfeldbruck)* (Frankfurt/M., 1998), pp. 77–78, 82. See also U. Kaminsky, '"Vergessene

Opfer"—Zwangssterilisierte, "Asoziale", Deserteure, Fremdarbeiter', in S. Baumbach, U. Kaminsky, A. Kenkmann, B. Meyer, *Rückblenden. Lebensgeschichtliche Interviews mit Verfolgten des NS-Regimes in Hamburg* (Hamburg, 1999), pp. 348–349.

8   J. Woydt, *Ausländische Arbeitskräfte in Deutschland. Vom Kaiserreich bis zur Bundesrepublik* (Heilbronn, 1987), pp. 60–134; A. Schäfer, *Zwangsarbeiter und NS-Rassenpolitik. Russische und polnische Arbeitskräfte in Württemberg 1939–1945* (Stuttgart, 2000), 21–130; N. Gregor, *Daimler-Benz in the Third Reich* (New Haven, CT/London, 1998), pp. 175–217.

9   Herbert, *Hitler's Foreign Workers*, pp. 96–97, 99, 130–131, 145–146, 157, 185–186, 220; Schäfer, *Zwangsarbeiter und NS-Rassenpolitik*, pp. 153–160.

10   Schönhagen, *Tübingen unterm Hakenkreuz*, p. 357.

11   J. Noakes and G. Pridham (eds), *Nazism 1919–1945* vol. 3: *Foreign Policy, War and Racial Extermination: A Documentary Reader* (Exeter, 2001), document 638, pp. 300–301. See also G. Corni, and H. Gies, *Brot, Butter, Kanonen. Die Ernährungswirtschaft in Deutschland unter der Diktatur Hitlers* (Berlin, 1997), p. 448, table 24.

12   *Statistisches Jahrbuch für das Deutsche Reich*, 1941/42, pp. 424, 426.

13   Ibid., p. 466; C. Tholander, *Fremdarbeiter 1939 bis 1945. Ausländische Arbeitskräfte in der Zeppelin-Stadt Friedrichshafen* (Essen, 2001), pp. 68–69, 104; R. Botwinick, *Winzig, Germany, 1933–1946. The History of a Town under the Third Reich* (Westport, CT, 1992), p. 88.

14   Corni and Gies, *Brot, Butter, Kanonen*, pp. 280–297, 433–445, 449; L. Elsner, 'Ausländerbeschäftigung und Zwangsarbeitspolitik in Deutschland während des Ersten Weltkrieges', in Klaus J. Bade (ed.), *Auswanderer—Wanderarbeiter—Gastarbeiter. Bevölkerung, Arbeitsmarkt und Wanderung in Deutschland seit der Mitte des 19. Jahrhunderts* (Ostfildern, 1984), vol. 2, pp. 527–557; Woydt, *Ausländische Arbeitskräfte in Deutschland*, pp. 10–51.

15   Kershaw, *Popular Opinion and Political Dissent in the Third Reich*, p. 286; Stephenson, 'Triangle: Foreign Workers, German Civilians and the Nazi Regime', p. 343.

16   Herbert, *Fremdarbeiter*, p. 11.

17   Tholander, *Fremdarbeiter 1939 bis 1945*, p. 67.

18   T. Schnabel, *Württemberg zwischen Weimar und Bonn 1928–1945/46* (Stuttgart, 1986), p. 572; Broszat, Fröhlich, Wiesemann, *Bayern in der NS-Zeit*, vol. I: 'Aus Monatsbericht des Landrats, 31.1.1942', p. 155; 'Aus Monatsbericht des Landrats, 30.9.43', p. 176.

19   Staatsarchiv Ludwigsburg, K110, Bü37, 'Betr.: Beschäftigung polnischer Landarbeiter', 1 March 1940. See also Tholander, *Fremdarbeiter 1939 bis 1945*, pp. 51–52.

20   U. Herbert, 'Apartheid nebenan. Erinnerungen an die Fremdarbeiter im Ruhrgebiet', L. Niethammer (ed.), *'Die Jahre weiss man nicht, wo man die hinsetzen soll'. Faschismuserfahrungen im Ruhrgebiet. Lebensgeschichte und Sozialkultur im Ruhrgebiet 1930 bis 1960* (Bonn, 1983); Corni and Gies, *Brot, Butter, Kanonen*, pp. 454–460; Bauer, *Nationalsozialistische Agrarpolitik und bäuerliches Verhalten im Zweiten Weltkrieg. Eine Regionale Fallstudie zur ländlichen Gesellschaft in Bayern* (Frankfurt/M., 1996) p. 156; Tholander, *Fremdarbeiter 1939 bis 1945*, pp. 50–53.

21 Kershaw, *Popular Opinion and Political Dissent in the Third Reich*, p. 287; Sauer, P., *Württemberg in der Zeit des Nationalsozialismus* (Ulm, 1975), pp. 417, 419; 'Aus Monatsbericht des Gendarmerie-Kreisführers, 29.9.1942', in Broszat, Fröhlich, Wiesemann, *Bayern in der NS-Zeit*, vol. I, pp. 160–161; Bauer, *Nationalsozialistische Agrarpolitik und bäuerliches Verhalten*, pp. 161–162.

22 Schnabel, *Württemberg zwischen Weimar und Bonn*, p. 572.

23 Broszat, Fröhlich, Wiesemann, *Bayern in der NS-Zeit*, vol. I: 'Aus Monatsbericht des Gendarmerie-Kreisführers, 30.12.1939', p. 136; 'Aus Monatsbericht der Gendarmerie-Station Hollfeld, 26.6.1940', p. 141; 'Aus Monatsbericht der Gendarmerie-Station Königsfeld, 27.6.1940', p. 141; commentary, p. 144; 'Aus Monatsbericht des Landrats, 28.2.1941', p. 147.

24 Schnabel, *Württemberg zwischen Weimar und Bonn*, p. 572.

25 Tholander, *Fremdarbeiter 1939 bis 1945*, pp. 51–52, 67; Bauer, *Nationalsozialistische Agrarpolitik und bäuerliches Verhalten*, pp. 166–167; Broszat, Fröhlich, Wiesemann, *Bayern in der NS-Zeit*, vol. I: 'Aus den Monatsbericht des Landrats, 28.2.1941', p. 147; 'Aus den Monatsbericht des Gendarmerie-Kreisführers, 29.4.1943', p. 172.

26 Tholander, *Fremdarbeiter 1939 bis 1945*, pp. 41–43; A. Grossmann, 'Fremd- und Zwangsarbeiter in Bayern 1939–1945', in Bade, *Auswanderer— Wanderarbeiter—Gastarbeiter*, p. 588; J.J. Delaney, 'Racial Values vs. Religious Values: Clerical Opposition to Nazi anti-Polish Racial Policy', *Church History. Studies in Christianity and Culture*, vol. 70, no. 2 (2001), p. 289; 'Social Contact and Personal Relations of German Catholic Peasants and Polish Workers (POWs, Civilian, and Forced Laborers) in Bavaria's Rural War Economy, 1939–1945', *Annali dell' Istituto storico italo-germanico in Trento*, vol. XXVIII (2002), pp. 393, 399, 403.

27 Quoted in Stephenson, 'Triangle: Foreign Workers, German Civilians and the Nazi Regime', p. 348.

28 A. Grossmann, 'Fremd- und Zwangsarbeiter in Bayern 1939–1945', in Bade, *Auswanderer—Wanderarbeiter—Gastarbeiter*, p. 588. See also Delaney, 'Social Contact and Personal Relations', pp. 398–401.

29 Ibid., pp. 618–619; Bauer, *Nationalsozialistische Agrarpolitik und bäuerliches Verhalten*, pp. 172–77; Stephenson, 'Triangle: Foreign Workers, German Civilians and the Nazi Regime', pp. 347, 349–350; Schnabel, *Württemberg zwischen Weimar und Bonn*, pp. 570–571, 573; C. Arbogast, *Herrschaftsinstanzen der württembergischen NSDAP. Funktion, Sozialprofil und Lebenswege einer regionalen NS-Elite, 1920–1960* (Munich, 1998), pp. 63–64, 219, 239; Tholander, *Fremdarbeiter 1939 bis 1945*, pp. 60–66; Schäfer, *Zwangsarbeiter und NS-Rassenpolitik*, pp. 160–173.

30 Ibid., pp. 163, 206–220, 259, 261; Bauer, *Nationalsozialistische Agrarpolitik und bäuerliches Verhalten*, pp. 179–180; J. Noakes (ed.), *Nazism 1919–1945* vol. 4: *The German Home Front in World War II: A Documentary Reader* (Exeter, 1998), p. 330.

31 Schönhagen, *Tübingen unterm Hakenkreuz*, p. 457 n. 460. See also Delaney, 'Racial Values vs. Religious Values', p. 286.

32 Ibid., p. 289; Delaney, 'Social Contact and Personal Relations', pp. 396–397; Weger, *Nationalsozialistischer 'Fremdarbeitereinsatz' in einer bayerischen*

Gemeinde 1939–1945, p. 83.

33 Grossmann, 'Fremd- und Zwangsarbeiter in Bayern', pp. 594, 605–606; Delaney, 'Social Contact and Personal Relations', pp. 400–401.

34 Bauer, *Nationalsozialistische Agrarpolitik und bäuerliches Verhalten*, p. 165.

35 Delaney, 'Social Contact and Personal Relations', p. 397; 'Aus Monatsbericht des Landrats, 31.7.41', in Broszat, Fröhlich, Wiesemann, *Bayern in der NS-Zeit*, vol. I, p. 151; W. Rinderle and B. Norling, *The Nazi Impact on a German Village* (Lexington, KY, 1993), p. 166; J. Stephenson, 'Nazism, Modern War and Rural Society in Württemberg, 1939–1945', *Journal of Contemporary History*, vol. 32, no. 3 (1997), p. 348; Bauer, *Nationalsozialistische Agrarpolitik und bäuerliches Verhalten*, p. 163.

36 Ibid., p. 160; Delaney: 'Racial Values vs. Religious Values', pp. 290–291, 293; Kaminsky, '"Vergessene Opfer"—Zwangssterilisierte, "Asoziale", Deserteure, Fremdarbeiter', pp. 329–330, 348–356; J. Stephenson, *Hitler's Home Front* (forthcoming), chapters 2 and 9.

37 Delaney: 'Racial Values vs. Religious Values', pp. 275–284; S. Drost, *Patronenwald. Dokumente zur Zwangsarbeit im 'Dritten Reich'* (Stuttgart, 1998), pp. 43–44; Stephenson: 'Nazism, Modern War and Rural Society in Württemberg', p. 352; 'Triangle: Foreign Workers, German Civilians and the Nazi Regime', p. 348.

38 Broszat, Fröhlich, Wiesemann, *Bayern in der NS-Zeit*, vol. I: 'Aus Monatsbericht des Gendarmerie-Kreisführers, 30.8.1944', pp. 187–188; 'Aus weltanschaulichem Bericht des Kreisschulungsamts Neustadt a.d. Aisch, 19.8.1943', p. 581; Tholander, *Fremdarbeiter 1939 bis 1945*, p. 71.

7: Did Hitler Miss his Chance in 1940?

1 On peace-feelers around this time, see Bernd Martin, 'Das "Dritte Reich" und die "Friedens"-Frage im Zweiten Weltkrieg', in Wolfgang Michalka (ed.), *Nationalsozialistische Außenpolitik* (Darmstadt, 1978), pp. 534–537; and, especially, Ulrich Schlie, *Kein Friede mit Deutschland. Die geheimen Gespräche im Zweiten Weltkrieg 1939–1941* (Munich/Berlin, 1994), chapters 10, 12.

2 Nicolaus von Below, *Als Hitlers Adjutant 1937–1945* (Mainz, 1980), p. 242; Max Domarus, *Hitler. Reden und Proklamationen 1932–1945* (Wiesbaden, 1973), pp. 1540–1559 for the speech, p. 1158 for the passage relating to Britain.

3 Winston S. Churchill, *The Second World War*, vol. 2: *Their Finest Hour* (London, 1949), pp. 229–230 for the British response.

4 Franz Halder, *Kriegstagebuch. Tägliche Aufzeichnungen des Chefs des Generalstabes des Heeres 1939–1942*, (ed.) Hans-Adolf Jacobsen, vol. 2, [= Halder, *KTB*, vol. 2], (Stuttgart, 1963), pp. 30–34 (22.7.40).

5 Halder, *KTB*, vol. 2, p. 49 (31.7.40).

6 Ibid., p. 33 (21.7.40).

7 Ibid., pp. 46–47 (30.7.40).

8 *Das Deutsche Reich im Zweiten Weltkrieg* [= *DRZW*], (ed.) Militär-geschichtliches Forschungsamt, vol. 4 (Stuttgart, 1983), pp. 9–10.

9 The naval leadership was not least anxious to emphasize that it had advanced an alternative which stood a good chance of success but had been spurned

by Hitler's insistence upon the attack on Russia: Erich Raeder, *Mein Leben*, Tübingen-Neckar, 1957, pp. 246-248 and Kurt Assmann, *Deutsche Schicksalsjahre* (Wiesbaden, 1950), pp. 211-212. Raeder had already claimed his opposition to the Russian war, with reference to his audience with Hitler on 26 September, in his testimony at Nuremberg: *Der Prozeß gegen die Hauptkriegsverbrecher vor dem Internationalen Militärgerichtshof, Nürnberg*, 42 vols (Nuremberg, 1947-9) vol. 14, pp. 117-119. See also Michael Salewski, *Die deutsche Seekriegsleitung 1935-1945*, vol. 1, (Frankfurt/M., 1970), pp. 271-272.

10   The title of the early postwar classic by Friedrich Meinecke, *Die deutsche Katastrophe* (Wiesbaden, 1946).

11   See Andreas Hillgruber, *Hitlers Strategie. Politik und Kriegführung 1940-1941* (2nd edn, Bonn, 1993), pp. 190-191; Lothar Gruchmann, 'Die "verpaßten strategischen Chancen" der Achsenmächte im Mittelmeerraum 1940/41', *Vierteljahrshefte für Zeitgeschichte*, 18 (1970), pp. 456-475; Gerhard Schreiber, 'Der Mittelmeerraum in Hitlers Strategie 1940. "Programm" und militärische Planung', *Militärgeschichtliche Mitteilungen* [= *MGM*], 27/2 (1980), pp. 69-99; and Gerhard Schreiber's contribution to *DRZW*, vol. 3 (Stuttgart, 1984), p. 270.

12   Explicitly demonstrated by Gerhard Schreiber, 'Zur Kontinuität des Groß- und Weltmachtstrebens der deutschen Marineführung', *MGM*, 25/2 (1979), pp. 101-171.

13   On the twin strands of German imperialism, see Woodruff D. Smith, *The Ideological Origins of Nazi Imperialism* (New York/Oxford, 1986).

14   See Jost Dülffer, *Weimar, Hitler und die Marine. Reichspolitik und Flottenbau 1920-1939* (Düsseldorf, 1973), pp. 492ff.

15   Bundesarchiv/Militärarchiv [= BA/MA] Freiburg, RM6/71, 'Gedanken des Oberbefehlshabers der Kriegsmarine zum Kriegsausbruch 3.9.1939'; cited in Salewski, *Die Deutsche Seekriegsleitung*, vol. 1, p. 91, and in English translation in Charles S. Thomas, *The German Navy in the Nazi Era* (London, 1990), p. 187.

16   See Hillgruber, *Hitlers Strategie*, pp. 242-255; Gerhard L. Weinberg, 'German Colonial Plans and Policies 1938-1942', in Waldemar Besson and Friedrich Frhr. Hiller v. Gaertringen (eds), *Geschichte und Gegenwartsbewußtsein. Historische Betrachtungen und Untersuchungen* (Göttingen, 1963), pp. 462-491; Klaus Hildebrand, *Vom Reich zum Weltreich. Hitler, NSDAP und koloniale Frage 1919-1945* (Munich, 1969), pp. 652-700; Salewski, *Die Deutsche Seekriegsleitung*, vol. 1, pp. 234-241; Gerhard Schreiber, *Revisionismus und Weltmachtstreben. Marineführung und deutsch-italienische Beziehungen 1919 bis 1944* (Stuttgart, 1978), pp. 288-297; and *DRZW*, vol. 3, pp. 250-271.

17   Salewski, *Die Deutsche Seekriegsleitung*, vol. 3 (Frankfurt am Main, 1973), pp.106-108; *DRZW*, vol. 3, pp. 254-255.

18   Salewski, *Die Deutsche Seekriegsleitung*, vol. 3, pp.108-114; *DRZW*, vol. 3, pp. 255-256. And see the two further memoranda from this period (Salewski, *Die Deutsche Seekriegsleitung*, vol. 3, pp. 114-118), and a further memorandum of 4 July 1940 (pp. 122-135) outlining the implications of the massive territorial expansion for the growth of the fleet.

19 BA/MA, RM6/83, printed in Schreiber, 'Zur Kontinuität', pp. 142–147; *DRZW*, vol. 3, pp. 257–258.

20 Andreas Hillgruber (ed.), *Staatsmänner und Diplomaten bei Hitler. Vertrauliche Aufzeichnungen 1939–1941* (Munich, 1969), p. 102 (Hitler's remarks to Serrano Suñer, at the time Minister of the Interior in Spain, shortly afterwards to become Foreign Minister, 17.9.40).

21 BA/MA, RM7/894, 'Studie Nordwest (Landung in England)', dated December 1939, considered possibilities of a landing in Great Britain, indicating beaches which might come into question, the geographical difficulties of the coastlines, and other factors. Raeder reported the findings—based, he said, on analysis that had begun the previous November—to Hitler on 21 May 1940: Karl Klee, *Dokumente zum Unternehmen 'Seelöwe'. Die geplante deutsche Landung in England 1940* (Göttingen, 1959), p. 239.

22 *Kriegstagebuch der Seekriegsleitung 1939–1945*, ed. Werner Rahn and Gerhard Schreiber (Herford/Bonn, 1989) (= *KTB der Seekriegsleitung*), vol. 10, Part A, (mimeographed reproduction from BA/MA, 7/13), p. 186 (18.6.40).

23 Hillgruber, *Hitlers Strategie*, pp. 157–158.

24 Ibid., pp. 169–171.

25 *KTB der Seekriegsleitung*, vol. 11, Part A, (= BA/MA, 7/14), p. 190 (15.7.40), pp. 219–224 (19.7.40). And see Salewski, *Die Deutsche Seekriegsleitung*, vol. 1, pp. 58–59.

26 *KTB der Seekriegsleitung*, vol. 11, Part A, p. 201 (18.7.40).

27 Ibid., vol. 12, Part A, (= BA/MA, 7/15), p. 3 (1.8.40).

28 Ibid., vol. 12, Part A, pp. 353–354 (30.8.40).

29 Ibid., vol. 12, Part A, pp. 354–356 (30.7.40), pp. 364–365 (31.7.40); *Lagevorträge des Oberbefehlshabers der Kriegsmarine vor Hitler 1939–1945*, (ed.) Gerhard Wagner, (Munich, 1972) (= *LV*), pp. 126–128 (31.7.40).

30 Karl Klee, *Das Unternehmen 'Seelöwe'. Die geplante deutsche Landung in England 1940* (Göttingen, 1958), p. 205.

31 Salewski, *Die Deutsche Seekriegsleitung*, vol. 1, pp. 259–260.

32 Ibid., pp. 275–276.

33 *KTB der Seekriegsleitung*, vol. 11, Part A, pp. 236–239 (21.7.40).

34 Salewski, *Die Deutsche Seekriegsleitung*, vol. 3, pp. 137–144.

35 Schreiber, 'Der Mittelmeerraum', pp. 78–79.

36 *Kriegstagebuch des Oberkommandos der Wehrmacht (Wehrmachtführungsstab)*, vol. 1, (ed.) Percy Ernst Schramm (Frankfurt/M.,1965) (= *KTB d.OKW*), pp. 17–18, 31–32, (9.8.40, 14.8.40); Schreiber, 'Der Mittelmeerraum', pp. 78–79.

37 BA/MA, RM7/233, Fols.78–85:'Kriegführung gegen England bei Ausfall der Unternehmung "Seelöwe"'; printed in *LV*, pp. 138–141 (6.9.40). See also Schreiber, *Revisionismus*, pp. 281–282;

38 BA/MA, RM7/233, Fols. 83–84.

39 On the destroyer deal, see Churchill, vol. 2, Chapter XX; also John Lukacs, *The Duel: Hitler vs. Churchill* (Oxford, 1992), pp. 225–227.

40 *DRZW*, vol. 3, pp. 192–194; Schreiber, ' Der Mittelmeerraum', p. 80.

41 *LV*, pp. 134–141 (6.9.40). This passage is not included in the translated *Fuehrer Conferences on Naval Affairs 1939–1945* (London, 1990), p. 135.

42 *LV*, pp. 143–146 (26.9.40); Schreiber, 'Der Mittelmeerraum', 81; *DRZW*,

vol. 3, pp. 199–201; Gruchmann, p. 463.

43 He nevertheless put the arguments for full co-operation with France less forcefully than they had been advanced within the Naval Warfare Executive. See BA/MA, RM8/1209, 'Die Bemühungen der Skl. um einen Ausgleich mit Frankreich und um die Sicherstellung des französischen Kolonialreiches in Afrika', draft analysis of Vice-Admiral Kurt Assmann. Compiled in 1944, this was intended to absolve the Skl. from responsibility for the disastrous course of the war. It nonetheless points up the divergence in strategic preference. In the introduction (Fol. 11), Assmann wrote: 'The problem of a French-German understanding and the upholding of the French colonial empire in North and West Africa was one of the fateful questions of this war. In dealing with this issue, the decisions and actions of the supreme German leadership were not in accord with the views of the Skl. The Skl. correctly foresaw the coming development, repeatedly warned against it, and tried to convey its view.'

44 *KTB d. Seekriegsleitung*, vol. 13, Part A (= BA/MA, 7/16), p. 352 (26.9.40), 'Führer agrees in principle with the ideas of the head of the Naval Warfare Executive' ('Führer stimmt den Gedankengängen des Chefs Skl. grundsätzlich zu'). See also Raeder, pp. 246–248 and Assmann, pp. 211–212, though, in fact, Hitler's reported remarks to his naval adjutant were ambivalent, that Raeder's comments to him had been most valuable in that it served as a control on his own views, to see 'if he was right'.

45 *LV*, pp. 143–144 (26.9.40).

46 Hillgruber, *Hitlers Strategie*, pp. 178, 190; Wolfgang Michalka, *Ribbentrop und die deutsche Weltpolitik 1933–1940* (Munich, 1980), pp. 247–259.

47 Wolfgang Michalka, 'Vom Antikominternpakt zum euro-asiatischen Kontinentalblock: Ribbentrops Alternativkonzeption zu Hitlers außenpolitischem "Programm"', in Michalka, *Nationalsozialistische Außenpolitik*, pp. 490–491.

48 Andreas Hillgruber, 'Der Faktor Amerika in Hitlers Strategie 1938–1941', in Michalka, *Nationalsozialistische Außenpolitik*, p. 513.

49 Schreiber, 'Der Mittelmeer', p. 80; *DRZW*, vol. 3, p. 194.

50 Hillgruber, 'Amerika', pp. 512–513.

51 *Staatsmänner*, pp. 112–513.

52 Reports of the discussions in *Staatsmänner*, pp.104–123; and *Ciano's Diplomatic Papers*, (ed.) Malcolm Muggeridge (London, 1948), pp. 395–399.

53 *Staatsmänner*, pp. 132–140; and see Paul Preston, 'Franco and Hitler: the Myth of Hendaye 1940', *Contemporary European History*, 1 (1992), pp. 1–16.

54 *Die Weizsäcker-Papiere 1933–1950* (ed.) Leonidas E. Hill (Frankfurt/M., 1974), p. 221 (21.10.40)—before Hitler's meeting with Franco.

55 *Staatsmänner*, pp. 142–149.

56 *Die Weizsäcker-Papiere*, pp. 220–221 (21.10.40).

57 Below, *Als Hitlers Adjutant* , p. 250.

58 Halder, *KTB*, vol. 2, pp. 163–166 (4.11.40), quotation, p. 165; *KTB d. OKW*, vol. 1, pp. 148–152 (4.11.40).

59 Walter Warlimont, *Inside Hitler's Headquarters 1939–45*, (Presidio edn, Novato, California, n.d.; original Engl. language edn, London, 1964), p. 120;

DRZW, vol. 3, pp. 205–206; Schreiber, 'Der Mittelmeer', pp. 84–85; Gruchmann, p. 466.

60 For the talks, see *Staatsmänner,* pp. 165–193.

61 *Hitlers Weisungen für die Kriegführung. Dokumente des Oberkommandos der Wehrmacht,* (ed.) Walther Hubatsch (Munich, 1965), pp. 77–82.

62 *Heeresadjutant bei Hitler 1938–1943. Aufzeichnungen des Majors Engel,* (ed.) Hildegard von Kotze (Stuttgart, 1974), p. 91 (15.11.40).

63 *LV,* pp. 151–155, 160–163 (14.11.40); Schreiber, 'Der Mittelmeerraum', pp. 86–87.

64 Schreiber, 'Der Mittelmeerraum', p. 87.

65 Below, *Als Hitlers Adjutant,* p. 253.

66 *KTB d. OKW,* vol. 1, pp. 208–209 (5.12.40).

67 Ibid., p. 222 (10.12.40); *Hitlers Weisungen,* p. 90.

68 *KTB d. OKW,* vol. 1, p. 255 (9.1.41). On 28 January (p. 284), he accepted that there was no possibility of renewing preparations to take Gibraltar, which he momentarily envisaged taking place in April, because troops were needed for 'Barbarossa'. Even in mid-February, he was exhorting Franco to reconsider his decision not to enter the war: Domarus, p. 1666.

69 *Hitlers Weisungen,* p. 96.

70 In the eyes of the navy leadership, the chance to exploit British weakness in the Mediterranean was still not exhausted in spring 1941, following the German landing in Crete and Rommel's successes in north Africa: *LV,* pp. 240, 258–262 (6.6.41); Gruchmann, pp. 471–474. By this time, however, there was not a shadow of doubt about Hitler's priorities. Preparations for the imminent 'Barbarossa' took such precedence that, unlike autumn 1940, any strategic alternative existed purely in theory.

71 Paul Schmidt, *Statist auf diplomatischer Bühne. Erlebnisse des Chefdolmetschers im Auswärtigen Amt mit den Staatsmännern Europas* (Bonn, 1953), pp. 516–517; *Heeresadjutant,* p. 88 (28.10.40).

72 By the end of 1940, when Mussolini had reversed his earlier objections to an increase in French strength in the Mediterranean, it was evidently owing to Hitler's own objections that nothing was done to further an arrangement between Germany and France: Gerhard L. Weinberg, *A World at Arms. A Global History of World War II,* (Cambridge, 1994, p. 214 note a). But by then the strategic situation was different to that of the preceding October, when Hitler and Pétain had met. Most importantly, the decision to attack Russia had been confirmed. The Mediterranean was now, for Hitler, a sideshow.

73 Warlimont, p. 115.

74 Ibid., pp. 257–258, for Jodl's uncritical admiration of Hitler; see also Ian Kershaw, *Hitler, 1936–1945: Nemesis* (London, 2000), p. 533.

75 Warlimont, p. 118.

76 Fedor von Bock, *The War Diary 1939–1945,* (ed.) Klaus Gerbet (Atglen, PA, 1996), pp. 197–198 (1.2.41); *KTB d. OKW,* vol. 1, p. 300 (3.2.41).

8: Shoot First and Ask Questions Afterwards? Wannsee and the Unfolding of the Final Solution

1 Readers seeking more detail on the points advanced here, as well as refer-

ences, may like to consult the author's recent study: *The Villa, the Lake, the Meeting. Wannsee and the final solution* (London, 2002).

2   Text of the invitation reproduced in Kurt Pätzold and Erika Schwarz, *Tagesordnung: Judenmord. Die Wannsee-Konferenz am 20. Januar 1942* (Berlin, 1992), p. 89.

3   The address for the meeting was initially given as the 'offices of Interpol, 16 Am Kleinen Wannsee'. A subsequent memo of 4 December altered the venue to an SS guest house, 56–58 Am Großen Wannsee. We do not know whether the first address was given in error or whether Heydrich changed his mind and sought a new venue. Peter Klein, *Die Wannsee-Konferenz vom 20. Januar 1942. Analyse und Dokumentation* (Gedenkstätte Haus der Wannsee-Konferenz, Berlin, no date [1995]), p. 8.

4   We deduce they telephoned because we know that until 8 December the participants still believed the meeting would go ahead. On that day Luther's subordinate Rademacher presented him with notes 'for tomorrow's meeting'. Hans Safrian, *Die Eichmann-Männer* (Vienna/Zürich, 1993), p. 169. Since the cancellation does not appear in the otherwise complete Foreign Office records of the meeting, the cancellation was probably made by phone. The written invitation to the delayed meeting reproduced in Klein, *Die Wannsee-Konferenz*, p. 38.

5   The epithet is John Grenville's. See his chapter 'Die "Endlösung" und die "Judenmischlinge" im Dritten Reich', in Ursula Büttner with Werner Johe and Angelika Voss (eds), *Das Unrechtsregime: internationale Forschung über den Nationalsozialismus* (Hamburg, 1986), pp. 91–121, here 108.

6   'Das Protokoll dieser Konferenz war lang, obgleich ich das Unwesentliche nicht einmal hatte stenographieren lassen', Adolf Eichmann, 'Götzen', (unpublished manuscript, Haifa 1961), p. 219.

7   The original is in the possession of the Haus der Wannsee Konferenz in Berlin. It can be seen online at http://www.ghwk.de/deut/proto.htm.

8   Unless otherwise stated, translations are the author's own.

9   This was the question posed to Robert Kempner by US Chief Prosecutor Telford Taylor. See Kempner's account of the discovery in Robert M.W. Kempner, *Ankläger einer Epoche. Lebenserinnerungen.* (Frankfurt/M./Berlin/Vienna 1983), pp. 310–311, here 311.

10 Kemper, *Ankläger*, pp. 310–312.

11 *Trial of the Major War Criminals before the International Military Tribunal* (Nuremberg, 1947–49), vol. 29, pp. 502–503.

12 Leni Yahil, 'Himmler's timetable', *Yad Vashem Studies* 28 (2000), pp. 351–362, here 352.

13 Dieter Rebentisch, *Führerstaat und Verwaltung im zweiten Weltkrieg. Verfassungsentwicklung und Verwaltungspolitik 1939–1945* (Stuttgart 1989), p. 439.

14 Interrogation of Lammers 8 April 1946 as a witness in the Nuremberg Trials; interrogation of Lammers as accused in the Ministries Trial, September 1948; interrogation of Wilhlem Stuckart by his defence attorney in the Ministries Trial, 6 October 1948 all reproduced in Kurt Pätzold and Erika Schwarz, *Tagesordnung: Judenmord,* pp. 132, 154, 156–158. On the first occasion, Lammers misremembered the date, referring to a meeting in 1943,

but it is clearly the Wannsee conference.

15 Goebbels's diary entry from March 7 suggests strongly that he was reading the protocol at just that time. See *The Villa, the Lake, the Meeting*, p. 103.

16 The full minutes of the March and October meetings are reproduced in Robert Kempner, *Eichmann und Komplizien* (Zürich/Stuttgart/Vienna 1961), pp. 165–180, 255–267.

17 See the discussion of Eichmann's remarks in Kershaw, *Hitler 1936–1945. Nemesis* (London, 2000), p. 493.

18 Bernhard Lösener, 'Dokumentation. Das Reichsministerium des Innern und die Judengesetzgebung', *Vierteljahrshefte für Zeitgeschichte* 19 (1961) pp. 262–312, here 297.

19 Kershaw, *Hitler 1936–1945*, p. 493.

20 Wolfgang Scheffler, 'Die Wannsee-Konferenz und ihre historische Bedeutung', in the brochure edited by Gedenkstätte Haus der Wannsee-Konferenz, 'Erinnern für die Zukunft', (Printed by the Gedenkstätte, Berlin no date [1992]).

21 Eberhard Jäckel, 'On the Purpose of the Wannsee Conference', in James S. Pacy and Alan P.Wertheimer (eds), *Perspectives on the Holocaust. Essays in Honor of Raul Hilberg* (Boulder/San Francisco/Oxford 1995), pp. 39–50.

22 Henry R. Huttenbach, 'The Wannsee Conference Reconsidered 50 years after: SS Strategy and Racial Politics in the Third Reich', in Hubert Locke and Marcia Littell, *Remembrance and Recollection. Essays on the Centennial Year of Martin Niemöller and Reinhold Niebühr and the 50th year of the Wannsee Conference* (Lanham, New York/London 1996), pp. 58–79.

23 Rebentisch, *Führerstaat.*

24 Jäckel, 'On the Purpose', p. 39.

25 It is impossible to do justice here to the huge literature on the evolution of Nazi policy. For further references on the development of policy in the Soviet Union, see Roseman, *The Villa, the Lake, the Meeting*, pp. 27–39.

26 Ibid., pp. 40–42.

27 On the Serbian example, see Walter Manoschek, *'Serbien ist Judenfrei.' Militärische Besatzungspolitik und Judenvernichtung in Serbien 1941/2*, (Munich, 1993).

28 On Galicia, see Dieter Pohl, *Nationalsozialistische Judenverfolgung in Ostgalizien 1941–1944. Organisation und Durchführung eines staatlichen Massenverbrechens* (Munich 1996), p. 140–143; Thomas Sandkühler, *'Endlösung' in Galizien. Der Judenmord in Ostpolen und die Rettungsinitiativen von Bertold Beitz 1941–1944* (Bonn 1996), pp. 151–152, 407.

29 Ian Kershaw, 'Improvised Genocide? The Emergence of the "Final Solution" in the Warthegau', *Transactions of the Royal Historical Society* 6th series (1992), pp. 51–78; Deborah Dwork and Robert Jan van Pelt, *Auschwitz. 1270 to the Present* (New York/London 1996), p. 294.

30 Amongst other recent work, see Bogdan Musial, *Deutsche Zivilverwaltung und Judenverfolgung im Generalgouvernement* (Wiesbaden 1999), p. 195; Sandkühler, *'Endlösung' in Galizien*, pp. 136–140; Bogdan Musial, 'The Origins of "Operation Reinhard": The Decision-making Process for the Mass Murder of the Jews in the Generalgouvernement', *Yad Vashem Studies* 28 (2000), pp. 113–153, here 116–118.

31 Gerald Fleming, *Hitler and the final solution* (Oxford paperback edition, 1986), pp. 70–71.

32 See Adam, *Judenpolitik*, p. 309, citing Serge Lang and Ernst von Schenk, *Portrait eines Menschheitsverbrechers. Aus den hinterlassenen Memoiren des ehemaligen Reichsministers Alfred Rosenberg* (St. Gallen, 1947), p. 129; and the discussion in Christopher Browning, *Nazi Policy, Jewish Workers, German killers* (Cambridge, 2000), p. 48–49 and Peter Witte et al. (eds), *Der Dienstkalender Heinrich Himmlers 1941/1942* (Hamburg, 1999), p. 262, note 46.

33 Cited in H.G. Adler, *Der verwaltete Mensch. Studien zur Deportation der Juden aus Deutschland* (Tübingen, 1974), p. 63.

34 Kershaw, *Hitler 1936–1945. Nemesis*, p. 485, citing Goebbels's diary.

35 Fleming, *Hitler and the final solution*, p. 104.

36 We can not pin this down to a specific date or instant. The evidence recently garnered by Christian Gerlach to suggest that such a moment can be found in early December is based partly on a misreading of a statement by Rosenberg, and partly on the rather unlikely premises that Hitler would make a policy announcement on this matter to a large gathering of Gauleiters. See Christian Gerlach, 'The Wannsee Conference, the Fate of German Jews and Hitler's Decision in Principle to Exterminate all European Jews', in Omer Bartov (ed.), *The Holocaust. Origins, Implementation, Aftermath* (London and New York, 2000), pp. 106–161 and Roseman, *The Villa, the Lake, the Meeting*, pp. 60–63.

37 Peter Longerich has argued that Heydrich was merely sketching out what would happen once the war had finished, and that it took subsequent decisions by Himmler in 1942 to bring these conjectures into the realm of wartime policy. See Peter Longerich, 'The Wannsee Conference in the Development of the "Final Solution"', (Holocaust Educational Trust Research papers, vol. 1, no. 2, London, 2000).

38 One of the flaws in Peter Longerich's approach, it seems to me, is the underplaying of this shift. However genocidal earlier territorial models had been, the recognition now that all must die or be killed manifested that a fundamental change had taken place.

39 A memorandum from Adolf Eichmann notes that following Friedrich-Wilhelm Krüger's visit on 28 November, it was decided to revise the list slightly. Memorandum reproduced in Pätzold and Schwarz, *Tagesordnung: Judenmord*, p. 90. These changes however do not support Christian Gerlach's contention that the meeting's scope changed fundamentally between December and January and became European. The guest list change was modest and took place very soon after the first draft. No one else with responsibility outside the Reich was added later (though some of Heydrich's own staff at the meeting did have responsibilities outside Germany, and it is possible they were brought in only in December). On the guest list, see the invitations reproduced in Pätzold and Schwarz, *Tagesordnung: Judenmord*, pp. 89–90; and above all Klein, *Wannsee-Konferenz*, pp. 29–30. See Gerlach, 'Wannsee Conference'.

40 On the emergence of this concept see Pohl, *Nationalsozialistische Judenverfolgung*, p. 165ff.; Sandkühler, *'Endlösung' in Galizien*, p. 134.

41   Heydrich, speech to top functionaries of the Occupation administration in the Czech Protectorate, 4.2.42, in Karl Heinz Roth, '"Generalplan Ost"— "Gesamtplan Ost" Forschungsstand, Quellenprobleme, neue Ergebnisse', in Mechtild Rössler und Sabine Schleiermacher (eds), Der "Generalplan Ost" : Hauptlinien der nationalsozialistischen Planungs- und Vernichtungspolitik (Berlin, 1993), pp. 25–48, here 40–41. Roth is citing Miroslav Karny et al. (eds) Protektoratni politika Reinharda Heydricha, (Prague 1991), dok. 61, pp. 212–224.

42   On Eichmann's testimony, see Kershaw Hitler: Nemesis, p. 493. On other testimony, see Pätzold and Schwarz, Tagesordnung: Judenmord, p. 57. Hans Mommsen, 'The Realization of the Unthinkable: The "final solution of the Jewish Question" in the Third Reich', in Hans Mommsen, From Weimar to Auschwitz. Essays in German History (Oxford, 1991), pp. 224–253, here 249; Hans Mommsen, 'Aufgabenkreis und Verantwortlichkeit des Staatssekretärs der Reichskanzlei Dr Wilhelm Kritzinger', in Institut für Zeitgeschichte (ed.), Gutachten, vol. 2, (Deutsche Verlags-Anstalt: Stuttgart, 1966), pp. 369–398, here 381.

43   An error reproduced in Martin Gilbert's Holocaust Journey, (London, 1998), p. 43.

44   See in particular Noakes's seminal essays 'Wohin gehören die "Judenmischlinge"? Die Entstehung der ersten Durchführungs- verordnungen zu den Nürnberger Gesetzen', in Ursula Büttner with Werner Johe and Angelika Voss (eds), Das Unrechtsregime : internationale Forschung über den Nationalsozialismus (Hamburg, 1986), pp. 69–89, and 'The Development of Nazi Policy towards the German-Jewish "Mischlinge"', in Leo Baeck Institute Year Book 34 (1989), pp. 291–356.

45   Something which a number of authors have observed: see Grenville, '"Endlösung"', p. 108 and Noakes, 'The Development of Nazi policy', p. 341.

46   On the history of these disputes see the two articles by Jeremy Noakes, cited above, note 44.

47   Noakes, 'The Development of Nazi Policy', p. 339.

48   See note 39 above.

49   Witte et al. (eds), Dienstkalender, p. 262, note 46.

50   Ibid., p. 265.

51   Ibid., p. 274.

52   Ibid., p. 277.

53   Testimony at Session 78 at the Eichmann Trial. Testimony viewable online at http://www.nizkor.org/hweb/people/e/eichmann-adolf/transcripts/Sessions/ index-04.html.

54   See Safrian, Eichmann-Männer, p. 143–147.

55   Raul Hilberg, Perpetrators, Victims, Bystanders. The Jewish Catastrophe 1933–1945 (London, 1992), pp. 48–49.

56   George C. Browder, Foundations of the Nazi Police State. The Formation of SIPO and SD (Lexington, 1990), p. 229; Lösener, 'Reichsministerium', p. 286.

57   On the Foreign Ministry's role see Christopher Browning, The Final Solution and the German Foreign Office. A Study of Referat DIII of Abteilung Deutschland

1940–1943 (New York, 1978), pp. 56ff.

58 On Himmler's concern, see Richard Breitman, *Official Secrets. What the Nazis Planned. What the British and Americans Knew* (London, 1998), p. 82.

59 Lösener, 'Reichsministerium', p. 310.

60 Cited in Gerlach, 'Wannsee', p. 129.

61 Letter from Heydrich, 25. Januar 1942 to Commander of the Security Police and the SD amongst others re. "final solution of the Jewish Question", reproduced on the website of the Gedenkstätte Haus der Wannsee Konferenz, www.ghwk.de/deut/chefsd.htm.

62 My translation from Johannes Tuchel, *Am großen Wannsee 56–58. Von der Villa Minoux zum Haus der Wannsee-Konferenz* (Berlin, 1992), p. 121; see also Gerlach, 'Wannsee', p. 130.

63 See Kempner, *Eichmann*, p. 182.

64 I see no grounds to follow Peter Longerich in assuming that Heydrich did not mean what he said and was merely talking about hypothetical actions after the war was over. See Peter Longerich, *The Unwritten Order: Hitler's Role in the final solution* (Stroud, 2001), p. 96.

65 Kempner, *Eichmann*, p. 148; Gerlach, *Kalkulierte Morde*, p. 755.

66 For the discussion of why this was so, see Roseman, *The Villa, the Lake, the Meeting*, pp. 100–101.

67 Herbert, *Best*, p. 320.

9: Auschwitz and the Germans: History, Knowledge, and Memory

1   Marianne B., 'Bericht über die Dienstzeit als Gymnasiallehrerin in Auschwitz (1.9.1943–21.1.1945)', Deutsches Tagebucharchiv, Emmendingen, Reg. no. 463. I am grateful to Dr Sybille Steinbacher for bringing these memoirs to my attention, and for generously allowing me to make use of them here.

2   Marianne B., 'Bericht', pp. 8f. Emphasis in the original.

3   Ibid., p. 10. Here the author is clearly mixing up personal experience with what she has picked up from later reading. 'Selections' did not take place in the station in Auschwitz. However, it is conceivable that the schoolchildren had observed the treatment of people arriving in the station at the hands of the SS.

4   Ibid., p. 29.

5   Ibid., pp. 46ff.

6   Ibid., p. 47.

7   Ibid., p. 16.

8   This and the three following sections are based on Norbert Frei and Sybille Steinbacher, 'Auschwitz. Die Stadt, das Lager und die Wahrnehmung der Deutschen', in Klaus-Dietmar Henke (ed.), *Auschwitz. Sechs Essays zu Geschehen und Vergegenwärtigung*, (Dresden, 2001), pp. 37–51; also the more detailed study, with supporting documents, by Sybille Steinbacher, *'Musterstadt' Auschwitz. Germanisierungspolitik und Judenmord in Ostoberschlesien*, (Munich, 2000). See also her concise overview, *Auschwitz. Geschichte und Nachgeschichte*, (Munich, 2004).

9   Steinbacher, *'Musterstadt' Auschwitz*.

10 A particularly significant example is the Erfurt firm of crematorium specialists, Topf & Sons, whose intensive co-operation with the SS, first in

Buchenwald, and then especially in Auschwitz, is currently being studied as part of a research and exhibition project on the part of the Foundation for the Memorial Sites of Buchenwald and Mittelbau-Dora.

11 On the Deutsche Bank in the occupied eastern territories and the role of the bank director, Hermann Josef Abs, see Harold James, *Die Deutsche Bank und die 'Arisierung'* (Munich, 2001); now also Lothar Gall, *Der Bankier Hermann Josef Abs. Eine Biographie* (Munich, 2004).

12 Bernd C. Wagner, *IG Auschwitz. Zwangsarbeit und Vernichtung von Häftlingen des Lagers Monowitz 1941–1945*, (Munich, 2000).

13 Peter Hayes recently offered an incisive survey of the research debate around this issue, in a review essay: 'Auschwitz, Capital of the Holocaust', *Holocaust and Genocide Studies* 17 (2003), pp. 330–350.

14 SS-Sturmbannführer Rolf-Heinz Höppner to Adolf Eichmann, 16.7.1941, quoted from Egon Kogon et al. (eds), *Nationalsozialistische Massentötungen durch Giftgas*, (Frankfurt/M. 1983), pp. 110f.

15 For a recent overview of this topic, see Ulrich Herbert (ed.), *National Socialist Extermination Policies. Contemporary German Perspectives and Controversies* (New York and Oxford, 2000).

16 Details to be found in Kogon, *Massentötungen*, pp. 111–145; Mathias Beer, 'Die Entwicklung der Gaswagen beim Mord an den Juden', *Vierteljahrshefte für Zeitgeschichte* (Frankfurt/M., 1983), pp. 110f.

17 See Franciszek Piper, *Die Zahl der Opfer von Auschwitz.* (Oswiecim, 1993).

18 At this point, I can only refer selectively to Yisrael Gutman and Michael Berenbaum (eds), *Anatomy of the Auschwitz Death Camp* (Bloomington, 1994); Waclaw Dlugoborski and Franciszek Piper (eds), *Central Issues in the History of the Camps*, 5 vols, (Oswiecim, 2000) (Polish edition 1995; German edition 1999); Debórah Dwork and Robert van Pelt, *Auschwitz, 1270 to the Present* (New York, 1996); see also our four-volume series 'Darstellungen und Quellen zur Geschichte von Auschwitz', which, apart from the monographs by Sybille Steinbacher and Bernd C. Wagner (see notes 8 and 12), contains the following two volumes: Norbert Frei, Thomas Grotum, Jan Parcer, Sybille Steinbacher and Bernd C. Wagner (eds), *Standort- und Kommandanturbefehle des Konzentrationslagers Auschwitz 1940–1945* (Munich, 2000); Norbert Frei, Sybille Steinbacher, and Bernd C. Wagner (eds), *Ausbeutung, Vernichtung, Öffentlichkeit. Neue Studien zur national-sozialistischen Lagerpolitik*, (Munich, 2000).

19 Garrison order No. 25/43 of 1[2].7.1943, in Frei et al. (eds), *Standort- und Kommandanturbefehle*, p. 306.

20 This emerges from the garrison and station command orders (see note 18), which served the Commandant as an instrument for communicating with the guards, and reveal many details of the everyday life of the SS in Auschwitz.

21 Garrison order No. 17/44 of 9.6.1944, in Frei et al. (eds), *Standort- und Kommandanturbefehle*, p. 454.

22 Cf. Bernd Wagner, 'Gerüchte, Wissen, Verdrängung: Die IG Auschwitz und das Vernichtungslager Birkenau', in Frei, Steinbacher and Wagner (eds), *Ausbeutung*, pp. 231–248.

23 Quotation from Walter Manoschek (ed.), *'Es gibt nur eines für das Judentum: Vernichtung'. Das Judenbild in deutschen Soldatenbriefen 1939–1944*

(Hamburg, 1995), p. 63.

24 Cf. the letter from Professor Hans-Martin Stimpel (Göttingen) to the *Frankfurter Allgemeine Zeitung* of 3.2.2004; interestingly, the writer passes on this information as the report of a younger fellow pupil, although the amount of detail given in the rest of the account suggests that the author himself was present.

25 Victor Klemperer, *Ich will Zeugnis ablegen bis zum letzten. Tagebücher 1942–1945*, (Berlin, 1995) p. 47.

26 Ibid., entry for 17.10.1942, p. 259.

27 Cp. the recollections of the historian Reinhart Koselleck, 'Vielerlei Abschied vom Krieg', in Brigitte Sauzay, Heinz Ludwig Arnold and Rudolf von Thadden (eds), *Vom Vergessen und Gedenken. Erinnerungen und Erwartungen in Europa zum 8. Mai 1945*, (Göttingen, 1995), pp. 19–25.

28 Cp. Piper, *Zahl*.

29 Ruth Klüger, *Weiter leben. Eine Jugend*, (Göttingen, 1992)[English version: *Landscapes of Memory. A Holocaust Girlhood Remembered* (London, 2003)]; Anita Lasker-Wallfisch, *Ihr sollt die Wahrheit erben. Breslau—Auschwitz—Bergen-Belsen*, (Bonn, 1997) [English version: *Inherit the Truth 1939–1945. The Documented Experiences of a Survivor of Auschwitz and Belsen* (London, 1996)].

30 Primo Levi, *Ist das ein Mensch? Erinnerungen an Auschwitz* (Frankfurt/M., 1961) (English version: *If this is a Man* (London, 1960)).

31 Elie Wiesel, *Die Nacht zu begraben, Elischa. Nacht—Morgengrauen—Tag* (Munich, 1961)(English version: *Night* (London, 1960)).

32 Ella Lingens, *Eine Frau im Konzentrationslager* (Vienna, 1966).

33 Cp. Hermann Langbein, *Menschen in Auschwitz* (Munich, 1999) (first published Vienna, 1972); Kerstin Robusch (Bochum) is writing a dissertation on Langbein's role in preparing for and carrying out the trials of National Socialists.

34 See in this connection the recent catalogue of an exhibition by the Fritz Bauer Institute: Irmtrud Wojak (ed.), *Auschwitz-Prozess 4Ks 2/63* (Frankfurt/M. and Cologne, 2004).

35 Hans Buchheim, Martin Broszat, Hans-Adolf Jacobsen and Helmut Krausnick, *Anatomie des SS-Staates*, 2 vols (Freiburg, 1965; paper-back edition Munich, 1999). On the role of the expert reports in the preparations for the trial, see my essay 'The Frankfurt Auschwitz Trial and research in German contemporary history', in Jahrbuch des Fritz Bauer Instituts (ed.), *Auschwitz. Geschichte, Rezeption und Wirkung*, (Frankfurt/M. and New York, 1996), pp. 123–138.

36 For detailed discussion, see my study, *Adenauer's Germany and the Nazi Past. The Politics of Amnesty and Integration* (New York, 2002).

37 Cf. Jahrbuch des Fritz Bauer Instuts (ed.), '*Gerichtstag halten über uns selbst. . .'. Geschichte und Wirkung des ersten Frankfurter Auschwitz-Prozesses* (Frankfurt/M. and New York, 2001).

38 Cp. the detailed study by Christoph Weiss, *Auschwitz in der geteilten Welt. Peter Weiss und die 'Ermittlung' im Kalten Krieg* (Sankt Ingbert, 2000).

39 The slim volume published by the Institut für Zeitgeschichte, *Studien zur Geschichte der Konzentrationslager* (Munich, 1970) remained the last contri-

bution to empirical research for many years. For an overview of research up until the mid-1990s, see Ulrich Herbert, Karin Orth, and Christian Dieckmann (eds), *Die nationalsozialistische Konzentrationslager. Entwicklung und Struktur*, 2 vols, (Göttingen, 1998).

40 Wilhelm Stäglich, *Der Auschwitz-Mythos. Legende oder Wirklichkeit? Eine kritische Bestandsaufnahme* (Tübingen, 1979). The book was placed on the index of the *Bundesprüfstelle für jugendgefährdendes Schrifttum* (national bureau for the scrutiny of publications likely to place youth at risk). My essay was broadcast by the *Deutschlandfunk* on 10.1.1979 with the title 'Die Dolmetscher der Unmenschen. Die Massenvernichtung im Spiegel rechts-radikaler Publizistik' (Interpreting the monsters. The mass extermination programme as seen by extreme rightwing polemics).

41 Hans Safrian, *Die Eichmann-Männer* (Vienna, 1993).

Contributors

EDITOR:

Neil Gregor is Reader in Modern German History at the University of Southampton. He is the author of *Daimler-Benz in the Third Reich* (1998), editor of *Nazism. A Reader* (2000) and the author of *How to Read Hitler* (2005).

CONTRIBUTORS:

Jane Caplan is University Lecturer in History and a Fellow of St Anthony's College, Oxford. She is, amongst other things, the author of *Government without Administration. State and Civil Service in Nazi Germany* (1988), editor with Thomas Childers of *Re-Evaluating the Third Reich* (1993), and editor of *Written on the Body. The Tattoo in European and American History* (2000).

Norbert Frei is Professor of Modern History at the University of Bochum. His many books include *The Führer State 1933–1945. National Socialist Rule in Germany* (1993), *Adenauer's Germany and the Nazi Past. The Politics of Amnesty and Integration* (2002), *1945 und Wir. Das Dritte Reich im Bewußtstein der Deutschen* (2nd edn, 2005) and the co-edited *Ausbeutung, Vernichtung, Öffentlichkeit. Neue Studien zur nationalsozialistischen Lagerpolitik* (2000)

Dick Geary is Professor of Modern History at the University of Nottingham. He is the author of numerous books, including *European Labour Protest 1848–1939* (1984), *Hitler and Nazism* (1993), *Aspects of German Labour* (1997) and co-editor, with Richard Evans, of *The German Unemployed. Experiences and Consequences of Mass Unemployment from the Weimar Republic to the Third Reich* (1987).

Robert Gellately holds the Earl Ray Beck Chair of History at Florida State University. He is the author, amongst other things, of *The Gestapo and German Society. Enforcing Racial Policy 1933–1945* (1990) and *Backing Hitler: Consent and Coercion in Nazi Germany* (2001), and the co-editor, with Nathan Stoltzfus, of *Social Outsiders in Nazi Germany* (2001).

Ian Kershaw is Professor of Modern History at the University of Sheffield. His many books include *Popular Opinion and Political Dissent in the Third Reich. Bavaria 1933–1945* (1983), *The 'Hitler Myth'. Image and Reality in the Third Reich* (1987), *Hitler* (1991), and the 2-volumed biography *Hitler. 1889–1936: Hubris* (1998) and *Hitler. 1936–45: Nemesis* (2000); most recently he published *Making Friends with Hitler: Lord Londonderry and the Roots of Appeasement* (2004).

Mark Roseman holds the Pat M. Glazer chair of Jewish History at the University of Indiana. He has published widely on twentieth-century German history; his recent books include *The Past in Hiding* (2000), *The Villa, the Lake, the Meeting: Wannsee and the Final Solution* (2002) and he is co-editor (with Neil Gregor and Nils Roemer) of *German History from the Margins* (2006).

Jill Stephenson is Professor of History at the University of Edinburgh. She is the author of *Women in Nazi Society* (1975), *The Nazi Organisation of Women* (1981), *Women in Nazi Germany* (2001) and *Hitler's Home Front. Württemberg under the Nazis* (2006).

Nikolaus Wachsmann is Senior Lecturer in Modern German History at Birkbeck College, London. His study of *Hitler's Prisons. Legal Terror in Nazi Germany* (2004) won the Longman/*History Today* Prize in 2005; in addition, he has published several articles on Nazi penal policy and practice.

Suggestions for further reading

The best introduction to the history of the Third Reich is the 4-volume set of readers produced by Jeremy Noakes and Geoffrey Pridham:

Jeremy Noakes and Geoffrey Pridham (eds), *Nazism 1919–1945. Volume 1: The Rise to Power 1919–1934. A Documentary Reader.* (University of Exeter Press, 1983; New Edition with Index, 1998)

Jeremy Noakes and Geoffrey Pridham (eds), *Nazism 1919–1945. Volume 2: State, Economy and Society 1933–1939. A Documentary Reader.* (University of Exeter Press, 1984; New Edition with Index, 2000)

Jeremy Noakes and Geoffrey Pridham (eds), *Nazism 1919–1945. Volume 3: Foreign Policy, War and Racial Extermination. A Documentary Reader.* (University of Exeter Press, 1988; New Edition with Index, 2001)

Jeremy Noakes (ed.), *Nazism 1919–1945. Volume 4: The German Home Front in World War II. A Documentary Reader.* (University of Exeter Press, 1998)

Those wishing to read further on the subjects covered by individual essays in this volume should consult:

1. Neil Gregor, 'Nazism – A Political Religion? Rethinking the Voluntarist Turn'

Michael Burleigh, *The Third Reich. A New History* (London/New York, 2000)

Neil Gregor, 'Politics, Culture, Political Culture: Recent Work on the Third Reich and its Aftermath', in: *Journal of Modern History* 78 (2006)

Wolfgang Hardtwig, 'Political Religion in Modern Germany: Reflections on Nationalism, Socialism and National Socialism', in: *Bulletin of the German Historical Institute* (Washington, D.C., 2001)

Jane Caplan, 'Politics, Religion and Ideology: A Comment on Wolfgang Hardtwig', in: *Bulletin of the German Historical Institute* (Washington, D.C., 2001)

Ian Kershaw, *The Nazi Dictatorship. Problems and Perspectives of Interpretation* (4th edn., London, 2000)

Richard Steigmann-Gall, 'Nazism and the Revival of Political Religion Theory', in: *Totalitarian Movements and Political Religions* 5 (2004)

2. Jane Caplan, 'Political Detention and the Origin of the Concentration Camps in Nazi Germany, 1933–1935/6'

Hans Buchheim et al, *Anatomy of the SS-State* (London, 1968)

George C. Browder, *Hitler's Enforcers. The Gestapo and the SS Security System in the Nazi Revolution* (New York, 1996)

Richard J. Evans, *The Third Reich in Power* (London, 2005)

Eric Johnson, *The Nazi Terror. Gestapo, Jews and Ordinary Germans* (London, 2000)

Harold Marcuse, *Legacies of Dachau. The Uses and Abuses of a Concentration Camp 1933–2001* (Cambridge, 2001)

Nikolaus Wachsmann, *Hitler's Prisons. Legal Terror in Nazi Germany* (New Haven, 2004)

3. Dick Geary, 'Working Class Identities in the Third Reich'

Ulrich Herbert, *Hitler's Foreign Workers. Enforced Foreign Labour under the Third Reich* (Cambridge, 1997)

—. 'The Real Mystery in Germany. The German Working Class during the Nazi Dictatorship' in: Michael Burleigh (ed), *Confronting the German Past. New Debates on Modern German History* (London, 1996)

Alf Lüdtke, 'The Appeal of Exterminating "Others": German Workers and the Limits of Resistance' in: Christian Leitz (ed), *The Third Reich. The Essential Readings* (Oxford, 1999)

Timothy W. Mason, *Social Policy in the Third Reich. The Working Class and the National Community* (Oxford, 1993)

—. *Nazism, Fascism and the Working Class* (Cambridge, 1995)

Tilla Siegel, 'Whatever was the Attitude of German Workers? Reflections on Recent Interpretations' in: Richard Bessel (ed), *Fascist Italy and Nazi Germany. Comparisons and Contrasts* (Cambridge, 1996)

4. Robert Gellately, 'Social Outsiders and the Consolidation of Hitler's Dictatorship'

Gisela Bock, 'Racism and Sexism in Nazi Germany: Motherhood, Compulsory Sterilisation and the State' in: Renate Bridenthal, Atina Grossmann and Marion A. Kaplan (eds), *When Biology Became Destiny: Women in Weimar and Nazi Germany* (New York, 1984)

Michael Burleigh and Wolfgang Wippermann, *The Racial State: Germany 1933–1945* (Cambridge, 1991)

Saul Friedlaender, *Nazi Germany and the Jews. The Years of Persecution 1933–1939* (London, 1997)

Robert Gellately and Nathan Stoltzfus (eds), *Social Outsiders in Nazi Germany* (Princeton, 2001)

—. *Backing Hitler. Consent and Coercion in the Third Reich* (Oxford, 2001)

Günter Grau (ed), *Hidden Holocaust? Gay and Lesbian Persecution in Germany 1933–1945* (New York, 1995)

Jeremy Noakes, 'Social Outcasts in the Third Reich' in: Richard Bessel (ed), *Life in the Third Reich* (Oxford, 1987)

5. *Nikolaus Wachsmann, "'Soldiers of the Home Front": Jurists and Legal Terror during the Second World War'*

Richard J. Evans, *Rituals of Retribution. Capital Punishment in Germany 1600–1987* (London, 1997)

Robert Gellately, *The Gestapo and German Society. Enforcing Racial Policy 1933–1945* (Oxford, 1990)

D. Majer, *'Non-Germans' under the Third Reich. The Nazi Judicial and Administrative System in Germany and Occupied Eastern Europe, with Special Regard to Occupied Poland 1939–1945* (Baltimore, 2003)

Michael Stolleis, *The Law under the Swastika* (Chicago, 1998)

Nikolaus Wachsmann, '"Annihilation Through Labour": The Killing of State Prisoners in the Third Reich', in: *Journal of Modern History* 71 (1999)

R.F. Wetzell, *Inventing the Criminal. A History of German Criminology 1880–1945* (Chapel Hill, 2000)

6. *Jill Stephenson, 'Germans, Slavs and the Burden of Work in Rural Southern Germany during the Second World War'*

Richard Bessel, *Nazism and War* (New York, 2004)

J.J. Delaney, 'Racial Values vs. Religious Values: Clerical Opposition to Nazi Anti-Polish Racial Policy', in: *Church History* 70 (2001)

—. 'Social Contact and Personal Relations of German Catholic Peasants and Polish Workers (POWs, Civilian and Forced Laborers) in Bavaria's Rural War Economy, 1939–1945', in: *Annali dell' Instituto storico italo-germanico in Trento* 28 (2002)

Oded Heilbronner, *Catholicism, Political Culture and the Countryside: A Social History of the Nazi Party in South Germany* (Ann Arbor, 1998)

Ian Kershaw, *Popular Opinion and Political Dissent in the Third Reich. Bavaria, 1933–1945* (Oxford, 1983)

Jill Stephenson, 'Triangle: Foreign Workers, German Civilians and the Nazi Regime. War and Society in Württemberg, 1939–1945', in: *German Studies Review* 15/2 (1992)

—. *Hitler's Home Front. Württemberg under the Nazis* (2006)

7. *Ian Kershaw, 'Did Hitler Miss his Chance in 1940?'*

W. Carr, *Poland to Pearl Harbour. The Making of the Second World War* (London, 1985)

Ian Kershaw, *Hitler: Nemesis. 1936–1945* (London, 2000)

Paul Preston, 'Franco and Hitler: the Myth of Hendaye 1940', in: *Contemporary European History* 1 (1992)

Gerhard Schreiber et al, *Germany in the Second World War* Vol. 3, *The Mediterranean, South-East Europe, and North Africa 1939–1941* (Oxford, 1995)

Gerhard Weinberg, *A World at Arms. A Global History of World War II* (Cambridge, 1994)

—. *Germany, Hitler and World War II. Essays in Modern German History* (Cambridge, 1995)

8. Mark Roseman, 'Shoot First and Ask Questions Afterwards? Wannsee and the Unfolding of the Final Solution'

Omer Bartov (ed), *The Holocaust. Origins, Implementation, Aftermath* (London, 2000)

Christopher R. Browning, *The Origins of the Final Solution: The Evolution of Nazi Jewish Policy September 1939–March 1942* (London, 2004)

Henry Huttenbach, 'The Wannsee Conference Reconsidered 50 Years After: SS Strategy and Racial Politics in the Third Reich' in: Hubert Locke and Marcia Littell (eds), *Remembrance and Recollection. Essays on the Centennial Year of Martin Niemöller and Reinhold Niebühr and the 50th Year of the Wannsee Conference* (Lanham, New York/London, 1996)

Eberhard Jäckel, 'On the Purpose of the Wannsee Conference' in: James S. Pacy and Alan Wertheimer (eds), *Perspectives on the Holocaust. Essays in Honor of Raul Hilberg* (Boulder/San Francisco/Oxford, 1995)

Mark Roseman, *The Villa, the Lake, the Meeting. Wannsee and the Final Solution* (London, 2002)

9. Norbert Frei, 'Auschwitz and the Germans: History, Knowledge and Memory'

Allen, Michael Thad, *The Business of Genocide: The SS, Slave Labour and the Concentration Camps* (Chapel Hill, 2002)

David Bankier, *The Germans and the Final Solution: Public Opinion under Nazism* (Oxford, 1996)

Yisrael Gutman and Michael Berenbaum (eds), *Anatomy of the Auschwitz Death Camp* (Bloomington, Ind., 1994)

Peter Hayes, 'Auschwitz, Capital of the Holocaust', in: *Holocaust and Genocide Studies* 17 (2003)

Primo Levi, *If this is a Man* (London, 1960)

Sybille Steinbacher, *Auschwitz* (London, 2005)

Index